RAGNELL the WOMAN who was A BEAST

A re-imagining of an Arthurian folktale

A Novel by

Raïna Manuel-Paris

CHIRON PUBLICATIONS • ASHEVILLE, NORTH CAROLINA

www.ChironPublications.com

Interior and cover design by Danijela Mijailovic
Printed primarily in the United States of America.

ISBN 978-1-68503-707-9 paperback
ISBN 978-1-68503-708-6 hardcover
ISBN 978-1-68503-709-3 electronic
ISBN 978-1-68503-710-9 limited edition paperback
ISBN 978-1-68503-711-6 limited edition hardcover

Library of Congress Cataloging-in-Publication Data

Names: Paris, Raïna M. author
Title: Ragnell, the woman who was a beast : a re-imagining of an Arthurian folktale / a novel by Raïna Manuel-Paris.
Other titles: Wedding of Sir Gawain and Dame Ragnell.
Description: Asheville, North Carolina : Chiron Publications, 2026. | Summary: "This novel finds its roots in Arthurian legends, specifically the medieval folktale, The Wedding of Dame Ragnell and Sir Gawain - a reversal of the well-known fairytale, Beauty and the Beast. In this retelling of the story, the Beast is the real Beauty. The Roman Empire has retreated from the British Isles, and the old druidic ways are losing ground to the new Christian faith. The dragons that once protected the kingdom have vanished or been enslaved. They are on the verge of becoming a thing of myth, even for the weavers from the Isle of Skye who knew them best. In this world, Ragnell, the daughter of a great lord, destined for marriage, falls prey to a terrible curse on the night of her fifteenth birthday, which transforms her from a beautiful maiden into a hideous beast. Reviled by those she loves the most, she escapes into the woods where she manages to survive for years, alone. Plagued by despair and moved by deep dreams, she seeks the help of the great druid, Myrddin Emrys, to discover who did this to her, why it happened, and whether solving a riddle to save King Arthur's life will help unmake the curse that befell her. In the process, she learns to navigate the magical and political landscape of the times. And more importantly, she comes to understand that in order to be her whole human self she cannot fully abandon the beast she has become - or the dragons she has come to know - and that letting go of who she is to fit into a society that scorns and censures female agency may not be a bargain she is willing to make" -- Provided by publisher.
Identifiers: LCCN 2026036748 (print) | LCCN 2026036749 (ebook) | ISBN 9781685037079 paperback | ISBN 9781685037086 hardcover | ISBN 9781685037093 ebook
Subjects: LCGFT: Fantasy fiction | Novels
Classification: LCC PS3616.A7431334 R34 2026 (print) | LCC PS3616.A7431334 (ebook)
LC record available at https://lccn.loc.gov/2026036748

LC ebook record available at https://lccn.loc.gov/2026036749

Inspiration and Writing Journey

Myths and legends from the world over have been an essential part of my life since I was a little girl. They gave me a metaphorical vocabulary to navigate life's challenges early on. They also taught me to listen to the world beneath the world.

The Arthurian Legends have inspired many scholars and many movies. What drew me in was a folk tale in which a cursed lady saved King Arthur's life and got a husband out of it. I thought this was a really smart woman but also someone who must be suffering. I wanted to put this female character at the center of the story, to know the how and why of it and what it felt like to be cursed at fifteen, on the cusp of womanhood. The irony that for centuries the visible sign of women's creative power, the onset of menses, was referred to as a "curse," did not escape me. This is such a fragile time for most women, learning to relate to their newly emerging bodies while navigating the external pressures of family, culture and society. Lady Ragnell was my guide through her epic journey, and I knew her story would sustain me through the entire process of writing this novel and beyond. Every character in the story wrestles to one extent or another with the concept of freedom (or lack of it) and what it means to choose your own life. This is a fundamental idea which is essential to my life, and I believe to most everyone.

The historical context, the end of the Roman Empire with the reshaping of its geography, internal wars that tore through Wales and its neighboring kingdoms and the newly arising Christian era gave me room enough as a writer to imagine situations and combine characters in a way that served the story that wanted to be written. While weaving history with myth, I did my best to remain faithful to the spirit of the era and of its people. Any errors are entirely mine. I chose to refer to Great Britain as *Briton* to create distance from the modern era, and from the Roman appellation of *Britannia*. It is also, for me, a reminder of the Brythonic languages of its local people, the *Cymri*, including the Welsh, Cornish, and Breton.

Though writing a novel is a singular endeavor, I am grateful for the encouragement and support I received not only from fellow writers but from Lady Ragnell herself who encouraged me to "write her". It was a gift from the imaginal winds of daydreams, and I couldn't say no to it. Finally, very special thanks to the brilliant writing coach and fellow dreamer Louise Rosager, and to the endlessly patient and dedicated managing editor of Chiron Publications, Jennifer Fitzgerald.

Contents

Chapter One

I was cursed on my fifteenth birthday. It was the night of the frost moon. My bed warmed with hot stones, which was essential from late fall into early spring in North Wales. Especially in a drafty castle.

Dinas Emrys was a fortress, my father's greatest holding, and the only home I knew. It stood on a craggy hill at the confluence of the Gwynant and Colwyn rivers, where they joined together to create the Glaslyn River in Gwynedd. The Glaslyn was impetuous like a young colt and moved fast between rocky terrain and wooded hillocks.

My brother Somer and I spent hours staring at the river from Pont Bren, the old stone bridge with the two arches. We'd cackle and shout like a couple of canny crows to scare off the lovers who dared venture onto it.

To the south, the hills rose toward the mountain peak of Snowdon, *Yr Wyddfa* in the Welsh. When I was a child, I wished to be a mountain fairy and fly above the valley. Instead, I became a monster.

Before my time, there were other monstrous creatures in Gwynedd. Two dragons got in the way of my father's building efforts. I thought perhaps our meddling with dragons caused the curse upon me. Years later, I learned that it was a foolish thought, for magical creatures are not evil. They only behave as they are or how they are forced to do so by humans. It is humans who can be evil, cause harm to each other on purpose. No animal does that, magical or otherwise.

On the night of my birthing day feast, I went to bed wearing my brand-new sleeping gown, made of gossamer white linen, weaved by the ladies of Skye, in the Outer Hebrides. It was my brother Somer's last gift to me. He'd accompanied me to my room *to bid a proper goodnight to his little sister on her big day*, and to give me his present in private. I loved him for doing so. I must admit to being somewhat jealous of his Lady wife despite my admiration for her beauty and allure. It was all the time he spent with her and so little with me. But they had been married less than a year. In fact, they were married three weeks after my father's death, as I endeavored to emerge from my terrible grief.

I woke up a nightmare. In the space of a single night, I became the shadow monster of my darkest dreams: hair brittle as twigs, skin leathery, nails turned into claws, hands and feet covered in coarse hair, the eyes and teeth of a wolf, and the temper and appetite of a wild boar.

My father felt compelled to assure me that I was a beauty, seeing as I had no mother to discuss such matters. I did have several marriage proposals by the time I turned twelve, even before he settled any dowry upon me. No more. I became uglier than a witch, fit only for the company of pigs in the pigsty of one of our tenant farmers. In a time when refinement and genteel manners were praised in the ladies of King Arthur's court, I was the image of revulsion. No suitor would sing poems of devotion to me, no one would go on a quest in my name or devote their chivalrous deeds to me. I became the opposite of all things elegant, or pretty. No one's Lady. A worthless filthy hag who must hide from all.

It was the first happy night I could remember since my father's death. I still knew myself, long brown hair brushed until it shone like silk, unblemished skin, hazel eyes, innocent of what awaited me. At dinner, I sat at the head of our table as Lady of the House of Gwynedd, the chosen heir of Lord Vortigern. During our feast, I was celebrated by my brother and his new wife, Lady Amunet, with many toasts and magnificent presents: a new saddle for my palfrey, Espoir, hand-tooled in the finest leather with carved leaves and grapes. It came all the way from Hispania with a matching saddle bag. A new winter cloak from the island of Eire, with the softest leather on the outside and thickest sheep's wool inside.

From Lady Amunet, I received two kinds of dates of the Hayany and Zaghloul varieties. She explained that they could only be found in Egypt, the country of her birth, and that they were the sweetest in the Middle East. I had nothing to compare them to since it was my first time eating such a fruit. But they tasted like honey, flowers, and the smoky flavor of wood bark, delicious. I also received camel milk. The lady insisted I drink some, right then, as I sampled the dates. *They're meant to be eaten together*, she said. So I did. The camel milk was a bit salty for my taste, and more filling than the sheep's milk I was used to. But I drank a small cup, not to offend, as she was my brother's wife.

The lords and ladies in attendance were cheerful and congratulated me on having reached this fortunate landmark of a birthday. I would be coming into my inheritance. Some of the lords crowding the hall hoped to bid for my hand in marriage and paid more attention to my brother than to me, intent on convincing him that they were the right match.

My brother urged me to dance with some of them. I was grateful for the lively music provided by our local players. The flute and the bodhrán kept us moving. I enjoyed the dancing but most of the lords seemed incapable of conversation, aside from commenting on my pretty face and elegant gown. *What lovely hair you have. What pretty eyes. Your gown is beyond compare. I haven't seen anything like it at court.* I would answer, *thank you. Yes. My ancilla is a gifted seamstress. She does all my gowns.* It became repetitious, a bore. I kept looking for my brother to come and rescue me, but he was too busy with his wife and with the guests.

I didn't care for any of the lords, except for the king's nephew, Gawain, who'd come with his mother and father, Lady Morgause, and her husband, King Lot of Okney. They were the only members of King Arthur's family present that night. I wondered if my brother had even invited them. Either he felt obligated in our father's memory or, more likely, they were here on King Arthur's behalf, and Somer couldn't refuse them entrance.

Our father was terribly upset when the king married Lady Guinevere. He thought Arthur was making a mistake and should marry me instead, but I was only eleven, still too young at the time. Somer thought our father was being ridiculous. He did have a point. But our father refused to see it and they got into one of their arguments. I hated that it was because of me. My attempt to stop their quarrelling failed as usual.

Our father reconciled himself to the event by deciding that Gawain could be a worthy suitor. Father thought him a boy with good manners and a sweet disposition, despite his *problematic mother*, Lady Morgause.

I kept asking what he meant by *problematic mother*. He explained that *the woman was a meddler, a busybody who thought too highly of herself, giving advice to Arthur on sensitive political issues*. To meddle in affairs not your own was inexcusable in our father's eyes. Certainly not worthy of a well-bred lady.

Still, I knew he wanted the best for me. I expected I would find happiness in being a lady married to a kindly husband. There was no other choice for me. It was the fate of all young girls of gentle birth, to become a wife and provide an heir, hopefully without dying. I loved life and didn't want to die as my mother had, in childbed. That was the frightening part, but I refused to dwell on it. And my ancilla assured me that I had a strong constitution despite my slender appearance.

Though I had not yet been formally introduced, I knew Lady Morgause was King Arthur's half-sister, like I was Somer's half-sister. My father's words would not leave me, how Lady Morgause was *problematic, thought too highly of herself.* I asked my ancilla about it before the feast while she helped me get dressed.

Lavinia always knew the best gossip, which is to say, the hidden truth of things. She wouldn't answer but I kept needling her, repeating, *tell me, what is it? Tell me, tell me!*

She relented, "Lady Morgause follows the old ways. She is a *bandrui*, a female Druid priest, and answers to no man, only the Gods."

I wanted to know more, for instance, if she, my ancilla, also followed the old ways, but she wouldn't say. It didn't matter because I'd seen Lavinia leave the castle one night, while I watched the moonrise from my window. Women from our nearest village were waiting for her. I knew she meant to join them in making offerings at the fairy mound to honor the cycles of the moon.

I had the urge to go with them, but what if I got caught? I didn't want Lavinia to get into trouble because of me. I stayed, inventing rituals in my room instead, dancing and singing to the light of the moon streaming down on me. I could hear the bodhrán keeping the beat for the dancers all night long, while the *cyhyraeh*, or *banshees,* as everyone else calls them, wailed and screamed, announcing the future dead. Flushed with the power of their frenzy, I was spinning in circles till I fell down, no longer in my room but on the fairy mound with the women dancing around me, holding witches' staffs of blackthorn wood.

I woke up in my bed with the sunrise, wondering if I had dreamed it all. When Lavinia asked me if I slept well, I answered, *as well as you.* She laughed deep in her throat, and I fancied myself her co-conspirator.

It would be years before Gawain and I met again after that cursed night, under very different circumstances. He was closest to my age, unlike the other suitors who seemed old enough to be my father, or my grandfather. But Somer didn't want me to dance with him. My brother had his reasons, and I obeyed him. I dared not defy him and create ill will between us, especially on my birthing day feast, and so soon after the reading of our father's will, an occasion full of bitterness for my brother. I knew his dislike of King Arthur and the royal family ran deeper than I understood, but I also remembered that our father thought well enough of Gawain to consider him as a suitor for me.

Gawain and I did manage to speak later that evening. He had the kindest smile and was most courteous, wishing me well on my birthday. I was mesmerized by the soft curls of his hair that fell haphazardly over his forehead, almost hiding his sky blue eyes. I had the urge to push the curls out of the way with my fingers, which went against everything I was taught as a lady of a great house. I had to restrain myself, cross my hands behind my back, but in my mind's eye I saw myself doing it. I felt a most agreeable shudder up and down my spine. I could not explain to myself whether it came from the desire to touch his hair, a desire so strong, it felt as if I'd done it, or from the violence in suppressing that desire. A verse from a Greek poem my brother taught me long ago arose in my mind. *Love shook my heart, like a mountain wind falling upon the oak trees.*

Gawain frowned, "What did you say? I didn't understand."

To my horror, I realized I had uttered the words aloud. "Nothing, some Greek verse my brother taught me."

Somer must have observed my fascination with Gawain for he rushed over to my side, grabbed my arm, and brought me to the dance floor for a lively spin. Part of me was relieved for the interruption and part of me felt bereft, as if I had been orphaned all over again.

Somer's dislike of the royal family was no doubt strengthened by the fact that they embraced the old ways still, whereas he had converted to Christianity. It had been another reason for our father and Somer to quarrel. Our father had nothing but contempt for the new God, *an upstart, a bad copy of our more ancient and powerful Gods, Celt or Roman*.

I was delighted when Gawain asked permission to give me a small present. Somer could not refuse. It was my birthing day feast and to refuse a member of the royal family was unthinkable. But he glared at poor Gawain who took it all in stride, staring right back at Somer. Not many people could keep their countenance under my brother's scrutiny. These days, with his wife standing by his side, none would dare. And Gawain was still a young man, barely three years older than me. His courage increased my regard for him.

The gift was a little wooden bird Gawain had carved and painted himself. "The bird is a wren, a *dryw,*" he said. "That's why I painted it brown on top and orange below with a dark bill and a white eyebrow stripe."

I picked up his offering gingerly into my cupped hands. Before I could thank him, he pointed out that he made it from a walnut tree. "The grain runs true, and the wood is sturdy but not too hard to carve. And the piece I used had some good knots on it." Then he laughed at himself, which endeared him to me even more.

"I can go on about wood," he said, "I like working with it."

"I can tell." I grinned. "Is it magical?"

"Well, my mother, Lady Morgause," he began to explain.

"I know who she is," I interjected, to impress him with my knowledge of the royal family.

Gawain didn't hold my bad manners against me. He smiled and I forgot to breathe.

"My mother says that the wren is an augury for the druids on the winter solstice. It's a symbol of hope and renewal." He leaned in closer, "And may you always keep your curious mind and courageous heart."

It was as if Gawain knew something true about who I was, inside. His closeness stirred me, and I blushed. Again, I had the maddening urge to shift his soft curly hair away from his forehead with my fingers. He bowed and I curtsied back.

The wren was a humble thing, but it was a treasure. "Thank you, Gawain. I will keep it with me always." And I did. I would hold the little wren close for many years to come.

Gawain walked back to his parents who greeted him with fondness. An arm around his from his mother. A comfortable hand on the back from his father. I noticed how Gawain and his mother leaned toward each other as they talked. I envied their familiarity.

I barely tore my gaze away when Gawain returned and asked if I wanted to meet his parents. I looked around and saw my brother engaged in conversation with one of the local lords, a baron of little consequence who fawned over my brother with flattery as excessive as his ambition. I said yes. We walked over and I curtsied to the lady. She dressed simply for the wife of a king, but her neck was adorned with a magnificent necklace made of amber, and she wore gold bangles on her wrists. They were inscribed with magical looking signs.

"These are runes, child," said Lady Morgause, observing my interest in her bracelets. "Yours will come to you if it is meant to be."

Her words intrigued me so. I was keen to question her further but watched my brother stride across the hall with thunder in his eyes. The lady noticed him too. She wished me joy on this day and best of luck in the future. I thanked her with a curtsy. I thought she was beautiful and longed for her to become my mother-in-law and blushed at such desire. What I couldn't put into words for myself then was: *This is a woman who has power of her own and will not hide it.*

Lady Morgause smiled as Somer pulled me away. His eyes were leveled at her as if daring her to speak. She managed to look both mocking and sweet. Her smile said *I couldn't care less who you are or what you think.* She turned her full attention to her husband without another glance at my brother. I had never seen anyone put Somer in his place so effortlessly.

Gawain left his parents' side to fetch them a drink, with the same smile on his lips. And I smiled as well when I placed the little wren carving on my bedside table, so I could have it in my sight as I fell asleep that night, oblivious to the fact that my world was about to end for a second time since my father's death.

Chapter Two

Though he was five years my elder, Somer and I were inseparable in play and study. I followed him everywhere, the typical annoying little sister. I would run too fast for my feet, trip and fall and skin my knees. I tried to follow him up a tree where he built his tree house, lost my footing, missed the branch I was attempting to grasp, fell and broke my arm. Father called on Hillel. The man had been a physician on the isle of Malta before he came to us. He set the bone, which hurt, but distracted me with tales from his homeland. Warm milk and honey helped too.

When the wood splint and wrap came off, Lavinia was so diligent with her ministrations of castor oil and calendula poultice with a little rosehip thrown in, the scar was barely noticeable. "We don't want anything to mar that perfect skin, do we?" she said, "Not on my little Ragnella, Nella, Nella," she cooed.

When Lavinia called me *Nella*, it never failed to soothe my spirit and calm my body.

"Not when the marriage proposals will start to pour in soon."

I blushed and smiled. The bone finally healed in time for my eleventh birthday. Lavinia had a gift for me to celebrate. I loved surprises and presents. It was a linen handkerchief she had sewn for me. The linen was very fine. It made me feel so grown up, and I walked through the halls with it in my hand, holding it up between three fingers. I was copying the lady in the tapestry that hung in my father's study. She was an ancestor of ours and by all accounts a great lady. I thought I was doing a fine job until Somer told me I looked a fool and confiscated it.

Somer was my champion and took responsibility for many of my pranks while we were growing up, taking the whip on my behalf. The last time was the worst. He was fourteen and about to be sent away to Cornwall as an apprentice to the duke and his sons. I was nine years old and a foolish child.

I felt so terrible about it, I confessed in the middle of his beating that I was the one who had broken our father's favorite standing urn, a present from Emperor Theodosius upon his marriage to Somer's mother. I tried to climb inside it while we played hide and seek, and it fell over and broke into a hundred pieces. It seemed like a good hiding place at the time. We had exhausted all the other ones by then, all the alcoves, and armoires, and cubbyholes. But our father said Somer had already confessed and that it was his responsibility to look after me and keep me out of trouble.

"It's time Somer learned how to be responsible, if he is ever to become worthy of Dinas Emrys," said our father.

I worried that Somer believed it meant he would never be worthy. I loved Somer exactly the way he was then. He spent hours reading Aristotle and Plato and Marcus Aurelius and often listened in to my tutoring in Greek and Latin when he was home. He had more facility with languages than I did and helped me with my homework, making games out of it as only my sweet scholarly brother could.

Somer had just read Plato's Crito, the part when Socrates is already in his jail cell. My brother decided we should amuse ourselves by playing Socrates and Crito. He'd play Socrates and I would be Crito.

"I don't want to be Crito. I want to be Socrates." I pouted.

Socrates was the wise one, that was clear from the way Somer referred to him with such reverence. That's who I wanted to be, a wise elder.

"You be Crito now. You can be Socrates next time," said Somer. "Tell me I have to submit to the laws of *bios politikos*, the good life, Athens's sovereign laws. By going against those laws, and subverting the youth of Athens, I have excluded myself from the good life. And because I threaten the order of the State, my crime is punishable by death."

"All right," I said. I tried my best impersonation of someone who represented the law. My father came to mind. I frowned the way I'd seen him frown. Skinny arms crossed over my scrawny chest, standing erect, I faced my brother, chin held high.

"Socrates, you put yourself above the law, you turn the youth of Athens against us. You must submit to the laws of the State." Then I shook my index finger at him. "Under our sovereign laws, your crime is punishable by death."

Somer sat back, one leg dangling across the back of his chair, as if he didn't have a care in the world. "Yes, Crito. I agree. I believe in the *bios politikos*. I have lived many years of the good life. To live a bare life, to live like an animal, alone in the woods, excluded from the community, is not what I choose. I do not want to be separated from my fellow citizens, from the work I love, from my students, and the many who love me. I yield to the sovereign laws, even unto death. For that is better than a bare life. I will drink the poison."

Somer leaned forward, picked up his cup and drank it to the dregs. It was only pretend. There was only cider in our cups, but I was spellbound. When he fell over, I screamed and seized his hand with mine. He opened his eyes and laughed at me. I was so relieved, I cried while applauding his version of Socrates, like I did everything my brother conjured. As Crito, I could do nothing but listen and agree with him, but Socrates's death troubled me. Dying from poison seemed particularly abhorrent to me because he must force himself to drink it. He was too wise and good and beautiful to die.

Though I was too young to fully comprehend it then, I suspected that Somer felt trampled by our father's sovereign power as *pater familias*, and that he saw himself as a creature alone in the wilderness. I wanted to shout that we were in this together and that I would never abandon him. We never played this game again. And I never got to be Socrates.

Somer was fond of guessing games and riddles. He'd start a quote, and I'd try to finish it and then he'd ask me who the author was. He'd say, *it is not death that a man should fear, but he should fear never beginning to live.* I'd continue, *Accept the things to which fate binds you, and love the people with whom fate brings you together but do so with all your heart.* And together we'd end, laughing: *Never let the future disturb you.*

"So, do you have the author?" he smiled.

"Plato."

"You know better, little sister."

"Then if it's not Plato, it must be Marcus Aurelius."

"Indeed, it is," said my brother.

And then it was my turn, though it scarcely challenged him. "*Ho dè anexétastos bíos ou biōtòs anthrṓpōi.*"

"That is too easy little sister. *An unexamined life is not worth living*. Plato's Apology. Give me something harder."

"Let me think. *If you have a garden and a library, you have everything you need.*"

Somer stroked his chin with a finger then grinned. "Cicero."

"Yes!" I clapped my hands together.

"Unfortunately, Cicero is mistaken. A man also needs power to control his own fate."

I retorted, "*Non nobis solum nati sumus.*"

"*Not for ourselves alone are we born*. Cicero again, and again I disagree."

I was determined to have the last word. "Well, you cannot disagree with this. *Dwell on the beauty of life. Watch the stars and see yourself running with them. Such thoughts wash away the dust of earthly life.*"

"Yes, little sister. A beautiful sentiment indeed. But we are not emperors like Marcus Aurelius and need our wiles and guiles to live in this unpredictable world."

I took his hand and dragged him into our courtyard with its small interior garden to play, determined, as only a child can be, to change his views on life.

We didn't see as much of each other after Somer was sent away for his apprenticeship. He would come home for short holidays, like Candlemas or Yule, in a surly mood. I tried to cheer him up by recounting some of what happened while he was away. I told him about the trapper who was caught in his own trap, screaming louder than his prey. And how Hillel said he would fix his foot if the scoundrel mended his ways. Of course, the lad said yes but once mended, forgot all his promises and went back to his old ways.

"Serves Hillel right for helping the rascal!" said Somer.

"But shouldn't we always try to help someone in difficulty?" I asked.

"Not if it goes against your own interest," he answered.

"Why not?" I protested. "Don't we all deserve kindness in our dark times?"

"Who tells you such rubbish?"

"My ancilla, Lavinia. And Hillel too."

"Nonsense. If you are dealing with a scoundrel or worse, a traitor, and you help them, you'll end up having to deal with the same situation later and you'll only have yourself to blame."

Somer's answer disturbed me. And with all the conviction I could muster, I said, "*Misericordia invicta, quandiu sine adulatione vel hypocrisi.*"

"*Kindness is unconquerable so long as it is without flattery or hypocrisy*, Marcus Aurelius. Yes a fine quote, little sister. But not in this world, which is *all* about flattery and hypocrisy."

Somer sounded so bitter, I barely recognized my brother. "If that's what they are teaching you in Cornwall, I wouldn't want to go there."

"You're right about that. You wouldn't," he answered, rummaging an aggressive hand through his hair, jaw set, eyes darker than midnight.

I saw plainly then Somer's discontent.

When he returned several months later, I was beside myself with happiness at seeing him again. He gave me a warm enough embrace, but the lack of luster in his eyes and the heaviness in his step troubled my heart.

Though I was dismissed after our family meal and should have returned to my rooms, I hid in one of the many alcoves gracing the central hallway, somber enough for bats to hang there in winter. Father and Somer walked right by me, as they came out of the dining hall. Their voices bounced off the stone walls. Somer told our father how he was being mistreated, how he hated every minute there, and begged our father to let him come home even though it had only been a year. Father said no. He would come home when his apprenticeship was done in three years' time. And he was always welcome for the holidays. Our father could not offend the Duke of Cornwall.

"Do you have any idea what the Duke of Cornwall actually thinks of you, father?" asked Somer, eyes like burning coals.

"I can imagine," said Father. "Which is precisely why I cannot let you come home."

"They laugh at me because I'm your son and because I know more than they do. They throw me around like I'm a serf, a slave. They say I hold my sword like a girl and tell me I have to prove I'm a man by ordering me to kill a wretch of a peasant who dared to protect his daughter from the duke's eldest son. And I have to slash his entrails like a pig or maybe they'll kill me instead. Do you know what it's like to have a man's warm entrails and blood spill out on your hands and hear him screaming? Of course you do. You've probably done it a hundred times. Well, it's not who I am. It's not what I want. Do you not care?!" he screamed, his voice raw.

Our father remained silent, walking away from his son. Somer went back to Cornwall. I could tell my brother was devastated by our father's lack of compassion. My eyes stung at Somer's wretchedness and our father's intransigence.

Before he left, I talked Somer into one more conversation about his favorite subject, his mother, plying him with questions. He protested that I already knew it all, that I had asked him the same questions a hundred times before.

"Let it be a hundred and one times," I countered.

I thought it would be a relief for Somer to bend his thoughts toward a gentler subject. As Marcus Aurelius wrote *take care that you entertain no notions unsuitable to virtue and reasonable nature.*

"Tell me about her, and how they met," I said.

This was my ploy: to remind Somer of a joyous memory connecting our father to his mother. Somer was the companion of my most playful times, he was my best friend, and I looked up to him like a god, radiant with wisdom and beauty, his dark eyes with their perfect almond shape, and lashes longer than mine, his lanky frame, like a young elm, his effortless charm, bright mind and endless wit in three languages, and most of all his love of poetry. I couldn't bear to see him so unhappy, what it could do to his sensitive soul.

We headed to his chambers in the western tower. It was the darker, colder side of the castle, except for radiant sunsets that sometimes filtered through and could momentarily leave one blind. I skipped and ran ahead. He walked. Once there, we dragged some of the furs and cushions from the bed, close to the fireplace for warmth. His rooms were bare except for his bed covered with a mess of blankets and furs, a big trunk for his clothes, a better one with a lock for his precious books, a chair and his desk strewn with half-filled pages of poetry and several books of philosophy and religion, some left open with a feather for marker.

I hung onto the most cuddly of our dogs, our Cardigan corgi who looked so much like a fox, one of her ancestors must have had a dalliance with the *vulpes genus* at some point. I named her Daffodil, which our father frowned upon. He considered all our dogs working dogs, not pets. Daffodil was excellent at herding, but she also enjoyed human company. The rest of the pack stretched out by Somer's feet.

He began, "Magnus Maximus was a Celt-Iberic."

"From the Astures tribe," I interrupted, "His real name was Macsen Wledig."

"Who is telling the story? Am I or are you, little sister?"

"You are." I covered my mouth with my hand, trying to be serious, eyes crinkly from withholding laughter.

"Fine." He cleared his throat, "He became emperor of the Roman Western Empire, taking the lands by force. He was a great warrior, and the following year became emperor of Briton and Gaul as well. He then decided to invade Italia, but his greed was stronger than his army and he was defeated by Emperor Theodosius at the battle of Poetovio."

Now came the good part, the part I was waiting for.

"Magnus Maximus had a baby daughter, Sevira."

"Your mother!" I exclaimed. I couldn't help myself.

Somer ignored my interruption. "Who was so beautiful, Theodosius decided to adopt her as he had one son, Arcadius, and wanted a companion for his little daughter, Pulcheria. Sevira became even more precious to him after Pulcheria's untimely death at only eight years old.

"Were Arcadius and Sevira close, like we are?" I asked.

"Not quite. Arcadius loved his real sister more. He named his own daughter after her," he answered. "A couple of years later, our father arrived in Rome as a soldier and in a few years, climbed to hold the post of centurion. He pleased Theodosius so much with his courage and clever ways that the emperor made our father a member, first of the equestrian class, and then the patrician class, which is how Sevira and our father finally met. The merciless arrow of Eros pierced our father's heart the moment he laid eyes on Sevira. It is a testament of the love Theodosius harbored for our father that he agreed to the marriage, even though our father intended to take Sevira away."

I interrupted my brother again. I wanted to stop the story there, in their moment of complete happiness. "Tell me, what was she like?"

In a mood more somber than our grey skies, he said, "I remember the bracelets on her wrists and how they jingled when she touched my cheek and kissed me. She loved to adorn herself with lapis, and her silk rustled softly on the stone floors. She hated wearing shoes, but it was too cold here to go barefoot. She had soft leather mules woven with gold thread and wore those everywhere. She let me slip them on once. It was not easy to walk in them. I stumbled but she caught me before I fell and gathered me in her arms. Our eyes locked and we were lost in laughter together. It is my favorite memory of us."

"Was she very beautiful?" I asked, for that was important to me then.

"The most beautiful woman. No one compared. But when our father insisted on taking her to Arthur's court, the ladies there judged her because she looked different, not dainty and pale like they were. She was tall. Her skin was dark and luminous. Her stare could turn any confident man into a clumsy boy."

Somer spit those last words out as if he hated the world.

"The following summer, I was born. She was happy then but as fall came and then winter, it took a toll on her. Year after year, our cold, rain-drenched climate seeped into her bones. As she held me in her arms and then helped me stand up and learn to walk, she deteriorated from a strong and beautiful woman to a weak and melancholy shade. She died on the solstice, at the height of our summer. It was my fifth birthday. I believe the sunlit sky of that day gave her soul the wings she needed to finally fly home."

We sat in silence but for the crackling of the fire and the quiet snoring of the dogs. I had a revelation: his mother had named Somer for the warmth of the summer months, and his birth had been a blessing and a guard against the sodden sameness of our winters.

"Our father remarried a few months later," said Somer, interrupting my oracular reverie. "But his new happiness was short lived. It lasted just long enough for you to be born, little sister."

It was a mistake. I yearned to bring a pleasing memory into Somer's mind and instead there was bitterness in the air as heavy and damp as a blanket left out in the winter rain. I asked him about my mother, but he refused to talk about her.

His jaw clenched with impatience. "Ask our father."

"Somer, I'm sorry. I've upset you," I said.

"It's not your fault," he said.

I suppose he meant it was our father's fault. Who could blame him for thinking so? A part of me was afraid to find out more than I already knew. My father told me that my mother was from a good family and was praised for her graceful manners and ravishing looks. He must have been too aggrieved to say more. But it was hard to know so little. All I had was my own likeness, since our father said I looked so much like her. Somer would tease me, *wouldn't you prefer to look like yourself?* But when he saw my sad face, he relented and agreed that, *yes, don't worry, you do look like your mother.* That was a comfort, and I hung on to that for years until Lady Amunet came into our lives and I was easily seduced, starving as I was for feminine regard and a helping hand into the mysteries of womanhood.

Barely sixteen, Somer thought himself a man grown. Both he and our father had the same righteous stubbornness. We were together for dinner, a rare occasion. Somer was home from Cornwall and so was our father, who traveled a lot to take care of his large holdings all over northwestern Wales. The holdings stretched from the Irish sea in the west to the mountains of Snowdonia in the east, including the counties of Caernarvonshire and Merioneth.

Our father mentioned that he had transferred some of our woodlands further south to Gawain, King Arthur's nephew.

Somer exploded. "Why do you keep giving in to this left-handed king and his druid family?"

"You do not speak of the king in this manner if you belong to this house," said our father, barely containing his temper.

I knew Somer was referring to King Arthur's birth. His mother, Igraine, stolen by Uther Pendragon from her marriage bed and from her husband, a former ally, Gorlois, Duke of Cornwall. Cornwall, where Somer was struggling with his apprenticeship. No one loyal to the king spoke of his ambiguous beginnings or his father Uther's faults. And the House of Gwynedd was loyal to the king.

"Isn't it enough that you surrendered our red dragon to him so he could do battle against the Saxons and take all the glory to himself?"

"You better stop now, Somer. Do not speak another word."

Our father's temper was nearing its threshold. He was half raised out of his seat. His hands, fists on the table. I wished Somer would stop talking but he wouldn't or couldn't. He was a youth of sixteen, full of strong feelings and stronger convictions.

"Isn't it enough that we made our *bed* with the Hengist traitor?" he yelled.

Somer's last remark was pointed in a way I didn't understand, but our father lost his composure then and cleared the table of food and plates with the wrathful sweep of one arm. The plates clattered on the floor. I pressed my hands over my ears. The noise was so loud, the dining hall resonated with it. Our hounds, crouched under the table for scraps, scattered in fear. Our little Cardigan corgi, Daffodil, hid under my skirts. Father and son stared at each other like wolves about to pounce in a fight to the death.

"Are you that ignorant, boy? Even your sister understands," he said, pointing at me.

I wanted to disappear, crawl into one of my hiding places.

"I'm doing this for your future. Placing you at a political advantage. Don't you get it? Our allies matter in this world. You know nothing of the king and his family. His friendship is more important to me than you can ever imagine. He accepted me at court when everyone else turned their back on me. In any case, it's my decision."

"It seems the king is more important than your children or you wouldn't be giving away their inheritance," said Somer.

"You best stop talking, or you'll have no inheritance at all," snapped our father.

"I know very well what you would do if you could."

I looked at our father, wondering what Somer meant, what our father's intentions were. Somer stood up then, vibrating with all the barely contained rage of an adolescent. I was so worried about what might happen next, I pleaded with both of them to end their quarrelling. They heard me, but they didn't listen. No one listens to an eleven-year-old girl. I loved them both and couldn't bear to watch them fight. It frightened me. They were the two pillars of my life and the glue to my heart.

I held my breath as our father untied his belt and started to hit Somer, but my brother would not submit to the punishment anymore. Though he was not as big as our father, he had filled out quite a bit in the last year and managed to catch the end of the belt as it was about to strike him. Somer wrenched it out of our father's hand, surprising them both. He held it for a dreadful moment when I thought he might hit our father back, then with scorn etched on his face, he dropped the belt between them, like a dead snake on the flagstone floor.

"I'm leaving for Rome. I've already made arrangements," said Somer.

"You owe the duke two more years," said Father. And then, he uttered those terrible words, "If you do not return to Cornwall to complete your apprenticeship, you're no son of mine."

"So be it," answered Somer. "I knew how it would be when I came home. I've taken enough abuse from the Duke of Cornwall and his foul sons *because of your loyalty to the king,* and I won't take anymore from you. I'm done. I'd rather die on a battlefield in some foreign land!"

He almost did.

Until his departure, Somer confined himself to his chambers, reading, and spent a great deal of time at the church, recently completed, in our neighboring village of Beddgelert, in the company of the new priest. I followed him in secret, like a new game of hide and seek, not as we had done before, in play, but a serious game, where I was spying on my own brother as if he was a stranger and I dared not come too close for fear he'd discover me.

The priest's surly face and gaunt appearance left me ill at ease. He wore a big cross on his chest that he fingered all the time like a charm. I couldn't imagine what attracted my brother to him. They sat and spoke together for hours, near Gelert's tomb, the faithful hound mistakenly killed by his master when it was protecting the master's baby son from a wolf. It was a well-known story, but I cried for the wolfhound whenever I thought of it and also for the master who was so sorry for his mistake, he never smiled again. Misunderstandings can create such discord as to ravage a family. I refused to believe this could happen to us, even though it was clear Somer and our father were deeply at odds.

I tried to coax Somer out on walks or on riding adventures and failed. I brought him my latest attempts at poetry on small scraps of pressed birch bark. He was studying the bible borrowed from his new best friend and put my poems aside on his desk with barely a glance. Later I found my efforts discarded on the floor, crumpled like wilted flowers. He preferred the company of the priest to mine.

Eventually I gave up and spent my time at the stables with Espoir, my new palfrey. We were getting to know each other. He was only a yearling but already showed a lot of promise. His strutting and bucking in the corral belied a kind and trusting heart. He nickered as I approached and let me braid his mane and nibbled bits of apple and choice grasses from my hand. Caden, our father's marshal, helped me. Caden was in charge of the stables, and he knew horses. He taught me that patience and kindness were far better tools than the whip to establish trust. He showed me how to praise and reward Espoir for any little try and ignore his mistakes. How to end a session on a good note even if it meant doing less.

Somer did not share another meal with us, nor did he speak to our father again until he left for Rome. He barely said a word to me. I clung to him anyway as he was getting ready to depart. I grabbed on to his boot and got on my toes. He gave in and bent down to give me a kiss on the cheek from the height of old Angus, his patient and faithful Shire warhorse.

"Don't be too hard on our father, please Somer."

"He's the one who is hard on me, little sister. You have his heart. I get his scorn and his belt. I cannot tolerate it anymore."

"He loves you. But you are his son. He has expectations. I just need to be pretty and find a husband." I was trying to be lighthearted but not succeeding very well.

"That shouldn't be too hard," he quipped.

"I don't know about that," I said.

"I do."

I couldn't tell if he was paying me a compliment or insulting me or both. Somer had wit enough to do that to people he regarded as fools. But he didn't do that to me, never to me, at least not until now. His quarrel with our father must be the reason.

"*Omnia Mutantur*," he said. It was his favorite quote from Ovid's Metamorphosis. It meant *Everything is changed.*

"*Nihil interit*," I answered with all the love in my heart. It was the rest of the quote: *Nothing perishes*. In a way, it was my prayer to all the Gods for my brother to return to us.

He yanked himself away, kicking Angus into a gallop. I watched him ride off until I lost sight of him on the other side of the hill. My heart ached for him and for our father.

Chapter Three

My child's mind assumed Somer would return in a few months, a year at most, and I would have contrived how to mend things between him and our father. But the weeks and months went on and on and I transformed from an eleven-year-old child into a fourteen-year-old rebel seeking to understand the mysteries of my own body, and how to become a woman.

I watched the tenants in our farms, how the women in the village walked with the menfolk, conveyed confidence or shyness with their step or a tilt of the head, how they could be tender with a familiar hand gesture, how they talked to their men, husbands, sons, brothers, able to change their moods, bring them back from anger or defeat, tease them in a way that brought smiles to their faces. How easily they created irrevocable bonds, connections, families. I knew nothing of this, how to do this. I had no example, no mother to show me the way.

I couldn't learn any of this from my ancilla, Lavinia. Her wisdom was of the crone. She understood the pain of menses though, and made me some decoction with catnip, skullcap, and hawthorn bark. The taste made my nose wrinkle and my mouth pucker, but it helped.

I missed Somer every day, hoping he was safe, knowing he had set aside his beloved philosophy and love poems for soldiering. I also envied him, getting to travel the world, visiting places we had both dreamed about, Hispania, Egypt and other faraway lands.

When I wasn't riding Espoir bareback through the woods, I studied relentlessly as if I had something to prove. I wanted Somer to be proud of me when he returned.

Lavinia spoke with my father, suggesting that it was time for me to learn more womanly arts, like sewing and dancing. That I needed to stop riding like a wanton child. We argued about it, and I lost. My time was not wholly my own anymore. I didn't mind dancing but found no value in learning to sew since others, like my ancilla, would make all my shirts and gowns for me when I became a proper lady with a holding of my own and a husband.

I also wanted to surprise my father, delight him again, make up for Somer's absence. The way he was surprised when I sat on his lap, a mere three-year-old, pointing a pudgy finger to a word on the parchment he was perusing and in my little piping voice pronouncing, *rop*. Father looked at my pointed finger and read the word *crop*. It was close enough and he was astounded. He immediately got me a tutor and a year later I could read and write. He then sent Hillel to Rome with a mission to hire the best philosophers and teachers.

Despite being slaves, some of them had high ranking positions in the best patrician houses, and even with the emperor. Our father told Hillel that he could promise them freedom, a paid salary and their own homes. No matter how well-regarded one might be, to be a slave is to be unsafe. Many of the upper class, the great Patrician families who claimed "founders of Rome" status, were jealous of the slaves, especially the ones who had the ear of the emperor. Being clever or intelligent could be a blessing or it could cost you your life in a dark alley of the city. They liked my father's offer and came to Dinas Emrys.

By the age of eight, my Greek and Latin were honorable. Somer had taught himself how to read and write and asked if he could attend my classes. Our father thought it was a waste of time for a knight but didn't actively forbid it. Somer became my partner in our lessons until his apprenticeship in Cornwall took him away from us for months at a time. He turned out to be the better student of the two of us and would always participate when he was home.

It was all about love poetry for Somer in those days. I would listen to him, enraptured, and clap afterwards as he made a sweeping bow. He taught me what became my favorite line from the great poetess

Sappho, *Love shook my heart, like a mountain wind falling upon the oak trees.* It gave me such a feeling though I knew nothing of romantic love.

My love went to my father and Somer, to my palfrey, Espoir, to Hillel and Lavinia, and to Daffodil, my little Cardigan corgi, her of the rounded ears and foxlike tail. She favored Somer, all the dogs did then, but I let her sleep with me sometimes and gave her treats. When I met Gawain at my birthing day feast, Sappho's line of poetry came to life in an entirely new way. I believed I finally grasped the fullness of its meaning.

My love for the night sky was in a special sphere of its own. Hillel told me that the stars were different in different parts of the world. He missed the night sky of Malta, *an infinite darkness pierced with numberless stars reflected in the ocean, like a god slashed through the night to make a great shimmering path.* He made it sound like heaven and the underworld were the same thing, a different path to follow to the same destination.

Hillel complained that there were too many clouds in Wales for good stargazing. But I thought the rarity of a cloudless sky made their appearance far more precious. The stars opened a vastness in my mind I didn't know existed. Most of the time my mind was filled with small thoughts, everyday concerns about my horse, my lessons, who was visiting and when the next feast would be. When I looked upon the night sky, my mind reached out into unfathomable spaces. I wondered about belonging to such strangeness; what people were doing on the other side of the world, if they had the same concerns, and if not, how were they different. I wondered about my place in the world and what choice I had in the matter. If I belonged to myself at all, or mainly to my father, to Dinas Emrys, to the lands of Gwynedd and to this time and place in our history. I would become dizzy contemplating all of this.

I preferred Hillel to any of my other more formal tutors. He had lived in so many foreign places from Malta to Egypt and Rome of course. In Egypt he was an apothecary for a time. He worked with precious stones like lapis lazuli. With him, I could talk about hidden things, difficult things, like the color blue, or the meaning of a starlit sky.

While Somer was away, soldiering in foreign lands, our father and I became inseparable. I was his second in command, after Hillel. We walked everywhere around Dinas Emrys, or he carried me on his destrier, in front of him, until I was able to ride Espoir on my own without the stubborn beast throwing me. I never got the knack of riding like a lady, side saddle. I rode astride. My ancilla, Lavinia, protested but our father dismissed it. I was still very young and so it didn't matter if I dressed like a boy to ride through the forest or accompany him to the farms, as long as I changed into a proper attire for supper, which Lavinia made sure I did. And I did like to wear a pretty dress once in a while.

On our adventures around the county, my father and Hillel talked at length about everything: the crops, our tenants, and shared stories from their time in Rome, sometimes forgetting I was even there. It was then I learned Hillel himself had been a slave to a Patrician family in Messina, serving as their overseer.

"Until your father freed me. He convinced the family to let me go, for a substantial price, I might add," he said, including me in the conversation.

During one of our journeys to Beddgelert, Hillel and our father recounted the building of Dinas Emrys. We were on our way to meet some new tenants. Hillel was riding his thirty-two-year-old mule, Camila. Our pace was slow out of respect for Camila's advanced age. The weather was a steady grey, white clouds held back the sun, and darker clouds held the rain that would come down later. The grass, a verdant green.

Hillel began, "Your father knew the hillock was the perfect place for a fortress. We'd be able to see for miles around and the Saxons would think twice about trying to attack it. Our troubles began right away. Every day the men would work hard erecting the first of several proposed towers; but the next morning they would return to find the masonry collapsed in a heap. This continued for many weeks. We were living in tents all around the valley. Finally, a local peasant said that there were two dragons living under that hillock, in an underground lake and they didn't take kindly to our building. He said there was no way to get rid of them except with the help of druids."

Father took over the telling. "Except the druids were of no help. They wouldn't come near the dragons. No matter how much money I offered."

"Your father didn't believe there were any dragons at all," said Hillel. "Until our local man took us to the entrance of the cave on the back of the hill and we found ourselves in the Underworld."

"The Underworld?" I asked, spellbound.

"Not the Underworld. You exaggerate Hillel," said Father. "It was a sizable underground cave with a vast lake at the center of it. And yes, there were two dragons living there. The screaming sound of a dragon is like nothing I have ever heard or ever want to hear again."

"We were as mice are to a horse," said Hillel.

"Yes, exactly so," said Father. "They chose to speak to me in my mind. A very peculiar sensation. They had been confined here for a thousand years and wanted to be liberated. Or else they would continue to prevent my building efforts. We didn't know how to negotiate with dragons. I didn't want to liberate them if they were going to go on a rampage. Unless of course, they could be used to our advantage, against the Saxons."

"Lord Vortigern, ever the wily commander," confided Hillel, with a side smile.

I sighed, wishing I could meet a real dragon.

Father resumed, "I spoke with the locals, and they said the only way to ensure the dragon's cooperation was to sacrifice a fourteen-year-old boy, born of a maiden and a devil, which they happen to have on hand and promptly delivered to me, tied up like a pig."

"They wanted to get rid of him because they were frightened," said Hillel. "They didn't understand his power and wanted him dead. And your father was to conveniently oblige them."

"What happened to the boy?" I asked.

"No harm came to him," said Father.

I was relieved to hear Father say so.

"He proved far too wise and gifted with a power beyond anything I ever encountered."

"You know him as Myrddin Emrys. Some call him Merlin," said Hillel.

My eyes opened wide at the name. His gifts were legendary throughout the kingdom.

"He's not a boy anymore. He has become the greatest druid of our time," said father. "This happened over twenty ago now. Myrddin

Emrys spoke the language of dragons even then. He could speak into their own minds. He told me he could bind the red dragon but only to a king. I replied, *that's fine with me as long as any rampage to be done is on behalf of the Celts, against the Saxons*. Which is what happened, after he was able to bind the red dragon to King Arthur."

"What about the other dragon?" I asked, enthralled that dragons existed.

"The white dragon wished to go home and so she did, to the northern country. She wanted nothing to do with the world of men. And Dinas Emrys was built."

"And the lake is still there," said Hillel. "There is a secret underground path from the lake all the way to the Glaslyn River."

"I know about that," I said proudly.

Father frowned, "How do you know?"

"Somer told me," I said, wondering if I got my brother in trouble once again.

"She might as well know," said Hillel to my father. "In case she ever has need of it." Hillel knew exactly what to say to placate my father's temper.

We arrived at our destination, and I heard nothing of our meeting with the new tenants. I suppose it went well because they took up residence at the farm. All I could think of were the existence of dragons and secret passages. I wondered, *how does one bind a dragon to a king?* It didn't occur to me that the *why* might be even more important than the *how*.

Chapter Four

Despite their falling out, Somer made use of our father's connections to advance rapidly in the Roman army. Father had been adopted into Emperor Theodosius's family because of his fight against the Saxons, in particular, his resistance against the Saxon leader Hengist and his brother Horsa. My father had then managed to convince Hengist to align himself with the Romans and Britons against the other Saxon tribes. Hengist had received the isle of Thanet on the Eastern coast of Briton in return for his cooperation.

It was incomprehensible to me that my father was considered a traitor by some of the local nobility because he had survived an attempt on his life on the *Night of the Long Knives*. The treachery was the Saxons' and Hengist's. After all, Hengist had taken advantage of the situation to proclaim himself King of Kent (Thanet was only separated from the province of Kent by the small channel of Wantsum) and it greatly offended the Romans.

The empire had grown so vast by then, they couldn't keep hold of it all. The Romans couldn't fight everybody everywhere. Father had saved their honor by pushing back against the Saxon invasion and winning a great victory on their behalf, right here at Dinas Emrys. I couldn't understand why Father wasn't more upset at the talk of his treachery, that he must have plotted with Hengist to get rid of the other leaders that night. He didn't even try to rectify the lies. He said it would be a waste of time, that people believed what they wanted to believe not what was true. The important people knew his honor.

"Important people?" I asked.

"Like you," he answered, pinching my nose. It was his way of showing affection and I reveled in it, despite my protestations.

"Like King Arthur and the royal family," I said, proud of my learning.

He nodded. "Yes, like that."

Many of Briton's leaders died on that fateful night, and some of the nobles thought my father should have too. But the Romans rewarded my father, granting him vast holdings beginning with Dinas Emrys and much more, so that his lands in Wales rivaled King Arthur's. The king was wiser than most. He valued a strong ally against the Saxon invaders. One of the only other leaders of their clan who survived that night was Lord Kay, King Arthur's uncle. But no one said anything about *him* being a traitor. My outrage only made Father laugh.

Perhaps what really irked these nobles was my father's vast holdings. They must be jealous of his wealth. Some people are. Father told me so before he died. *They will covet what you possess and sometimes attempt to kill you for it.* I didn't want anyone to covet what I possessed or try to murder me for it. I would rather have nothing at all.

Somer returned to Dinas Emrys about a year before our father's death. His campaigns with the Roman legions had spanned the Mediterranean, from Hispania all the way to Egypt. Somer had made a name for himself as a leader of men. Knowing him as I did as a gentle soul, a poet, who preferred letters to swords, I never thought my brother would follow in our father's footsteps. But his apprenticeship in Cornwall had ignited a change in him, the consequences of which would alter all our lives forever.

Like our father, Somer came home with a foreign lady who brought her wealth and her ways with her. But the lady was not like Somer's mother had been, languishing for her own country, its blue skies and white sand. Lady Amunet had spent a great deal of time traveling and living in other countries, in Hispania, in Rome and Roman Gaul, as her father had many commercial interests, on top of being one of Emperor Theodosius' personal physicians.

There was a thaw between Somer and our father when my brother first returned from warring on the continent. They seemed relieved to be able to discuss their war time experiences, one soldier to another.

That they both encountered berserkers during their soldiering was a bond they could share. I never heard our father refer to warriors with such a mixture of horror and awe. It wasn't fit conversation for the dining hall, not with a young lady present, but they had forgotten about me. I endeavored to make myself invisible, barely taking a breath for fear of being noticed.

Our father sat back in his chair, lost in thought as he spoke. "These worshippers of Odin, who attach themselves to kings and noble courts and fight, like the wild bears they are named after. They are clad in nothing but bear skin, and they fear nothing, not even death. They bite their own shields in a frenzy of rage as they attack. It's the most frightening experience I've ever had in combat."

He leaned in as if daring Somer to come up with his own story of the berserkers. Lady Amunet walked in, interrupting the conversation. She took my breath away, gliding over the stone floor with the carriage of a queen and the languid step of a cat. I secretly admired her painted face and elaborate costumes, but our father frowned upon them. Nevertheless, he got up and offered his hand to lead her to the table. He was treating her as an honored guest, but she stepped away as if affronted by his solicitude. He was only doing his duty as head of the household. There was no insult intended. And he certainly didn't covet my brother's wife. That was clear to me. But she seemed offended anyway. Somer stood up and rescued his wife, showing her a seat next to his. After she was settled and graciously accepted the cup of wine my brother offered, he asked our father on what occasion he'd had the misfortune of meeting the berserkers in combat.

"They were Hengist's hired men," our father answered. "I met them on the battlefield when we were fighting Hengist. But my worst memory comes from the Night of the Long Knives. They surged out of the darkness and into our camp like devils. It was during peace talks with Hengist, so we weren't prepared. They cut the throats of so many of us with their knives, I barely had time to unsheathe my sword. I shared a tent with Lord Kay and a few others. We fought side by side and back to back, forming a defensive circle to protect ourselves with our shields, until reinforcement arrived. Lord Kay and I saved each other over and over again. His men were only due the next day but arrived early. They rescued us from certain death. It was the most harrowing night of my life."

Somer stiffened. "A smart move from the traitor not to get his own men involved." He abruptly changed the subject, "Your great friend, Emperor Theodosius, has been baptized."

Somer was goading our father. Did Theodosius's conversion mean he was no longer the friend he had been?

"I hear he found his new faith after a serious illness," said our father. "But tell me, what of your own encounter with the berserkers?"

"In Gaul, fighting the Alemanni, and against the Sarmatians in the Balkans," Somer answered. "Each time was a blood bath. The last battle I fought, I was severely wounded across my chest. The cuts were so deep as to expose the bones. I could see my own heart barely beating. I was certain I would die."

My brother had faced death. I could see the image in my mind. My eyes filled with the shock of it: *I almost lost my brother.* But he recounted the whole event with a dull voice, as if it meant nothing at all. I wondered if it was to impress our father or if it was too unbearable to remember. I thought the latter.

"I was taken to the emperor's tent," he said. "His doctor looked after me until I was well enough to travel, then sent me to his house in Thessaloniki to convalesce. That is how I met his daughter, Lady Amunet." He reached across the table and squeezed his lady's hand. The confidence in her smile said it all. She harbored no doubt of her significance in my brother's life.

My stomach clenched. My mouth went dry. I worried that Somer would not have any love left over for me but reassured myself that our familial bond was unbreakable.

Our father received Lady Amunet graciously even though she was not yet married to Somer. I hoped Somer understood our father did that for his benefit but every word out of my brother's mouth was like a challenge to our father. "Lady Amunet and I were officially engaged back at her family home in Thessaloniki. Her family celebrated with a sumptuous feast in our honor. Princes and priests were in attendance. But I wanted us to come home, to be married here, at the church with our local priest officiating."

Father grumbled about the church and home being two different things. I was the only one to hear it because I was seated next to him. My brother and his wife were seated at the other end of the banquet table. Somer continued, "Theodosius has called the council of Constantinople. All pagan practices are now forbidden, including the Olympic Games."

"It's his prerogative," Father snapped. "A mistake I wager he'll come to regret."

My brother's affection for Christianity had grown more entrenched and he, more devout, as far as I could tell. It was another wedge between Somer and our father.

Our father confessed to me that he found the lady problematic. *Like Lady Morgause*, I thought. Even her name irritated him. It was all the trouble he had trying to pronounce it, calling my brother's wife *Lady Amenut* or *Lady Anemut*. Never her proper name.

I, on the other hand, was captivated. I invited myself into Lady Amunet's rooms and plied her with questions about the world, since I knew none of it. Somer would walk in on us and scold me for pestering his lady. She was kind and bid me stay.

I asked about the meaning of her name. She whispered in my ear that it was a secret and asked if I could keep a secret. I said yes, of course. A secret always contained magic and anything to do with magic enthralled me. That's why I loved our home so much. It was built on the magic of dragons. Lady Amunet's was not a Christian name even though the family was baptized by the bishop of Constantinople at the same time as the emperor.

"I was named for the Hidden One," she said. "The Egyptian primordial Goddess, mother who is also father of the before time, the invisible obscurity." Her voice as dark and warm as the perfume of musk and honey in her hair.

In my mind, she *was* the Goddess or at the very least, her priestess. She gave me a long silk scarf of a color I had never seen, different from the blue I had learned about in my studies. She said it was turquoise like the Mediterranean Sea. I wore it every day for a while and then not at all, after my ancilla remarked that if I kept wearing it, it would not last very long.

My ancilla, Lavinia, was practical and wise in a way I wasn't. She had been with me since the beginning. She had too many duties and no time to coddle me, but she was kind. She would attend to me on special occasions when we had visitors, and I needed to be more than merely presentable. She'd help me dress and comb my hair then. Otherwise, I was left to my own devices.

My appearance was of concern to me. My father told me it was one of my assets as well as the fortune he would bestow upon me when I came of age. So, I took care as best I could, especially with my hair, which fell down my back. I spent time untangling and combing through it with my fingers.

Lady Amunet's arrival changed things for me. She lent me some of her creams and potions, made with myrrh, frankincense and other aromatic oils like the helichrysum, named after the Sun God.

"Not only does it beautify the skin," she explained, touching her face lightly with two fingers, "But it can heal it too."

I believed it. Her skin was flawless. And I felt privileged that she would share her beauty treatments with me. She showed me how to wash my face with rose water at night, and she gave me a comb with ox horn teeth and a carved silver handle for my hair. It was so beautiful I was afraid to break it.

Lady Amunet spent hours sitting in front of her mirror, painting herself, adorning herself, and showing me how to do the same. The mirror was unique. It had a slight green tinge and was only a little rounded, with no distortion that I could tell. It was brought all the way from Rome. A renowned craftsman from Moorish Hispania had put the finishing touches on it. Great care was taken in the unwrapping and installing of it in her rooms. It was a most exciting occasion. I did spend quite a lot of time looking at myself in her mirror, becoming enamored with my likeness, whenever she allowed me to visit.

After studying her applications, sitting at her feet like the most ardent of followers, I went back to my rooms with a few pots of my own, to try it on my face. The results on me proved less than ideal and my ancilla laughed at my painted face, red lips, and black kohl rimmed eyes. I defended myself, citing Lady Amunet, *black and green kohl have medicinal and sacred properties.* For some reason, this made my ancilla laugh even louder. My pride injured, I turned my back on her and refused to speak with her after that. My silence toward my dear Lavinia continued for far too long, I'm ashamed to say. But she was patient with me. I was barely fourteen years old and desperately needed the attention of a great lady to look up to. Lady Amunet was the only one I knew.

We made a habit of the lady brushing my hair when we met in her rooms. She'd sit behind me, both of us facing the mirror, and we would talk about things. She told me of her mother and their relationship.

"My mother would brush my hair in just the way I am doing now," she said. "We were, and still are, very close. We did everything together. Planned our future for our family. How to best support my father to become the most important physician in all of the Roman Empire. My mother comes from a family of traders in medicines and rare spices, so they were a good fit. We moved from Egypt to Thessaloniki where Emperor Theodosius had his main residence."

"What is Egypt like?" I asked, thrilled with her every word.

"Egypt is the sacred land of the most ancient gods, with hot winds, white sand and blue skies as far as the horizon goes. There are outdoor markets, which are called *souk* in our border cities, made of mud bricks from sand and water."

"*Souk.*" I repeated the word to taste its strangeness on my tongue.

"At the end of the day, you can see the Tuaregs, the men of the desert tribes, in their blue robes and turbans, fly home to their oasis on their black horses, across the desert. The sun turns the walls of the city to flame then."

Her description took my breath away. I *was* the Tuareg. I *felt* the hot desert wind like a caress on my skin. I could hear the exaltation in her voice when she spoke of her home. It sounded so entrancing. She must miss it, I thought.

"What was it like when you arrived in Thessaloniki?" I asked.

"It was like a game," she said, her eyes bright with the memory of it.

Her answer was unexpected. Lady Amunet was full of mystery, like her name.

"We plotted together and found out which were the important people to meet, what must be sacrificed or taken off the board completely, what must be cultivated and kept close. It was a thrill to be at my mother's side and observe, as she knew exactly what to do. I was glad to help her achieve our goals in any small way I could. Our family always came first."

I was spellbound and amazed that she confided in me this way. I was entirely in agreement with her that family must come first.

"I'm sorry," she said. "Does it hurt you when I speak of my closeness with my mother? I forgot you grew up as a motherless child."

"No," I rushed to answer, worried she might stop telling me stories. "On the contrary. I like hearing about your relationship with your mother. It sounds so exciting."

"Yes, it was exciting, and I will always remember that time. But as I grew up, becoming a young woman, as *you* are, learning how to adorn myself and wear the right clothes was just as thrilling in a different way."

We could speak like this for hours. As the weeks went on, she started asking me about the castle, the lands, the crops. She was interested in everything, the type of crops, the weather patterns, the rotations of the crops and so I told her everything I knew, including all the innovations Hillel had brought to our lands and how it had improved everyone's lives.

One day, several weeks after her arrival, Lady Amunet looked at me pensively through her mirror and asked, "What if your brother Somer took over the affairs of Dinas Emrys, instead of your father? Wouldn't you say it's time?" With a lop-sided smile, she said, "Perhaps Lord Vortigern should set his sights on more quiet endeavors. He is getting quite old. I know Somer thinks so."

It seemed a very odd suggestion to me. My body grew rigid with disapproval under her ministrations. I no longer wished for her to brush my hair, but she held on to it and kept doing so. I felt caught in her gaze in the mirror, and in her hands at the same time.

"Somer has mentioned none of this to me," I said. "He knows very well there is nothing old about our father." I freed my hair from her hold, got up and faced her. I went on a bit of a rant then. I couldn't help myself. "His stride is swift and confident. The miles he rides or the walks he takes across our lands with our overseer, would exhaust men half his age. Our father is indestructible. He could spend half the night carousing with his men yet be fit to ride at dawn. It would take Arawn, the God of the Underworld himself to stop him."

Arawn was one of the only Welsh Gods I knew. He had taken my mother. I wished I could unspeak his name, but it was too late for that.

Lady Amunet waited until I was done with my tirade and spoke between tight lips, "I think we are done for today. Why don't you return to your room and your little amusements."

I left, feeling as if I had failed a test, as if I had damaged my relationship with Lady Amunet beyond repair. My stomach churned with it or perhaps it was all those rose flavored sweets I had eaten. Lady Amunet called them *Rahat Lokum* and always offered me some when I visited with her. They came all the way from Turkey, and I couldn't say no.

I was avoiding my dear Lavinia at the time because of my friendship with Lady Amunet, so I went looking for Hillel instead. Hillel ben Avram was our overseer. This Jew from Malta was the smartest man I knew, besides my father and my brother. He managed to thrive under both Arab and Norman rule until he was forced to leave or convert to Christianity. He chose to leave.

I came upon our father pacing back and forth in Hillel's office near the stables. Hillel could have had grand rooms in the castle. Our father had offered them to him long ago. But Hillel preferred his office outside the castle proper, behind the stables, and his own house nearer the woods. He said the distance helped him think better.

Father's pacing was short in strides, as the space was cramped with coffers full of treasuries accounting notes and papers and reduced to a few feet in any direction, but energized with his furious temper nonetheless. I didn't see Hillel right away. He was quietly sitting behind his small desk, waiting for our father to address him.

I squeezed myself in the shadowy recesses of the hallway, hoping they wouldn't notice me, and I'd hear the real story.

"Dinas Emrys is not for her and her family to expand their *trade*. It's not her land. That's final. I told her no."

I knew they were speaking of Lady Amunet which was a strange coincidence since I had come seeking Hillel's advice about her.

"We might be able to put *some* land aside, My Lord," suggested Hillel.

Hillel thought as I did, there was a possible compromise, but I knew my father wouldn't take it. Dinas Emrys was too important to him for any kind of conciliatory move, unless it involved the King. Then it was a different matter.

"Out of the question. I do not bargain with my lands. Somer needs to reign that woman in, or I will."

They were silent for a moment, then both turned to me at once, and I came out of hiding. I knew better than to add to the discussion. I smiled and asked our father if he would like to go for a ride. He found it a splendid idea:

"A good ride will certainly help get all that murky business out of this body." He slapped the sides of his body, his big stride propelling him out of the room.

Hillel gave me a look, for he knew I'd come to see him. I shrugged my shoulders, to let him know it could wait. And I ran out to catch up with our father. A ride was always something to look forward to. He didn't mind if we raced. He found my prowess on a horse gratifying. And he always beat me anyway. Not by much, since I turned fourteen.

The stables being right around the corner, we soon had our horses ready with the help of our stable hands.

"Race you to Beddgelert?" I challenged.

The village was not very far. Only a few miles but the trail could be treacherous, up and down hillocks, around waterfalls and wooded areas. It took skill, not just mindless speed, which is what my father and I loved best.

"Done," he said. What do I get when I beat you?

"The first dance at my birthing day feast," I answered.

"That's not a real prize, since I'm getting the first dance anyway," he laughed.

It was a year out, but we had already started to make plans.

"The second dance then," I offered.

"You'd better give that one to your brother or he'll be offended, and I won't hear the end of it."

It was my turn to laugh. We got on our horses and rode off. It was a wonderful afternoon even though he still beat me. I told him I was sure to beat him by the time I turned fifteen.

He pinched my nose, as was his habit. "No doubt, my little Amazon. No doubt."

Chapter Five

Perhaps my curse really started when our father got sick. He wouldn't get better no matter what the doctors tried. I heard him yelling at them through his chamber door, calling them incompetent, quacks and other choice epithets like *good-for-nothings fashioned from the dung heap*. I would slip into his room after they had gone and lie next to him on the bed. I told him stories, about the fractious new stallion our stable marshal, Caden, was training for him, about our old nanny goat, Marybelle, and how she had been more ornery than usual that morning and poor Jasper, who worked at the stables, had taken such a kick in the shins, he kept hopping about like a chicken on one leg. Father guffawed like his old self at my silly tale, and it was such a relief to hear his boisterous laughter, I thought I would cry.

My brother stayed away, and I know our father was sad though he wouldn't speak of it. He would ask, "How is your brother? Is he well? Is he happy with his lady?"

"Yes father. He is. And very busy with all the farms," I'd answer. Though we both knew it wasn't true. The farms had reliable tenants to care for the arable lands. And we had our trusted overseer.

Hillel was good at everything he did. He was a healer who could actually help people. He listened to them. And everything he planted grew. He listened to the plants the same way he listened to people, with quiet reverence. When he crossed paths with my father in Messina, they recognized and valued each other. They shared a passion for finding ways to improve the life of people, with better crops, food, education.

After he paid for his freedom, my father convinced Hillel to come work for him, and Hillel ben Avram accepted the offer. It was clear that he was his own person and would not tolerate being anyone's slave ever again and father respected that. They made a deal. Hillel would oversee father's farmlands, but he would also have some land of his own to do with it as he pleased and a home of his own.

They would often go on long walks together discussing more than crops. I tagged along because my father thought Hillel was the smartest man he knew. On those walks, they were equals. There was no lord and serf. Hillel talked about the importance of not just weather, rainfall and the nature of the soil, but the spirit of the plant. How certain plants grew better in the presence of other plants, compatible or friendly plants who created more harmony and enhanced each other, and how some needed to be avoided as they would fight with each other over sun, soil and rain. Just like some people harmonize well together and others do not. He called it companion planting. Lettuce liked strawberries. Squash and pumpkin were friends with marigolds, radishes, and nasturtiums. He also recommended fast growing vegetables such as lettuce or spinach next to slower crops like our little purple carrots. As the first crop was harvested the slower growing plants had more room to grow and mature. He domesticated our wild vegetables like turnips and parsnips and cabbage, so we had more steady supplies during the winter months.

Father praised Hillel to the skies. To hear him talk about it, Hillel was a revolutionary of farming, a genius of agriculture, but he did it in such simple ways, made minor suggestions, like *why don't you plant some celery next to the cabbage, or those lettuces would do well with a strawberry plant next to it.* And when it worked, the farmers were more inclined to listen to overhauling the entire system.

Farmers tend to be set in their ways so it's not always easy to open their minds to new ideas. But Hillel did it. And in five years' time no one starved in Gwynedd anymore. Everyone had enough to eat even through the worst of the winter season. Word got around. And the lords from neighboring counties asked to borrow Hillel so he could show their tenants what to do. My father agreed, for a price, which was a tenth of their next harvest. It worked out, as Father knew it would, since the yield from their harvest was greater than previous years.

I was desperate for Hillel to come to my father's bedside. But Father didn't want to bother him, didn't want to take Hillel away from his duties, which were many. Father kept saying it was nothing, that he would get better. I wanted to believe it. We both did. Neither one of us wanted to face the truth of it because he was never sick.

The doctors were useless, just like they had been before, when Somer's mother, Sevira, was languishing. Useless when my mother, Rionach, died in her own blood, giving birth to me. My father was the great Vortigern, a warrior who could go for days without rest, giving his own rations away to his men. I knew the stories his soldiers repeated, how he would sooner get off his own horse, so one of his wounded men could get on, than keep riding himself.

Some of his men would come to the kitchen door asking for news. I never knew what to say except, "He lives." I made sure the servants knew to welcome them with ale and bread. And if for some reason I was not at home, I asked my ancilla, Lavinia, to take care of them that day and serve as I would. I loved it when they talked about him. He was such a man. I wanted to hear them tell any and all those tales. How he had saved Lord Kay's life the Night of the Long Knives when Hengist had turned his coat again as traitors do. How Lord Kay had been an honorable man and recommended him to King Arthur. Lord Kay remained a friend their whole life. This was how King Arthur and my father became acquainted, before my father gifted the Red Dragon to the king, and Myrddin Emrys as well. You could say the Emrys and the dragon came together as a pair. Kings tend to have short memories, but King Arthur remembered Lord Vortigern.

I watched my father fade away from the vital force of nature he had been to a shade of himself. He couldn't eat or drink much of anything. I would rinse a cloth in a small basin of cold water and bring it to his lips. He would close his mouth around the edge of the cloth and suck the dampness from it like a babe. I fed him broth with a small spoon. He finally agreed to my pleas and Hillel came to his bedside. But by then it was too late. Hillel asked Lavinia to make Mother of Thyme tea for my father and that did ease his breathing a bit. But Hillel shook his head, saying that at this point, nothing could cure him.

"I'm very sorry, My Lady," he said. His eyes filled with sadness. "My skills have limits. Lord Vortigern is past my help."

When I pressed for an answer as to what could have rendered my father so ill, after examining my father's darkened lips and tongue, Hillel suggested my father must have been poisoned.

"What poison?" I asked. Hope dawned in my mind. Perhaps an antidote could be found.

"It could be anything," he answered. "Arsenic, Hemlock, Aconite, Mandrake or Henbane, or a combination. These substances act as medicine or as poison depending on the dosage and preparation. Apothecaries use them all the time."

It could be anyone of those fools, doctors or the apothecaries who served them. I threw them all out, all the doctors; I didn't care that Somer hired them. Some of them fought me, said I had no right, demanded to speak to my brother, and who was I to speak to them in this way, a mere girl. I didn't care. I told them I was the Lady of Dinas Emrys, and they had better not touch my father. Looking back on that time, I was so beside myself with worry about my father, I wasn't thinking clearly. I should have put them all in one room and had Hillel examine all the content of their vials, draughts, and various medicines for poison until the culprit was discovered. Instead, I confronted them with poisoning my father. They stopped arguing with me and left quickly. I stopped all medicine except for Hillel's Mother of Thyme tea, which Lavinia prepared daily. It calmed my father's hacking cough a little. Hillel said my father would need something stronger for the pain. There was nothing else to be done. I collapsed into Hillel's arms then.

When Somer found out I told all the doctors to leave, he stormed into my chamber. "How dare you dismiss the doctors without consulting me first? Were you thinking at all about our father? How could you do this to him?"

I had never stood up to my brother before, but our father was sick. “Because one of them poisoned our father,” I answered, standing as tall as my short stature allowed. “Whether it was by mistake or deliberately, I don’t know.”

“And how would you know this?” he asked. “Are you a specialist in poisons all of a sudden?” he said, sarcasm dripping from his lips.

“Hillel recognized the signs immediately, but apparently none of the doctors did.”

“That’s nonsense. I don’t believe it,” he said. “One of them would have noticed.”

“If they were looking for it. Someone has poisoned our father,” I repeated.

Somer’s response was to throw a chair across the room. It was odd to see him do this. It was something our father would have done.

“That’s absurd,” he shouted. He ran his hand through his hair like a nervous child, then shook his head to calm himself down. “How could this happen?”

“You mean how they did it or how they missed the signs?” I asked. I didn’t wait for him to answer. I shouted back at him, “Useless, murderous doctors who know nothing of healing.”

“You exaggerate, little sister.”

“Our father is dying,” I roared. “Do you truly mean to tell me I am exaggerating?” I was seething with anger. It burst out of me, taking me by surprise. I don’t remember ever being angry at my brother. I was always the peacemaker between him and our father. I don’t think Somer expected it either. I admit a part of me blamed my brother even though he had nothing to do with the doctors’ incompetence.

“I was healed by such a doctor,” he said quietly.

“You were lucky,” I answered. “And I doubt you can put these charlatans in the same category as the emperor’s physician, your *father-in-law*.”

“If this is true and our father is poisoned, he must be in pain,” said Somer. “Since you dismissed all the doctors, who will ease his suffering?”

"Lavinia and Hillel are taking care of him. I trust them. And I'm with him. I will not have anyone else approach him. I'm sorry, brother. I can't. Not without knowing which of those doctors did this."

Somer said nothing. He kept looking at me as if I spoke a foreign tongue, as if I was a stranger.

"Since you hired them, you must go to their homes and interrogate them," I urged. "Find out who gave him what. We can't even try an antidote without knowing the exact contents of the poison. Hillel said it could be more than one."

"I don't know that I'll be able to convince any of them to cooperate, after your accusations. I am not inclined to roam all over Gwynedd for nothing."

"For nothing?" *This can't be my brother speaking.* "Then hire someone else to do it. Don't you want to find out the truth? How it happened? What if there is a chance to find an antidote?"

"Didn't Hillel say our father was too far gone?" he asked. "Why don't you concentrate on easing his pain instead, since you know better than the doctors?" he added, then walked away.

I stayed with our father day and night after that. I couldn't leave his side. I willed him to live on. I stopped sleeping for fear his spirit would leave his body during the night. I exhausted myself. Lavinia begged me to take some time away from father's bedside. I refused. She enlisted Hillel's help to convince me to rest, to go breathe some clean air outside the bedchamber. Hillel scolded me, saying it served no purpose to put my own health at risk. I relented only when they both assured me that she and Hillel would take turns staying at my father's side while I went out. I surrendered, got on my horse, and galloped into the woods. I saw the wisdom of their words then. I cried and breathed a full breath of air and touched green moss and smelled green leaves and let rain fall over me and cried some more at how helpless I felt. It should have prepared me for what came next, but it didn't, not really. No one is ever prepared for the calamities that befall us. That's why they are calamities. They're things, events, that come to us by fate, that we cannot escape, or change, but that change us so completely we're barely recognizable to ourselves.

On one of my outings, I saw my brother riding and caught up to him. He was on his way to Beddgelert but after a slight hesitation, changed his course so we could spend time together. We didn't speak. Instead, we raced across the river valley, until our mounts were breathing hard and so were we. It was exhilarating and reminded me of happier times. It was good to be brother and sister again for a brief moment, to put aside all the bitterness of the business with the doctors, to not think about my father dying in his bed.

I couldn't help noticing his wife's absence, which was unusual these days, and wondered why Lady Amunet didn't ride with him.

"She has a superstition about horses," said my brother.

"A superstition?" I was curious. Horses were a gift from the Gods to me. I wondered that anyone could be scared of them. If that was the case, they simply must be taught properly. And their ignorant assumptions corrected.

"That she could die from a fall or else be hit by a horse, so she stays away," he explained. "But I think I can convince her otherwise and get her over it. I will try anyway."

A part of me was glad she didn't ride so we could meet like this again, the two of us. I found myself grateful for her superstition, though to my mind, it was pure silliness. I hoped my brother would fail in his attempt to change her mind. My heart always leaned toward the joyful memories of us as children. They were anchored in the fabric of my being, no matter what.

We took a leisurely stroll through the woodlands along the Glaslyn. A wan afternoon sun pierced through swollen clouds, as it sometimes did before dusk, beaming its particular magic onto the hilly landscape. It had been a long time since it was just the two of us. I asked my brother if he had fully recovered from his wartime injuries. The health of my family was foremost on my mind, with our father so ill.

It was difficult for me to see my brother as a man fashioned into a hardened soldier, a centurion no less, like our father had been. I couldn't believe that the flame of him as a poet and philosopher had been irrevocably snuffed out. He answered, *not extinguished but rather forged into something stronger, a philosopher informed by religion and faith*. He was talking about the Christian faith, and, like our father, I was suspicious of a religion that needed to banish all other faiths, make them illegal.

"When I was taken off the battlefield in the Balkans, I resigned myself to die," he said. "I couldn't face another battle. I felt soiled to my core. Diminished and dirty from all the blood I spilled and all the killing I witnessed. I did want to make my own fortune, not depend on my father's will, or Dinas Emrys. All this had been a means to an end, but I knew I would lose my soul if I continued, unless I died of my wounds first, which seemed more and more certain as I lay on a cot in my own blood, my chest torn open to the winds."

I wanted to ask my brother a million questions but kept quiet for fear he would stop talking. I wanted to know everything that happened to him, especially the difficult things. I wished to help soothe his soul as I believed only I, his little sister, could.

"The doctor who took over fixing my body, Theodosius' physician, was smart. He told me that he had done all he could to mend my body but that my spirit was still wounded. He recommended a three-month cure at his house outside Thessaloniki. I found out then that my doctor was also a skilled merchant, even though he belonged to the Patrician class. He turned out to be the greatest importer and exporter of all kinds of herbs, precious spices and rare medicines, from south of Constantinople to Hispania and Gaul. When I was well enough, he even offered me a place in his business. I haven't said yes or no, yet.

"His wife was an excellent apothecary. They worked closely together and so did their daughter. After the wounds got healed, I still ended up with a fever. Mother and daughter were the ones who restored me to my best self, body and soul. The family welcomed me like a long-lost son, like their prodigal son."

I could hear the rest of the words he did not utter, *like our father never did*. I could hear how grateful he felt, how important these people had become to him, but my thoughts were on our father. "Perhaps your Lady could help with our father's condition then?"

"I think not." His answer was so terse, it was a jolt. I couldn't hide the shock from my face, and he strived to explain further. "She doesn't have her medicines with her, and I doubt any of what she knows would work on our father."

It was disappointing to hear. And to my mind, more an excuse than a reason. He went back to praising the doctor's home, how it was a palace for the mind as well as the spirit. On many evenings all sorts of luminaries from philosophers to astronomers and bishops from Constantinople would gather together. They spent hours in literary and religious discussions or listening to music from accomplished musicians and singers. Lady Amunet herself was accomplished in music and singing.

It sounds idyllic, I thought. *I wonder why Somer bothered to come home at all.*

It was as if he'd heard my thoughts because he said, "I missed Wales and I wanted to show Lady Amunet where I came from. I wanted to come home because it's my rightful inheritance."

Somer got quiet for a moment, "I didn't want her to think I was just a soldier of fortune."

"She must have known you were more than that," I said. "After all, the emperor wanted you to have his best physician."

I deemed my remark to be quite sensible, but he dismissed it with a wave of his hand and went on with his story. "Their hospitality was beyond compare. I wanted to show my future wife I had something of value to offer."

"You mean Dinas Emrys?" I asked.

"Yes, little sister."

"Do you love the lady?"

"I do," he answered. "She is the most impressive person I know. More knowledgeable than any physician, and as clever as any politician, everything a man could want."

It was an odd turn of phrase, but it was sincerely meant. We were back at the stables. And my worry for my father returned with full force.

"Will you not come visit our father with me? He asks after you."

Somer shook his head. "I doubt it. I do not think it will do either of us any good. I'm sorry." Somer turned toward his squire and gave him his horse's reins. A gift from Emperor Theodosius after Angus was killed in battle. The new horse was a magnificent destrier, fast and fiery, with great conformation, but he wasn't Angus.

When I asked about Angus, Somer explained with both real admiration and sorrow, that his warhorse had continued to fight, to protect Somer, while standing in his blood, mortally wounded, until his master was safe and then collapsed with one last breath. There was no horse braver or kinder than old Angus. I would miss him. Somer would too, though he didn't say. He would never forget the manner of his death. His eyes were shiny with held back tears at the retelling of it. He patted the destrier's neck absentmindedly. Beautiful horseflesh is not a measure of character or heart.

Over the next few weeks, I saw our father decline even more rapidly. I took shorter turns with Lavinia after Hillel made it clear the end was fast approaching. Hillel did what he could to make our father comfortable. But I could tell he was suffering despite almost hourly doses of poppy syrup that Lavinia came in to give him. My own hand wasn't steady enough to hold the spoon to his mouth. It was terrifying to watch my father try to catch a breath, excruciatingly, haltingly. I wished I could breathe for him. His hands curved into fists around the bedsheet with the effort of it all. A sheen of sweat covered his face, framed by damp hair, all turned white in less than a month. His breath became a rasp, accompanied by a low whistling sound. He could hardly breathe until the day he stopped breathing altogether.

It took three months for him to die. I could not fathom it and became unwell, frozen in grief, taking to my bed for weeks after the funeral rites were over. I walked through our father's death ritual like a ghost myself. Lavinia dressed me and combed my hair and fed me. I paid no attention. I barely noticed who was in attendance. I knew it must be a grand occasion. The king arrived with members of the court. Lord Kay was there of course, and many others I don't remember. Lord Kay and the king himself were of the party who lifted my father's casket in procession all the way to his resting place on the highest hillock facing west.

Following my father's design, Hillel had created a kind of mausoleum carved straight into the rock and surrounded by gardens. No church burial for our father, even though Somer insisted on his priest speaking. This was not done for our father who never liked the man, but to reaffirm the hold of the church in these parts. It was truly an odd mixture of Celt and Christian ritual.

The king's magician, Myrddin Emrys, requested by our father before he died, gave his blessings. He wore a ceremonial cloak with the hood up and was mostly hidden from the people. He must be protecting himself from the priest who voiced his complaints loudly against the druid's presence, saying that *it imperiled Lord Vortigern's soul.* Fortunately, the priest was ignored. Except my brother tried to placate him and invited him to stay a few days, saying something like, *you would honor us with your presence* and the priest, mollified, answering, *if you insist.* It set my teeth on edge.

I wished I was more myself so I could speak with the druid, but my grief was too great and my mind too weak. Still, a feeling of peace momentarily enveloped the assembly after the Emrys spoke, weaving the protection of the runes around my father's tomb. I felt it release my father's soul from his death and all the pain that came with it. Like a sigh. Myrddin Emrys left right after the ritual, before they all came over to kiss my hand and felt obliged to share with me their version of my father.

Somer never left Lady Amunet's side. He seemed to vacillate between an unnatural agitation and a frozen air about his face and body, like a ghost. He still managed to perform his duties as son and heir of Dinas Emrys, aided by his wife at every turn. And though she leaned on him with her arm about his, and appeared the picture of a grieving daughter-in-law, she seemed the stronger of the two.

Neither the king nor Myrddin Emrys stayed for the feast but everyone else did. Lady Amunet took charge of the evening entertainment and made sure that all the lords and ladies were taken care of and had suitable lodgings. She did all this effortlessly as if she had done it all her life. Her family was used to entertaining princes.

I was grateful that she performed the duties I was too distraught to take on myself. And it helped me to witness how upset Somer was. I was afraid he didn't care at all. He had not paid one visit to our father while he was dying. He came too late on the last day, after I sent Lavinia to beg him to come to our father's bedside. Our father was gone by the time Somer arrived. He kneeled silently next to me by the bed and put his arm about me for a moment. I wanted to stay on my knees next to him longer, but he got up and left me there to grieve by myself until it was time to take our father's body away to prepare him for the funeral.

The reconciliation I hoped and prayed for between our father and Somer never came to pass. For a while, I hoped that my brother's return with his lady meant that he wanted to make up with our father, but he didn't, not really. Somer chose to keep himself and his lady at a distance. I even got mad at him wondering why he bothered to come home at all if not for us to be a family again. He answered that he had a real family now, *his wife's family*.

I couldn't have felt worse if he hit me full in the face with his fist. My body grew weak, and I had to sit down. He must have seen me turn pale.

"You'll see," he said, "It will be the same for you when you marry. You'll discover a whole new family, a place where you'll always belong." Then he took me in his arms and said I was his little sister always. But his words left a scar on my heart.

Chapter Six

I closed myself off in my rooms after the funeral. I wanted no part of the world without my father in it. It took a month for Lavinia to coax me out of my bed and urge me to return to my life, my studies, my hobbies. Perhaps my blood was too wild to remain unstirred for very long. I was not yet fifteen, after all. And the thought of Espoir being stuck in his stall gnawed at my conscience. I knew Caden, our marshal, would look after him, but Espoir was my responsibility and my father's gift to me. I could hear his voice scolding me for not taking better care of my equine charge, my best friend, next to my brother. *If this is how you treat your horse, how can I trust you with more responsibilities, and how will you ever look after a household?* It was comforting to hear his voice even if I was the one conjuring it in my mind.

"Nella, you have to get up now. Nella. You have to get dressed."

I had a fitful night's sleep and was struggling to open my eyes. I could sense the urgency in Lavinia's voice.

"They are waiting for you down in your father's office. And your brother and Lady Amunet are married now."

My eyes opened wide then. They were married and I wasn't there. "I missed my brother's wedding?" I asked. It was my own fault. Nobody wants a grieving child at such a joyous occasion.

"Don't worry. You didn't miss much," said Lavinia. "They had a simple ceremony at the church."

By *simple*, I knew she meant dull.

"They are waiting for you to begin the formal reading of your father's will."

"Right now?" I exclaimed. Lavinia nodded. The thought of our father's will being read jolted me out of bed. I barely got the comb through my hair, entangled as it was from so many days and nights without caring for it. We were both trying to dress me quickly. Normally, we would be joking about how clumsy and slow trying to hurry made us. But there was no humor in it for either of us that morning.

"Lord Kay has brought his own notary. Hillel and I were brought in as witnesses for your father's last will and testament, as well as Lord Kay. He put his notary in charge because of all the numerous formalities and legalities associated with such a large estate."

"I didn't even know about that," I said. Much had gone on while I hid in my room.

I ran down the stairs of our eastern tower where most of the women's quarters were, Lavinia's and my chambers and some of our house servants. My bedroom faced the sunrise, and I'd loved every morning until our father's last breath seemed to take all the sunrises away. Our central hallway was lit with a hundred torches in their sconces. It didn't dispel all the darkness, and the dancing light threw long shadows on the stone walls, including my own. Part of me still felt ghostly, not real to myself since my father's passing into the underworld. It was as if I didn't know who I was without his loving gaze upon me.

Two guards in Lord Kay's livery and a young man with close-cropped hair and serious eyes stood in the entrance hall. The young man nodded as I passed by. I stumbled in my haste, and he caught my arm. I thanked him and hurried on. When I walked in, they all stood up. Hillel was there. I saw him first. His kind eyes sought mine. He gave me a smile and my smile back at him was as tentative as my steps, as if

I'd forgotten how to walk properly in these last weeks of mourning. I barely acknowledged Lord Kay and the notary, instead I ran straight to my brother, and threw my arms around his neck.

Somer gave me a squeeze, then detached himself from my arms and said, "Aren't you going to greet your sister-in-law?"

I stood back and examined my brother. He had changed in one month. He had grown a beard since I last saw him. He was a married man now.

"Good morrow, Lady Amunet," I said.

She stepped close to him and interlocked her arm with his. It was a natural enough gesture and yet in my mind she was saying, *he is mine now, no longer yours*. I felt a pang of jealousy but then silently chided myself, *they are newlyweds*. I curtsied. She nodded, without letting go of Somer's arm. She was from foreign lands after all and must need the reassurance of his nearness to feel more at ease. It was only a year since she arrived at Dinas Emrys.

We all pulled our chairs around my father's prized oak desk. The notary greeted me in the traditional Welsh, *Sutmae*. It was obvious by his pronunciation that he was from the south. He said *shoe-my* instead of *sit-my*. His demeanor was humble but to the point. It was all about the business of reading the will for him. He sat down in my father's seat behind the desk. I almost cried out at his audacity and had to remind myself that our father was gone and there was no disrespect intended. I looked to Somer to see if he had noticed but he said nothing, only stared out to the Glaslyn River. I felt so nervous standing there, I kept my hands behind my back, fingers locked.

The notary began listing the lands and farms and various properties and households. "Lady Ragnell will receive the castle of Dinas Emrys and all its surrounding lands with all the adjoining farms and their tenants coming under her authority. Furthermore, she will have sovereignty over all the Gwynedd woods, and villages from Beddgelert to Caernarfon."

I glanced over at Somer. He looked like a horse ready to bolt, nostrils flared, breathing labored. The notary kept going on and on, citing names of tenants I didn't know, farms I had never visited. I wanted him to stop. It was too much.

"Also included are Ynys Mo and Ynys Enlli, the islands off the coast of the Llyn Peninsula. The Isle of Anglesey. And of course, the port of Colwyn Bay, as well as Deeside, Rhyl, Bangor, Llandudno, Caernarfon, and Pwllheli."

My heart kept sinking as I watched my brother. Somer was visibly upset. Jaw tight. His hand going through his hair repeatedly. As the reading continued, it became clear that our father meant to disinherit my brother entirely and I was to receive it all. It was so shocking, I could hardly breathe myself.

After the notary was done, the room echoed with all the names and places, and the power of our father's will. No one said a word for a very long time.

Lord Kay broke the silence to offer his congratulations. "You are now the greatest lady in the land. I will be at your service if you need any help. But I know master Hillel has things well in hand," he said, gesturing toward Hillel. "With such riches, there will be no dearth of suitors, and I can help you manage that situation as well. If I may, I would put forth my own suit on behalf of my son Edwin."

I nodded in a daze. The young man in the hall was his son.

"Of course, the choice is yours in the end, My Lady. And you'll want to consult with your brother, no doubt."

"Thank you Lord Kay. You are most kind." I looked over at Somer and the rage etched on my brother's face frightened me. His hands were white from holding on too tightly to the sides of his chair. Lady Amunet was stroking his forearm slowly, like one would a pet.

Somer stood up, pulling his arm away from his wife. "This is my inheritance. There is no precedent. It goes against everything we know, every law."

Lord Kay tried to speak. "I realize this comes as a surprise."

"A surprise? It's a travesty, an abomination." My brother was outraged.

"What Lord Vortigern chooses to do with his lands is his right and the only law that matters," said Lord Kay firmly, yet as gently as he could.

Somer laughed. It was a bitter sound. "His right? What about my rights? I am the eldest and I am his son. I am the rightful heir, whatever this fabrication of a will says!"

Lord Kay was so shocked by the outburst, he must have felt the need to defend his honor as well as the will. His hand went to his side, looking for his sword which was not there. He had left it outside, with his son, presuming the reading of a will to be a peaceful endeavor. "I can assure you this will is no fabrication and was witnessed and approved at the highest level."

Somer demanded, "When? By whom? I was not informed. Why was I not informed? When was it done?"

The notary went back through the will, clearing his throat, visibly uncomfortable with the situation, and said, "I believe the will was ratified under complete secrecy, per Lord Vortigern's request, on the fifteenth day of August."

"Two weeks after my return," said my brother. "Two weeks. That's all it took for my father to disinherit me and my family."

I couldn't bear to watch my brother so upset. I spoke up then, addressing the notary. For the first time in my life, I was too frightened to speak to my brother directly.

"Sir, I believe our father went too far and was too harsh in his decision, and I wish to rectify it. If I am permitted."

"My Lady," said the notary, bowing awkwardly behind the desk. He was sweating, despite the coolness of late fall weather. "You can rest assured, as soon as you turn fifteen, and come into possession of your full inheritance, all the holdings and lands are yours to do with as you wish. Your father made it clear that he trusted your ability to manage all dealings regarding Gwynedd Province."

I wished the man had not said the last words, that my father trusted me in this way. I knew it must make it worse for my brother to hear it. I loved Somer with all the innocence of my childish heart. I turned to him then and looked into his long-fringed eyes, full of fury and despair and other things besides I couldn't fathom.

"Brother, you have my solemn promise that upon my birthing day, which is a mere six weeks away, I promise to give you half of all the lands and holdings of Gwynedd, including Dinas Emrys. I believe in this way to remedy a great wrong done to you. And come closer to my father's truest intentions."

Somer took hold of himself with a little shake of his head, pulled wayward strands of hair out of his face, and turned to look at Lady Amunet, as if waiting for a sign of her approval. She remained quiet as ever, eyes looking down at her hands folded on her lap, the picture of a dutiful wife. He approached, still trembling from our father's betrayal, and I was tempted to take a step back. He gave me a kiss on the forehead and said, "Thank you little sister. That is most generous."

I thought it was fair, that he would be pleased. But the fact remained that he was the eldest son, and I was only his little sister, half-sister at that, and our father had chosen me. It was the final blow from our father to his son. I couldn't divine how deeply my brother's pride might be hurt. He was a commander of men, a husband, and still, he would owe his fortune to a mere girl. It troubled me and I hoped Lady Amunet would help him put some of that hurt aside so we could enjoy our lives together. *Love the people with whom fate brings you together but do so with all your heart.* If it was good enough for Marcus Aurelius, it was good enough for me. Half of everything was still a lot. I would find a good husband and Somer would find some peace.

I sought my brother's wife in her chambers the next morning.

"May I come in?" I asked politely.

"You need not ask. This *is* your home," she answered.

I wasn't sure if it was a pointed remark. But maybe not. Everything felt challenging and raw and overly significant at the time.

"I want him to be happy," I said. "I want us to be happy here together."

"I know you love your brother. And your offer was commendable," she said as she applied the dark kohl around her eyes, staring into the mirror, without shifting her gaze to look at me. "But if you want him to be happy, why not surrender it all to him and let *him* take care of *you*? He *is* the eldest son. Shouldn't it all go to him by rights?" She placed her beautiful kohl rimmed eyes upon me.

She smiled sweetly but her words cut through me like a knife. My hand covered my throat, and I stammered like a child caught in a lie. "I've not considered—It's not—It's not what our father wanted. I will not go against all of our father's wishes for Somer's sake." I struggled to find the words and say what I really meant. "I do love Somer. I always will. I believe I came up with the best compromise under the circumstances. I thought you might understand that and encourage my brother to make peace with it. I do want us to be happy."

"You want me to tell him that half of his inheritance is good enough, whatever his little sister determines for him?" she asked.

"Yes," I replied. "Though you make it sound like a despicable fate."

"I support him in receiving everything he deserves," said Lady Amunet.

I remembered how Somer talked of Lady Amunet as his new family. It was true for her as well. My brother was her family. Not I. I must have looked thoroughly dejected because Lady Amunet sounded more conciliatory when she spoke again.

"I'm sorry, Lady Ragnell. Perhaps it's best if we do not mention this again, or better yet, pretend we never did. Let us instead focus on your birthing day feast. I will assist you with it if you desire it."

"I would like that. Thank you Lady Amunet." I was grateful for her kindness in that moment. I took it as a sign that things might improve, that my birthing day feast would be an opportunity to bring us together after all. I was forever hopeful in those days, tenacious in my hopefulness. It was the most salient trait of a naïve and foolish girl, full of learning and no experience of the world.

Chapter Seven

Preparations for my birthing day feast got underway and the excitement and anticipation of it all took precedence over everything else. It was a reprieve from the grief I'd felt day in and day out since my father's death, and from the awkwardness of the reading of the will.

Lady Amunet was so helpful with organizing the theme of the feast, the frost moon, which was obvious once she pointed it out, and also what dress to wear. She even lent me some of her more dainty jewelry. It seemed all had truly been forgotten.

The whole castle sparkled with candlelight, adorned in bows of evergreen and silver-white fabric, a dream. I could sense my father's presence watching over me when my brother requested the first dance. Perhaps my wishing made it so, but it lingered in every room, around every corner. Somer felt it too. He looked over his shoulder more than once while we danced.

In my mind, the night of the feast meant I would be coming into my inheritance, would share it with Somer as promised, and soon after that, would be wed to a noble man my brother would help choose for me. My brother loved me so I knew he would do right by his little sister. Despite my affection for Gawain, I wanted to defer to Somer's judgment in this, to make up for what father had done, to give him back some of the authority father had taken away from him by bestowing so much upon me.

Somer's gift was so exquisite. I wanted to sleep in the linen gown that same night since it was my birthday present. Somer smiled his approval, and I threw my arms around him and told him I couldn't wish for a better brother, indeed he was the best brother in all the world. He gave me a goodnight kiss on the cheek and left. I put on the gown, gazed upon Gawain's little carved wren, and thought myself the luckiest fifteen-year-old as I fell into a darkness deeper than sleep. It was like drowning. There were no dreams.

My ancilla woke me as she came in with breakfast. I looked up at her from my bed and our eyes met. She dropped the platter and fainted dead away at the sight of me. I grabbed the silver tray from the floor, caught a single glimpse of my reflection and saw a demon. It couldn't be me. It couldn't. But there was no one else in the room. There was no one beside me or behind me. I was alone. It was *my* reflection in the mirror, not some unearthly creature that had wandered into my bedchamber by mistake. It was me, somehow. I had become a demon, a monster.

I howled like an animal at the slaughter. In a matter of moments, the entire castle from kitchen hands and squires to the nobles visiting my brother, all knew what fate had befallen me. The cries of "She's cursed! She's cursed!" reverberated throughout. All the guests left quickly. No one was allowed into my chamber. My brother only came in once and quickly left. He couldn't bear the sight of me. I couldn't. No one could. No one should.

My brother called on the best doctors, urging them to find a solution to my unfortunate condition by any means necessary. They all tried to outdo one another in the administration of the foulest potions, which left me retching and heaving for days. They were the same ones who had tended to my father, though not as many. I had not the smallest hope that they could help me.

Then others were summoned who consulted amongst themselves until they came up with the idea of cutting pieces of my skin off for closer examination. Strangely, the skin grew back overnight as leathery as before. It didn't make it any less painful. I screamed at every cut.

They didn't care. To them, I had become an animal, to experiment on freely. They carved into my flesh, starved me, and pulled out my fur and hair and tortured me for weeks.

When the doctors finally, mercifully, gave up on me, I slinked back to my room, and stayed hidden from everyone. A young kitchen maid, sent to my room with a meal, dropped the tray, shrieking, and ran out as fast as she could.

I was on the floor, eating with my hands, putting as much into my mouth as I could—I had not eaten in weeks—when my brother walked in. He couldn't hide his disgust as he took a brief look at me then turned his face away. I felt shame to the core of my being then. I stopped gorging myself. What I wanted to say to him but couldn't was *I'm still me. It's still me, inside*. Instead, I asked him where my ancilla, Lavinia, was.

"With Lady Amunet," he answered.

Did I hear guilt in his voice? Maybe. Or wishful thinking on my part.

"She requested Lavinia," he said. "She needs someone skillful to help with her dresses."

I knew he meant that with my recent transformation, I didn't need Lavinia's help anymore. He was wrong. I needed her more than ever. I was desperate for my ancilla's presence, her wisdom, her caring. If anyone could see beyond this foul skin, it was her, despite the initial shock she experienced. I knew her kindness was not something superficial or convenient but ran through to the deepest part of her being.

It took a while for Somer to find the words he wanted to say next. He kept fingering all the little pots of cream and precious oil on my dressing table. The ones borrowed from Lady Amunet. All ridiculous and useless now. Eventually he said, "There is one last hope. I will call for the priest. Perhaps he can banish this devilry from your body."

He was talking about an exorcism, like I was the devil. Was I the devil, or some other demon from hell? I didn't know. I couldn't tell. All I knew was that my brother was abandoning me to his Christian God. I thought that was the worst of it. Then he said, "If the priest cannot help, it is best if you do not linger in the castle. You will frighten the servants as well as any guest who comes. You will be better off out of the castle. There are many places on our lands. I can have Hillel arrange for a farmer to let you stay in their stables. I can also have servants leave food for you outside the castle. And you can take Espoir with you, if he can accept you as you are now. You understand, don't you?"

I had no words. My brother was telling me I didn't belong in my own house anymore. And he was bringing in the priest because to him I was no longer his little sister. I was a demon, perhaps the devil himself.

The priest from Beddgelert came soon after. I dreaded his ministrations most of all, even though he was my brother's confessor and advisor. He took one look at me and ordered his helpers to bring me to his church and make me lie down on my stomach, naked, on the cold floor. My hands and feet tied down to nails hammered in the flagstone, facing the altar. I was left alone like this for hours.

He came back in the dark. I heard the woolen robe scraping the floor, the shuffling of his sandal clad feet on stone. Out of the corner of my eye, I could see the shadow of the torch tremble and move until he set it in an alcove. He approached quietly, carrying the whip trailing the floor, and whispered close, *this is for your sins. We must beat them out of your monstrous body. May God forgive you.* The lashes came down on my back with a crack accompanied by the words *repent, repent.* The priest went on and on, repeating the words *repent, repent,* and he whipped and whipped as if caught in a frenzy. The whip slashed into my body, cutting strips of flesh. I howled and begged for mercy. My blood surged out, warm on my cold skin, and ran down my legs and sides. It felt as if it went on for days. I remember thinking I must be a terrible sinner to be punished by God in such a way. I wanted this God to take me away for I couldn't bear to live another day like this. But I was too wretched a beast for Him to take notice or care.

It became clear that nothing and no one could heal my affliction. Even the priest gave up on me, or he just got tired of whipping. No doubt he informed my brother that I was beyond help. Part of me hoped that

Somer would come to my rescue, that he'd take me in, and tell me, *you will always be my little sister, no matter what. We will not stop until we find a cure. And until we do, I will protect you.* But that was a fantasy. He'd made it clear he wanted me out of the castle, out of his life. Still, I couldn't make myself believe it. We were bonded, motherless children. I'd forgotten that he had a new family now, a new mother, father, wife. He didn't need me anymore.

I fell into a darkness beyond my body. I fell beyond my mind. I floated weightless in a starlit sky. I saw great beings as tall as mountains, with taller hats, covered in dark veils, floating in a celestial breeze. They peered over a giant book made of infinite stardust, it was the Book of Life, and it was open at my page. They spoke to me in my mind and chided me for giving up too soon, that it wasn't my time yet, that there was more to be done. With a flick of a finger, they threw me back to earth, down onto that church floor, into that wretched cursed body.

I woke up with a voice speaking inside my head, dark and strong. Perhaps it was the devil after all. It had one clear message: *Run before they kill you dead with their experiments*. And then I thought, *if I am to die, let it be by my own hand, not theirs*. These were far from the wise meditations of Marcus Aurelius, urging me to *take care that you entertain no notions unsuitable to virtue and reasonable nature.* My life, my being, had been torn apart and there was nothing reasonable or natural left in me. I was now the sinful incarnation of unsuitable. I could almost laugh at the absurdity of it all if not for the abject terror and pain holding me in its grip.

What was left? What could I do? My palfrey had his hand tooled saddle worthy of a king's ransom, and I had my cloak, befitting a lady of the highest rank. Hillel or Lavinia could sell these for me. I preferred to ride bareback anyway. I would live in abandoned animal enclosures or stables nearby and steal into the castle at night for warmth and food.

I could get in unseen. I knew the passage from the river into the lake under the castle.

I figured it all out in my head, but I couldn't even move an inch without a scream escaping from my lips, let alone drag myself to the church entrance, shackled as I was to the stone floor. My back was ribbons of flesh, seeping with my blood, pooling on the ground around me. I thought I would die here and a part of me felt enraged, like a trapped animal. I suppose that is exactly what I was. I heard the door creak open and feared the worst. This was my time. I surrendered in my heart to the eternal forces of life and death, to Arawn.

It was my ancilla, Lavinia, not the priest. She knelt next to me and spoke softly, while she untied my wrists and ankles. And tears of relief came to my eyes. She cleaned my wounds and applied her poultice all over my back as gently as she could, all the while cooing, *Nella, Nella*. I winced and whimpered at her every application of the mixture, and she apologized again and again. She came to me in the middle of the night even though the priest said it was forbidden, that I needed to stay there alone in contrition for my sins, for at least another three days and nights. I didn't look at her. I kept my eyes closed. They were so many leaking sores on my body, she had to make several batches. But eventually I was wrapped up like a dead body in a shroud.

I begged her to bring me Espoir and a saddle bag with provisions before the priest came back. She brought Hillel instead. He looked at Lavinia's work thoroughly. Then he nodded but said nothing.

"Will the mixture heal me?" I asked, my voice a whisper, hoarse from howling in pain.

He shook his head. "It will heal what you have become. It will not restore what you were. What was done to you is beyond my human skill. I'm so sorry, child."

My body trembled and shook, then I took a breath, "Please bring me my palfrey and saddle, and my cloak. I cannot stay. My brother doesn't want me here. He made that plain."

"We will look after you for a couple more days to give Lavinia's poultice a chance to work. Then we'll do as you ask," said Hillel.

I was grateful that he didn't argue.

"In the meantime, I will stay close," said Lavinia.

Her kind words brought me back from the terrified wildness of my mind. She did stay close. Every night she brought me blankets and food and water. Cradled my head while I drank. I could hardly bear being so helpless. I asked about Somer. Lavinia said he had gone away with his wife to visit her family at their residence in Hispania. That is why she was able to attend me.

"I told Lady Amunet that traveling made me so sick, I would be unable to assist her at all," she explained. "And I would be better off at home, working on a new gown."

My clever Lavinia.

Finally on the third day, what was going to heal healed. My new animal skin had unforeseen powers of restoration. When Lavinia took off the wraps, there were no scars. I was whole in my monstrous way. The hunger which had abated with the beatings came back even more overwhelming than before. Lavinia brought me food, some chicken and bread and fruit. I snatched it from her like a starving lunatic and devoured it in an instant. I looked up when I was done and saw them staring at me. I recognized the look of pity on their faces. My eyes opened wide and filled with tears. Lavinia took me in her arms. I let her hold me for a moment because I needed it so desperately but then pushed her away, ashamed of my unhinged hunger, my appearance, my fate. I did feel sorry for myself then. Who wouldn't?

Hillel brought my horse to the church already saddled. In a corner of my mind, I did understand that Hillel and Lavinia cared about me even now, despite my outer form, and remembered who I was, and I could trust them. *And love the people with whom fate brings you together but do so with all your heart.*

My palfrey, Espoir, took some time to get used to the change in my appearance. Hillel suggested I keep cooing to him and touching him like he was used to. I tried. I kept calling to him softly, *Mon Espoir*, but he kept backing away, rearing up, trying to protect himself from this creature I had become. It was hopeless. I gave up, my head hanging down with even deeper despair. Espoir calmed down then. He took a few tentative steps and came close, putting his nose against my chest, snuffling like he always did. Hillel had wisely brought Espoir's favorite cookies made with flax seed and bran. He handed one to me and I gave it to Espoir, careful to keep my claws out of the way. He lipped it carefully. My smile was no more than a grimace but a welcome feeling after the last few weeks.

Chapter Eight

Hillel warned me that despite his efforts to regulate the hunting and trapping on our lands, there were poachers in the forest who set traps and snares and that I needed to be careful. He shouldn't have worried. I was too fearful to venture anywhere in case a hunter might mistake me for an animal and kill me. Once I settled into the old stone hut which had belonged to a hunter, there I stayed for the most part, deep in the Gwynedd woods, hidden from prying eyes.

In the beginning, I didn't even stay inside the cabin. There was a small stable in the back for Espoir and I stayed with him. That first night, after I took off his saddle and bridle, Espoir knelt down on the ground without me asking, sighed a big sigh and laid on his side. I snuggled up against his back, wrapped in my fancy cloak, using my saddle bag for a pillow. I fell asleep, grateful for the warmth of his big body.

For many weeks, I sneaked into the castle late at night, through the delivery door and into our kitchen, to avoid an encounter with any of our servants, to avoid terrifying them. I was ravenous for food and raided our pantry, even eating the dogs' food. I looked up from one of their bowls and found our dogs staring at me with surprise in their eyes, and more than a little fear at this strange creature stealing their food. The boldest of them tried to fight me for their bowl but one growl from my curled lips kept them at bay. Not even my little Daffodil recognized me. Perhaps my smell had changed with my skin or perhaps I was too dreadful even for a dog.

I didn't die then. I forgot I wanted to. I was too hungry all the time. My appetite had no bounds. It was insatiable. Since no one would come near me, it wasn't long before I sought the company of pigs. My grunts echoed theirs. Though I could still walk upright, I preferred to be on all fours with the other farm animals, unless I was riding. Riding Espoir, more than anything else, kept my humanity in mind. What was left of it.

All the tenant farmers turned their eyes away when I approached to beg for some food or drink. They couldn't bear to look at what I had become but they didn't betray my whereabouts, not even to my brother. It was a kindness I would not forget. Perhaps they pitied me, remembering what I once was, the heiress to my father's holdings, large enough to rival King Arthur's. After a while, I found food set aside at the delivery entrance. My brother must have given his orders to Hillel after all, unless Hillel had taken it upon himself.

The Gwynedd woods were like a book I read faithfully growing up. I learned the streams and the names of trees, the field elm and the silver birch, the oak, the walnut and the goat willow, eating the summer berries with Somer, avoiding the wayfaring tree with its creamy white flowers in spring and poisonous dark berries in fall, sampling the red berries of the guelder rose that the bullfinches loved so much. Always accompanied by either Somer, Hillel, or with my ancilla to collect mushrooms, and on more rare occasions my father when he was home. I was never truly alone until the curse.

It was bound to happen at some point. I came face to face with a poacher as he was setting up his snare in a little clearing, not far from my hut. Before I had time to run and hide, he took one look at me, dropped everything and escaped into the woods, screaming. The man's response stunned me. It was a revelation and gave me some confidence. I was a creature to be feared. *I* was the scary one, and so perhaps I didn't need to be so scared all the time. And in this world of the forest, I could, I would, survive.

I learned to track the poachers. Their route was fairly predictable. I learned their routine, what time of day they came, how often. They were three regulars. I did take advantage of the traps when I found a rabbit, or some other small creature caught in a snare. I would take it and make a meal of it. Frustrating for the poachers. Most of them were trapping for food. But there was one who trapped for fur. He was a big man, not so easily frightened, unpredictable in his comings and goings. I stayed away from his traps, until one day, I heard deafening cries. I had to cover my ears. I crawled toward the place, hiding amongst the hedgerows. And saw the fox, so fearful, so angry, so desperate to get away. He reminded me of Daffodil.

I couldn't stop, despite the teeth, sharp as blades, despite the scratching and the cries. I cried back. I echoed the fox's every plea in his fight for freedom, until he finally escaped. He stared at me for a moment, then yelled at me and ran off, and I yelled back: *Ungrateful wretch. See if I care next time!* But I always did. I rescued quite a few more foxes over the next three years. It became another sort of compulsion for me. Their desperation, their fierceness to fight for their lives while in a trap, to not give up, biting and screaming, often tearing at their own leg or foot. We were alike. Creatures caught in men's snares. At least I could help them even if I couldn't help myself. And each time I liberated one, I felt as if I was freeing some tiny corner of my being, even if it was only temporary. It helped me feel less frightened of myself, my ungodly appetite, my face, my body. I would clean the blood on my hands in a stream afterwards and scramble the water to avoid the mirror of my awfulness.

The only creatures not deathly afraid of my appearance, aside from my horse, were the animals in the forest. A squirrel would forage next to me, and there was a bit of solace in that. A creature's acceptance of me brought up feelings in my heart, where I believed I had none left. I would start grieving my fate, feel sorry for myself, and that in turn would bring up such a rage, I wanted to kill something. I would slap and scratch myself until I bled and howled. I must have looked like the devil himself. I vacillated between wanting to kill the beast I had become and killing the one who had done this to me. I was like one of those berserkers my father and Somer talked about, biting their own shield in rage, bloodthirsty and fearing nothing, not even their own death. I knew I couldn't live like this for much longer. And if I didn't kill myself, then something in this forest would. I always believed it would be a hunter or a trapper who'd had enough of me liberating their catch.

I never saw it coming. I was working as fast as I could to free a fox while unsuccessfully trying to avoid its sharp teeth. I was having a conversation with the said fox, mostly growling and grunting at him to *stop biting me you idiot, I'm trying to help you.* I finally managed to free the animal who ran off limping into the thickets when a slow shiver ran down my spine. Someone was observing me. I thought for sure that the hunter had caught up with me. I turned around and was transfixed by what I saw: a huge beast, the kind legends are made of, the kind even great knights do not face alone but with a whole company of squires.

A wild boar, its beady little eyes fixed on me, was brimming with rage, offended by the sight of me. Stamping the ground with its black cloven hooves, foam dripping from its long mobile snout, the boar lowered its tusks as it prepared to launch itself at me. Terror flowed through my veins. I held my breath, trying to control the rising panic, then my legs took over and I ran to the nearest oak tree like it was my salvation. And it was, if I could reach it in time. I could already feel its breath on my back, its tusks about to plunge into my cursed flesh. I did not want to die this way, gored by a wild boar, too new and insecure of my own beastly nature to know my limits, or to withstand such an attack. I wanted a death of my own choosing by all the gods! *Not this way! Not this way!* I kept telling myself. I climbed faster than I ever climbed a tree before, thankful, for once, for my clawlike nails that easily found purchase on the bark.

The boar pranced around the tree for a long while before it gave up or smelled a new prey and decided to move on. It took me longer still to stop shaking and find enough strength to let myself down the tree. I put my forehead against its bark and thanked the oak for saving my wretched life. I vowed to never be this scared again in these woods. They were *my* woods, and that creature was another of *my* vassals. That is what I told myself. I didn't quite believe it, but it helped me get over the attack, though I never forgot it.

A year and a half into my confinement in the Gwynedd woods, I finally caught sight of my brother on one of our trails. He was riding with Lady Amunet. A carriage followed at a distance. He must have gotten her over her fear of horses after all.

They did not see me. I thought I must be far from their minds. I got as close as I dared and followed them from the hedgerows. They were talking about an upcoming visit of her parents. Lady Amunet was concerned that her parents be treated as well as possible. She wanted a grand feast arranged for them with the right kind of entertainment, and to show off the lands of Dinas Emrys to their best advantage. Somer was trying to reassure her.

"My dearest, they know they are visiting Wales and that it won't be Thessaloniki or even Hispania. I'm sure they'll adapt. Your father is a smart man."

"I know. I want to show him our progress with the new plantings. But it doesn't seem to be going as well as expected. Can we trust this man, Hillel? He was your father's man, after all, and a Jew. Perhaps we should get rid of him."

"I've told you, Hillel is the best at what he does. It would be a mistake to let him go."

Somer sounded short-tempered as he spoke. As if they argued often about Hillel.

They walked past me without seeing me. I blended in with the foliage quite well but disturbed an owl sitting in the yew tree behind me. She flew off suddenly with a loud hoot. The horses shied a bit. Lady Amunet shouted in fear. My brother got hold of her horse's bridle and calmed the animal down quickly. It was nothing really.

"Calm yourself. You're making it worse," he said to his wife.

My thought exactly.

"I'm not making it anything," she said. "I don't know why I even agreed to come out with you. I hate this. It serves no purpose."

"Not everything has a purpose, Amunet. The purpose, if you want to call it that, is to be with the horse. To ride in the countryside. To enjoy the beauty of this fall day."

"It's not for me. It never was." The lady slid off her horse in a rather ungainly fashion, which almost made me laugh, and called to the carriage following them. The boy sitting next to the driver came off and took over, climbing on the horse while she stepped into the carriage.

"My horse needs to run. I will meet you at home," said Somer.

"As you wish," she answered.

Lady Amunet ordered the carriage to turn back, followed by the steward on her horse. My brother stood there for a moment, watching the carriage diminish in the distance. Then he fixed his gaze at my hiding place in the hedgerow.

"I know you are there," he said.

It took me by surprise. It shouldn't have. We played hide and seek throughout our childhood, and he always found me out.

"Do not show yourself. You'll frighten my horse," he said.

I was used to hiding myself from everything and everyone by now, but his remark still stung. It wasn't about scaring his horse. He didn't want to lay eyes on what I had become. Once had been enough for him.

"Hello, brother," I said from my hiding place, as if it was just another day.

"You speak. You know who I am."

He sounded astonished. Like he assumed I had lost my mind, forgotten him, forgotten who we were.

"Yes, brother. Did you expect me to be deaf and dumb as well as a monster?"

"What do you want?" he asked.

To be as we were. Your love and affection. To come home, I thought. But those were the thoughts of a sad little girl. It was much too late for that. "Nothing from you. That much is obvious," I said. "Your Lady seems pretty worried on a horse."

"She is getting better," he said. "She can do anything she sets her mind to."

Such fervor. He must worship the lady. Our conversation was almost casual. It was an odd sensation, but I was still a beast hiding in the hedgerow and Somer was bristling with discomfort, his horse dancing under him in response.

"Why are her parents visiting?" I asked.

"It is *not* your business," he said. "They want to see how we are doing."

"Are they coming to meet their grandchildren?" It was an honest question. I thought there would be children by now. But Somer almost fell off his horse then. He *never* fell off. I saw such emotions pass over his face, one after the other: anger, regret, determination, despair, and I know not what else. It occurred to me then, neither of us knew what the other had become.

"There are no grandchildren. Again, *not* your business," he said.

"I would have liked to be an aunt," I said, "Tell them all about my big brother Somer, the one I know to be kind and thoughtful and caring."

"You made that brother up in your mind, little sister. It was an illusion."

Somer talked between clenched teeth, as if he was trying to convince himself. *He did call me little sister*. A part of me clung to that. But it may have been simple force of habit.

Somer looked up in the distance where dust still rose from the carriage as it headed back to the castle. As if he was looking for his guiding star. He said, "I will not listen to any more of your drivel. You have no idea how to make difficult decisions."

I could have answered, *No, I don't have any idea, because no one showed me how*. Instead, I asked, "And your wife does?"

A part of me was intent on provoking him. I wanted to shake him out of his worship for Lady Amunet and back to himself, back to my brother, the one I loved. He didn't take the bait.

"Being cursed hasn't made you any cleverer," he said.

I could hear the scorn in his voice as he spoke. I realized I made him angry, just as I had in the past. But this time, I didn't care. "And being married hasn't made you any kinder," I said.

My brother sounded almost contrite when he changed the subject and asked me how I was faring. He regretted doing so as soon as the words passed his lips.

"How am I faring? You're asking your little sister how she is faring, your cursed little sister, abandoned by her only family, her brother, alone in the woods? Really?" I screamed at him and ran out of my hiding place in the hedgerow, like a berserker, with blood filled eyes, ready to tear the world apart with my teeth, as mean and vicious as the boar that had attacked me. "Take a good look, brother. This is what I am become!" I tore at my own flesh in a frenzy.

He pulled his horse away from me as it began to spook. I don't know who was more horrified at my appearance, my brother or his horse. But they were both soon gone at full gallop, down the trail. I stopped, panting, exhausted. I was mad and bitter and wished my brother back all at the same time.

My rage surged, unsolicited, but it was always fueled by the same thoughts, like a rondeau, over and over again in my head. *Someone cursed you, turned you into this. Someone did this to you. May they die a thousand terrible deaths for doing this to you*. Revenge was like a goad on my mind in those days. It kept me alive, like my temper and my ravenous appetite. Those were armor, like my foul skin, and my best protections against despair, hopelessness and oblivion. All those things that precede the ultimate capitulation into the arms of death.

ᚨ

ANSUZ

Chapter Nine

The curse worsened over time. The animal quality of my appearance, the wildness of my battered heart. Every day, every week and month that passed, I was sinking further away from civility, from community, from anything resembling humanity. I learned to survive in the woods by hiding from all people and all things and in doing so, I became a strange thing, not human, not quite animal either, a creature of the in-between. My favorite times were dawn and dusk when everything is tentative, not so clearly marked as in the light of day, not so stark as in the light of the moon. Not even the darkness of a moonless night could appease the torn shreds of my spirit.

One such night, I sought oblivion, running as fast as I could through the woods. I ran and ran with all the strength of the beast I had become propelling me forth, until I lost track of myself, my pain, my fear. I ran like the mad creature I was and found myself at Snowdon Mountain, *Yr Wyddfa*, a place full of memory: my father and my brother pointing out hidden trails or encouraging me to jump across a stream. I fell, breathing hard, exhaustion overcoming even my rage. I dragged myself to a rock to sit down. I looked up and saw a brilliant starlit sky. The air smelled sweet with the early summer fragrance of alpine meadow rue, roseroot, and the rarest flower of them all, the Snowdon lily rising from the dark earth toward the night sky. I envied their certainty. Without a thought, I clawed through a bunch of lilies and shoved the white petals in my mouth. I tasted the dampness of the night on my tongue and shivered.

In the stillness of the mountain, wrapped in the arms of a sidereal heaven, I heard a melody rise from the ground itself, one I doubt a human ear could ever perceive. It was the song of the mountain, a call and response between her and the plants and animals who lived with her. My own creature body was vibrating with it, answering the same call. It was not of this earth, and it was this earth. It was a song made of stars and wind, plants and roots, and my body knew it before my mind could comprehend it. It was a song of such love and beauty I never heard before, but it soothed my tattered soul and I lived another day.

The only human who still sought me out on a regular basis was Hillel. He considered himself my overseer as Lord Vortigern's chosen heir, despite my brother's claim. Hillel came about once a month. He brought me dresses my ancilla had modified for me to accommodate my new body and circumstance. My dear Lavinia continued her work as seamstress for my brother's wife and was unable to visit me. She could not leave the castle unchecked.

The dresses would get stuck on bramblebushes and tear. Or I would rip them myself with one of my sharp nails to make room for my legs and arms. This animal body needed to move freely and fast through the forest, chasing prey, climbing a tree for a piece of fruit, or to get away from bears and boars. I'd crawl on the forest floor looking for mushrooms, jumping from stone to stone to a pool for drinking or cleansing my clawing fingernails from spilled blood.

Hillel also brought me food. There was never enough food. He stayed on one side of the wall by the stable behind my little hut, and I stayed on the other. I didn't want to frighten him though he said he didn't mind. I was afraid he would not return if he saw me now, the wildness in my eyes, the darkness of my leathery skin, the fur, the claw like strength and length of my nails, the teeth. I could not forget how aghast Somer had been.

The only one who still knew me, and I knew him, was Espoir. His eyes turned white at the horror he saw, when I approached. He couldn't help himself. But he remembered my touch and the sound of my voice, though I rarely used it anymore. He schooled the trembling of his graceful limbs and let me ride him. That he still carried me was his great gift to me and a clear sign of his courageous heart. He was my only solace, and I roamed our woods around Dinas Emrys for hours when I wasn't foraging for truffles or gorging myself on rotten fruit with the pigs, in one of our tenants' farms. That I still had my wits, my mind, was part of the curse. I knew what I was and could do nothing to change it.

It was almost three years to the day. The frost moon of my birthing day was almost full.

Hillel and I were in the habit of meeting once every full moon in my little hut. He always managed to bring a bag of oats for Espoir, some bread and cheese, fruits and vegetables from his personal garden, whatever was in season. He had given up on the dried goods since I didn't cook. It was the occasion to give me news of the castle, and of my brother. He seemed hesitant to broach that subject. I urged him on.

"Lady Ragnell," he began. That he still called me *Lady* seemed incongruous and endearing at the same time. "Your brother is full of talk against the king. And Lady Amunet encourages him."

"He's always been full of talk against the king and his family," I said, dismissing the whole thing as old news.

"True," he acknowledged. I could see Hillel was not convinced but I refused to believe my brother would go against our father's sworn fealty to King Arthur. Then again, our father was dead, and I was now a monstrous secret.

Hillel hesitated, then added, "Your brother has officially stepped in to reign upon your lands."

I believed it was as it should be, for the sake of Dinas Emrys, our tenants, and the people of our county. In my current state, I was useless. I had no purpose.

Hillel continued, "Lady Amunet takes the lead in everything. Part of the eastern tower of the castle, where your own chambers are, has been turned over to the apothecary trade, and that's not all."

He explained that a great deal of our arable lands had been appropriated for the cultivation of spices and herbs. I worried that meant our tenants might starve, like my father had said. Hillel worried about the same thing and went against the lady's wishes. He ordered the farmers to keep enough of the root vegetables essential for surviving the winter. The farmers had colluded with Hillel, acknowledging his wisdom and their own interest in it. He had assured them that he would take responsibility for the decision and say the fault was his if it came to that. I was glad Hillel cared as much about Dinas Emrys as I did. It made me feel better about the decision to end my life.

I chose to do this on the night of the frost moon, on my eighteenth birthday, three years after it all began. I told Hillel that if anything happened to me, he must take care of Espoir for me. He said of course he would, but he must have suspected something because he kept telling me that eighteen was a lucky number, because in the Kabbalah, using gematria, which assigns numbers to letters, when you added up the two letters *chet*, and *yud*, which made up the word *chai*, alive or living, you got eighteen. Eighteen meant Life. Good change would come then. Hope would not give up on me, like Espoir had not either.

I gathered chains from the old traps I had dismantled. My plan was to bind myself with them and jump in from Pont Bren, the Glaslyn bridge so favored by lovers. The Devil's bridge, over the river Mynach, would have been more appropriate, but Ceredigion, where it was located, was simply too far to walk while dragging chains.

I didn't drown myself in the river that night. I waited until morning instead. I don't know why. Perhaps it was Hillel's hopeful words, his talk about gematria, that made me wait another day. But that is when I had the dream that changed the course of things for me. I sought Hillel out since he was in the dream and I needed his help interpreting it. I trusted things might come to light in the retelling of it.

I wouldn't enter his rooms, so he suggested the stables. Hillel sat on a stool inside the entrance and I on a log outside. I began the retelling. It seemed important to speak it as if it was happening now, in the present, like in the dream, "It's a winter night. The landscape is covered in snow. There is a path, barely visible. I try to follow it as best I can. I look up and realize I'm walking behind you, Hillel. In my dream, you are here to save me, as you did when you came to my aid at the church with my ancilla. We keep walking for a long time. Snow begins to fall again. I'm hungry, so hungry, like I always am these days. I could have eaten the snow. I see people walking off the path, heading in a different direction.

I ask them where they're going. They answer to an inn to get some food. They urge me to come along. I'm eager to follow but you say it won't satiate my appetite. It's the wrong kind of food. I battle with myself for a long time before I finally agree to stay with you. And then you turn into a dog. It seems like the most natural thing in the world at that moment. Our footsteps sink into thick pristine snow. Not another soul in sight. Not a sound. I'm filled with doubt, ravaged by hunger. I think I made the wrong decision. Suddenly you, as the dog, leave our path, make a right turn and head into an empty square that appears out of the darkness. The full moon makes a circle of light in its center. I can see the outline of buildings in the distance, not buildings, more like tall standing stones. I can't tell. I can't see. The air shimmers in the light, crystalline and cold. I stand back and wait. You, as Hillel the dog, meet up with an enormous wolf, a wolf of myth. Like Fenrir, the beast of the Norse apocalypse. I hope it's Lupa, the she-wolf who nourished Romulus and Remus. It's itself, entirely unknown. You and the wolf converse silently for a while, nose to nose. Though the dog-you is much smaller than the wolf. Then, by some mutual understanding, you break your silent conversation, and the dog-you scampers over to me, barks once, turns your head back toward the wolf, as if to indicate that it's my turn into the circle and then trots off, leaving me alone with this mythic creature.

"I walk over slowly and enter the circle. I feel its power, a circle of protection, of mystery, and healing. I look down at my body and see I am my human self, no longer a beast. The wolf saunters toward me. He is three times my size. My head could fit into his mouth. And yet I feel more curiosity than fear. He begins to speak to me in his own language, intently. Part of me knows I should be able to understand him and yet I can't. He is my answer, my helper, my liberator from the curse but I'm unable to communicate with him. I wake up knowing I must find him and learn his language, and that he can help me."

By the end of my retelling, we both knew who the wolf was, and Hillel agreed to help me arrange a meeting. I was so relieved I rushed into the stable to hug him, but I remembered my ugliness and stopped myself. I thanked him instead with as much feeling as I could, hoping he heard the gratitude in my voice.

There was only one person in the world who could help me, King Arthur's own magician. The druid, *Myrddin Emrys*, or Merlin, as some called him, spent the majority of his time at King Arthur's court since the coronation. After all, Arthur would not have become who he was without him. I couldn't show myself in my condition. The archers would have killed me on sight alone. Hillel said he would endeavor to communicate with Myrddin Emrys and let him know of my desire to meet with him.

Hillel reminded me that Myrddin Emrys was first and foremost a druid, that such a man needed to commune with the spirit of nature, away from court, to keep his own connection to the great mystery alive. The full moon of the winter solstice was a good time for it and in accord with my dream. We both agreed.

I was attuned to the rhythms of nature by now, listening to the wind, looking up at the movement of the stars in the night sky and observing my fellow creatures. I knew when the hawks made their circles and cried above, there was rabbit or some other small game to hunt below. I knew to follow the deer to find the closest stream and the bears for berries and honey in the springtime. They always left something for me behind when they were done. And I knew where to find the druid on the solstice. I'd seen the place and thought it best to keep my distance.

Chapter Ten

In a glade, deep in the forest, there stood a stone circle by a small brook. I knew the druid would be there at the next winter solstice, and I'd be waiting for him. I was wrong. As I approached, *he* was waiting for *me*, sitting in the middle of the circle on a flat rock, illuminated by the long night moon. Like my dream, the landscape was bright with snow. This part of the forest was filled with our most revered and ancient trees, thousand-year-old rowan and ash and blackthorn, like the supporting characters of a sacred play.

I hid from him behind one of the standing stones, towering over the clearing. They were covered in moss and luminous with lichen, like elemental ancestors, imposing in their stillness. I wanted to see him before witnessing his reaction to what I had become. I wore my cloak with the hood up to hide my face, as I always did.

I was curious of him and wanted to observe him without being seen. I should have known he wasn't a man easily fooled, if he was a man at all. There were stories about him, that he was half human, half devil born. He was making little drawings in the snow with his blackthorn staff, a wood prized by such as he for its ability to ward off evil. A little brown wren with its white eyebrow stripe flew across the space between us. It was as if he was waiting for the bird to show up, a signal, in order to start conversing with me.

Without looking up, he said, "No need to hide yourself from me. I have met far worse monsters than you."

I barked my answer at him, "How would you know what kind of monster I am?" I stepped out of the shadows and removed the hood from my face. It was a defiant gesture to show him I wasn't afraid of anyone. But any shock I hoped to impart was lost on him.

He nodded. "Lady Ragnell, well met, on this solstice eve."

"I'm no lady. Not for a long time. Hillel does the same. Insists on calling me that."

I had grown mean-tempered as a fox caught in a trap over these last three years. I liberated enough of them to know.

He wasn't what I expected. I saw a man of youthful appearance despite his age which must be nearing forty. Being eighteen at the time, forty was ancient to me. He wore peasant clothing with a good woolen cloak, none of the court glamor about him. No beard covered his face. Unruly brown hair fell about his shoulders. He raised his head and the blackest eyes I have ever seen, filled with star fire, peered into my being with such fathomless love, I felt like the innocent vulnerable child I must be at my core. I couldn't bear it for long. My shame and self-loathing ran too deep. When I recovered, his arms opened wide, in a welcoming gesture. What I could see of them was flecked with drawings, runes or something similar, including his hands. He made no attempt to hide them. I couldn't tell if there was a pattern to it, like a map of the heavens, or if it was random. I thought his body must also be marked in this way. Oddly, a sense of kinship rose up in me because of it, though my body was cursed and his blessed by the gods with protection against spells and curses such as mine.

"You have been looking for me for a while, isn't that so?" asked Myrddin Emrys, as serene as could be. "Master Hillel told me of your urgent desire to meet me. He is a good man."

His calm helped me slow down my heart to a manageable pace. "He is," I said.

"And he keeps faith with you." A statement, not a question.

"He does." I nodded.

The druid stood up with a stretch from his stony seat, as if he was lifted up by some invisible hands. It was a slow and graceful thing to watch, and I saw the wolf in him then. "Follow me," he said.

I did follow, down a path I didn't know, to a cabin I had never seen, despite my roaming. I stopped on the way to gather nuts, and to eat some mushrooms. I couldn't help myself. I ate whenever I saw food.

He waited quietly for me to be done, then only said, "You know your mushrooms."

I looked up at him, my pockets and my mouth filled with them. I stopped my foraging, and we walked on until we reached the cabin. It was buried beneath thick foliage and included an unexpected front porch. I could have passed by it many times without seeing it. There must be some spell or enchantment over the entrance, I was sure of it.

"You know good hiding places, Myrddin Emrys. I've never seen this cabin before."

He chuckled, "We all need our solitude sometimes."

"Speak for yourself. You spend your time at court, surrounded by people," I retorted.

He sat on a stool in the little front porch and said, "You're right. I apologize. Your solitude was not chosen." He took off his shoes, stretched his feet and asked, "So tell me, why have you come?"

I stood in front of him with my arms crossed and grumbled, "You know perfectly well why. There is no one else who can help me."

"Master Hillel knows quite a lot," said the druid.

"Not enough to help me get rid of it," I replied, pointing at my beastly self.

"Your curse hasn't faded in all this time. It must be very strong. How long has it been?"

"Three years to the day."

"How do you keep track of time so precisely?" he asked.

"It was my birthing day, the night of the frost moon. The long night of the winter solstice," I sighed.

"I cannot promise you I can take the curse away," said the druid.

I slumped down on the ground, my hopes of a quick cure dashed.

He crouched down next to me and said, "I need to know all the particulars first. Tell me everything that's happened the day of the curse, everything that led to it and what happened right after. Do not skip any details."

He made me go all the way back. What it was like knowing my mother died in childbirth. The guilt I bore as if it was my fault. Growing up without a mother. The need for someone to see me, to listen to me, to know me. My father's love as intermittent as his presence, his erratic temper and how to placate him, make him laugh, make him proud, be the prettiest and smartest girl I could be. My brother also being motherless. His pain. What it was like for me when my father died. How angry I was at my father for leaving me. That was unexpected. My father and brother's relationship falling apart despite my best efforts. The terror of that, like another death. Like being twice orphaned. The pillars of my life failing, and my heart ripped apart. How I must always be strong for my brother, do everything in my power for us to remain close, together. Without him I would fall into oblivion, be a frozen fallen leaf in the wintering Glaslyn River.

Did I carry *all* these feelings within me the night of the curse? Some of them, undoubtedly. No one had ever asked me how I felt before. Had taken the time to listen. And in the telling of it, I felt feelings I didn't know were there. Myrddin Emrys was my witness through all of it, as still and present as one of the ancestor stones from the solstice circle. He never tried to touch me or stop me. And when I was done, a lightness buoyed my body that made me want to laugh. I was not quite so hungry as I had been.

Afterwards, he asked for the mushrooms I still carried in my pockets and cooked them with eggs. The first human meal I had eaten in three years. I ate it like the beast I was. He said nothing. Only then did we come to the particulars of the birthday feast.

"I was bored with most of the suitors wanting to dance with me. They had no wit and no conversation except for Gawain, King Arthur's nephew. He was interesting."

Myrddin Emrys nodded. Of course, he knew who Gawain was. Probably did the blessing ritual at Gawain's birth.

"But Somer doesn't like the royal family. Wouldn't let me dance with him. We did speak briefly later. I was given a beautiful hand tooled saddle for my palfrey, Espoir, and also a handsome well-made cloak from the Isle of Eire. I wear it to this day. Lady Amunet gave me dates from Egypt and urged me to drink this thick camel milk at the same time. She told me they go together, like bread and butter. It was my first time for both. I liked the dates, but the camel milk tasted a bit salty and was richer than the sheep's milk I'm used to."

Myrddin Emrys nodded. I resumed, "That's it really. When I went to my rooms, Somer followed to give me his particular birthday present. It was a white linen sleeping gown woven by the women of the Isle of Skye. It was so beautiful, I wanted to sleep in it right away. We said good night then. I told him that he was the best brother, and he kissed me on the cheek and left. I put on my new sleeping gown and shivered at the feel of it. It was so fine, like wearing a caress. I don't remember anything after that. I didn't drift into sleep as I usually do, thinking about the events of the day and evening. It was more like falling into a black pit of nothingness."

"Telltale signs of a strong sleeping draught," he said.

The druid's comment startled me, but it made sense. I should have known. Why didn't I think of it? I remembered how difficult it was for me to rise from sleep the next morning, "I was struggling to wake myself, like trying to separate myself from sticky dough, when my ancilla came into my room with the breakfast tray. Lavinia screamed and fainted when she caught sight of me rising from the bed. I screamed too after I picked up the tray from the floor and saw what I had become. At first I couldn't believe what I was seeing. I thought there must be a devil in the room with me but no, there was only me, no one else. I remember looking down at my body and noticing that the linen was changed and had become incrusted into my body like a new foul skin. After doctors and priest tried for weeks to break the curse, which was almost the end of me, I left, and my brother took over the running of Dinas Emrys."

I fell silent then, spent from all the retelling.

"There are substances which, because of their purity, can be manipulated for good or ill depending on the will of the maker," said the druid. "Such a substance is linen, and such is milk. Milk is magic, the purest magic you can find. It is the perfect nourishment for most new life. It contains everything for a baby to grow and be healthy, whether a fox, a whale, or a human child. All babes born of a womb live and thrive from the milk of the mother. The camel milk was such a substance which when disturbed by the sleeping draught and the intent of the maker, strengthened the depth of your sleep and circumvented the will of the body and of the mind to fight against the spell taking root. It also strengthened the intent of the curse. Not only does it make it near impossible to break but it increases its power over time."

"Lady Amunet is the one who insisted on my drinking the milk with the dates," I said.

"As she should," he answered. "They taste better together."

"You are missing the point," I said. *He's being obtuse on purpose.*

"Is she the one who poured the draught into the milk? Or did she serve you the milk?"

"I don't know. I remember looking at her. I didn't notice who served me," I admitted.

"Right now, we don't know," said the druid. "It could have been anyone of the servants or guests that night. We must focus on what can be known, such as the intent of the curse. That's the important piece."

"And what was the intent?" I asked.

"We can deduce what it is from its consequences," said Myrddin Emrys. "First, the curse has rendered you unmarriable, and second, you let your brother take charge of Dinas Emrys, effectively making him the unofficial heir instead of you. Therefore someone, or some people, wanted to make sure you wouldn't become the greatest lady in the land through a combination of an illustrious marriage and the vast holdings you would bring to such a marriage. It is also interesting to note that they didn't deem it necessary to kill you."

There was something despicable and vile about the fact that cursing me was enough, that it would fulfil their purpose, whoever they were. And it had, completely and absolutely. Now that I thought of it, I was furious with myself. I had not fought a single moment to hold on to Dinas Emrys. I only wanted to hide and felt unfit to take care of my home. I fully believed my brother to be the best, the only choice under the circumstances.

"Motherless children are more vulnerable to enchantment," said Myrddin Emrys.

"What did you say?" I asked. Every word out of the druid's mouth frightened me. It struck my body and rang it like a bell. But I wanted to hear more.

"The safety, protection, and nurturing of a mother's love are absent," he explained. "Their need for love and safety will thrust such children into terrible troubles."

His words rose up in me like a flame, and I wanted him to burn to cinders.

"Are you saying what happened to me is my fault?" I barked, claws itching to strike.

"No, I'm not," he replied. "Only that you were more susceptible to enchantment because of what happened to you. Now, to contravene the first intent of such a spell…"

"You mean how it made me unsuitable for marriage," I interrupted.

"Yes. A man would have to agree to marry you now, as you are, of his own free will. It may not spark a full reversal but, with some luck, it might break at least part of the curse. On the solstice would be best. There is another aspect to this which I cannot fathom yet. It must be for you to discover."

Myrddin Emrys had explained it all so matter of fact, like doing a sum with numbers instead of my life. What kind of magician was this druid anyway?

"No one will ever marry me of their own free will, in any case," I said in anger, willing my tears not to spill.

"You do not know this for certain," he said.

"I do, Myrddin Emrys," I answered. "A man will never choose a foul creature like me with nothing, if he can have a pretty one with a dowry."

"The lands are still yours by right," said the druid. "There is hope. The Auseklis must be with you somehow."

He was talking about the guardian star, the protector from malice and misfortune. It was one of our most powerful and ancient symbols to banish the darkness and drive away evil spirits.

"You are joking," I said. "Look at me!" I growled.

"I see someone who has managed to keep her mind and her wits about her," replied the druid. "An extraordinary feat under such circumstances. So yes. Specially since you have been living with the curse for as long as you have. Three years makes it practically irreversible. In general, time is of the essence with such a spell. The longer it lasts, the stickier it gets and the harder to break. The linen gown is your skin at this point."

His words sent shivers up and down my spine.

"So, I am lost. Is that it?" I asked.

"Well, something has acted as a protection, otherwise your mind would be gone too by now. I haven't discovered what it is yet," he said, a frown etched on his brow.

He sounded so calm, so logical. It drove me mad. My whole body trembled as I kept myself from scratching his eyes out. I crossed my arms around my body and held on tight. Dreadful thoughts, thoughts I couldn't bear to contemplate, were invading my mind, going round and round, that my brother had a hand in my misfortune. He was the one who presented me with the linen gown that night.

Myrddin Emrys interrupted my thoughts, "Are you sure you told me everything?"

I tried to think but Somer's face kept rising up in front of me, like an apparition. The linen gown was his gift. I battled with my mind. *He would never. Not his little sister. He wouldn't.*

Myrddin spoke as if he knew my mind. "You're thinking it may be your brother. You may be right, but it could also be the weaver and not the giver, or someone else entirely who might be connected to both. And it is probable that more than one person was involved."

Relieved beyond measure, I repeated out loud, "The weaver not the giver."

"Yes, My Lady," he said.

I snarled, "Stop pretending. I'm a beast not a lady."

"No matter what your appearance or how wretched you feel, you are still Lady of Dinas Emrys. If you don't know that, no one else will," he said.

"I'm so mad, I wish I was dead. But I'm much too hungry all the time to die," I said.

Myrddin Emrys chuckled. "Then let us bless your hunger then. You're much too precious to die quite so soon."

I didn't think it was funny but there was some very dark humor to my situation.

He made us a broth with dried herbs hanging from the eves. The sweet and spicy aroma was familiar. I inhaled deeply, nostrils flared for a better grasp of the scent.

"It's fennel, isn't it? Lavinia uses it as well."

"Yes," he replied. "Very good for digestion."

We watched the hearth, waiting for the herbs to steep. He sat in a chair. I crouched by the fire. Eventually, I broke our silence. "There is something else, but I don't think it's anything."

Myrddin Emrys waited for me to speak again. He was patient. Not like me.

"I received another present, a small thing, the night of the curse." (That's how I thought of that night now. It was no longer my birthing day. It was *the night of the curse.*)

"Do you have it with you?" he asked.

"Yes," I replied. "It was from Gawain."

"May I examine it? I will give it right back to you," he murmured.

The idea of handing my little wren to the druid made me nervous. I fiddled with the carving in the hidden pocket of my cloak. I could scarcely part with it even with his assurance. Finally, I brought it out of its hiding place. I had only glanced at it since that day. I just rubbed it inside my pocket whenever I felt particularly wretched. To my surprise, it hadn't changed at all. It was still this perfectly carved little bird with the brown body and orange chest. A reminder of something beautiful and good. I handed it over to Myrddin. He took it carefully into his hands as if it was alive and examined it thoroughly, delicately, like a precious jewel.

"Clever boy. Takes after his mother. Did you know your father made a nuptial agreement on your behalf with King Arthur? You were to become betrothed to young Gawain on your birthing day. It was going to be announced at the feast, but only if you liked him well enough. Your father insisted."

I was so stunned by this revelation I had no words. *Gawain of the lovely curls, beautiful, smart, sweet Gawain was meant to be my betrothed.* It was bitter news indeed. My fate galled me all the more.

Myrddin Emrys handed the carving back to me, "It was a closed agreement between the parents with the king's approval. Such a wondrous bird. Poor little wren. The Christians twisted her meaning to an evil thing so they can kill little wren every year in the name of their Saint Stephen. I was right by the way. Look underneath. There is your Auseklis."

I turned the wren upside down and I stroked the star carved into it as gently as I could with the pad of my thumb, long with claw. "Gawain," I breathed in his name, bereft beyond measure.

I felt like this little bird, like great hands had grabbed me and turned me upside down. The loss of Gawain before I even had a chance to love him. A wedding gone with the rest of my life before I could even contemplate its possibility. There was nothing I could say to that. I was angry no one told me, when I still had a chance at, at what? Saying *Yes I like this boy very much. He suits me. I will keep him forever, for a night, for an hour.* I wanted to throttle Myrddin Emrys for telling me now when there was no chance at all.

Bitterness dripping from every word, I said, "Well, if it was supposed to ward off evil, it didn't do a very good job, did it? Maybe this Gawain is no great loss after all."

I shoved the wren back in its hidden pocket, jaw clenched on everything I would never say to Gawain, everything I hadn't done, like touch the curls tumbling down on his forehead.

"Oh, it did its job," said the druid. "It mitigated the repercussions of the curse. You would have lost your mind without it."

"I thought I did."

"Maybe for a while," he acquiesced. "But not really. It has served you well."

I bared my teeth in disagreement.

"And your ancilla helped too," he said, ignoring me. "When she fainted, she took the first wave of the curse upon herself. She didn't mean to of course. But thanks to her you were not the first to see yourself. She was."

"Didn't you say linen is also supposed to ward off evil?"

"Yes," he replied, "When it's pristine. But if subverted for evil purposes, it is even more treacherous, because its origin is so pure. What is innocent is also what is most easily bewitched. Though it is a great sacrilege to do so. To subvert it takes skill and will. A great weaver."

"But that would mean traveling to the Isle of Skye. I can't. I can't travel like this. It's too far anyway."

"You've got anything better to do? Raid a few pantries or ransack a few pigsties perhaps?" he asked, mocking me.

Anger burned my eyes. I was ready to attack him again, plunge my teeth into his neck, when he said, "I will go with you."

"Why?" I barked.

"Call it professional curiosity."

I laugh-snorted for the first time since I can remember. I probably sounded like my horse. We both sipped our broth for a while. My eyes strayed back to the runes on his hands and arms.

"Ask," he said, as he followed my gaze.

I knew better than to equivocate with such as he. "These are runes, aren't they?"

"Yes, they are," he nodded.

"Did you trace them yourself or did someone do it for you?" I asked.

"Neither," he answered, "They appear on their own. When it's time."

"Does it hurt?"

"Like fire inscribing itself into flesh," he answered. "Similar to what happened to you."

"I don't remember it hurting," I said.

"Because of the sleeping draught. A strong decoction of valerian root and poppy in the milk, I wager. Otherwise, you would have been screaming all night long."

"I did scream, for days and weeks after, when the doctors worked on me. And the priest."

"I can imagine," he said.

I thought he could imagine it, if what he said of the runes inscribed on his body was true. What a pair we'd make if we traveled together. I was still hesitant about attempting such a journey in my condition, traveling across the country, all the way to the Isle of Skye, with no certainty that we would find this weaver, or even if we did, that we would learn anything from meeting her. The weavers were all women on the isle. My brother had told me so.

I had been hiding from the world for so long, the world had become my enemy. I couldn't contemplate the idea of travel without fear rushing through my limbs like a cataract. The idea scared me so, I went back to my inquiry about the runes instead.

"What did you mean, 'When it's time'?" I asked.

"I meant that exactly. They arrive at the precise time they are needed. Like the runes that sang their song when you came into the clearing."

"The ones you were inscribing on the ground?" I asked.

"Yes. Those runes," he replied.

"What were they?"

"You will not understand if I tell you," he said.

"Tell me anyway."

"*Ansuz. Ehwaz. Sowelu.*" The sound reverberated through the snowy night, calling out to the stone circle and ended with a crystalline ping in my ear. Like my dream: the wolf speaking in a language beyond my grasp.

"I don't understand," I said, in spite of myself. "What do they mean?"

"It is your path, what you must discover," he answered.

"It sounds important," I said. "Why don't you enlighten me?"

"To explain the runes is to miss their meaning," he said. "The knowledge is revealed as you experience the path."

I detested his answer. It reminded me of some of my teachers, including Hillel, who would answer in a cryptic fashion, so I would be left to solve the problem on my own. I wanted to tell him that if I could have figured out my path I would have done so by now.

"You are like one of my old teachers who covers his lack of knowledge by asking me to answer what he cannot." It was a snide comment from the beast I was and which he overlooked.

"If you do not stop clinging to what you were and keep hiding from what you are, you will never grow into what you're meant to become."

I heard the truth behind his words like a hammer ringing on an anvil between my ears. I lost my balance and sat back on my haunches. How was I meant to become anything? I could see no future for myself.

I could only hang fast to what was left of my friends, Hillel and Lavinia, and to my memories of my brother and my father. There was no future, only this curse that had swallowed me whole. What little hope I had was wrapped up in the past, the life I could still remember, like torn pieces of fabric floating in the wind, as thin as that vile piece of linen I wore on that dismal night. It was not much but I needed it and held onto it fiercely.

Myrddin Emrys bore his black eyes into mine, his face so close, I heard him breathe. No one had come this close to me since the curse. I was frozen, caught in the fierce love of his wolf stare like a prey. He smelled of tree sap and thunder and snow.

"Stop hoping at all until you can start hoping for the right thing," he said.

His words sizzled like lightning inside my skull, sending their little spiderwebs of light everywhere. I had not met a man who could speak so plainly and so wisely at the same time. Not even my father came close. And he flattered himself for his understanding of human affairs. Hillel might be the only one who could approach such stark clarity of mind.

My body started to shake as I asked, "What is the right thing?"

"You won't know until you stop."

"I like you *not at all* Myrddin Emrys," said I, enunciating each word.

"Most people don't." He was nonchalant in his answer, as if he didn't care one bit what I thought, what anyone thought of him. He was Myrddin Emrys after all, the greatest druid of our time. I wished I was more like that. But how could I be, looking the way I did? To be honest, even before the curse, I always worried about what others thought of me, always striving to make a good impression, to please my father, my brother. I suppose it is what children do, maybe more so what girl children do, when there is no loving mother to bridge the world.

I stood up, planted my feet and crossed my arms on my chest, a combination of a spoiled child and a surly beast. "I will not move until you tell me something of what the runes mean."

My petulance amused him. He smiled, "I will tell you of the first. *Ansuz* is the messenger. It brings sacred knowledge, a gift, usually from a chance encounter, particularly when it comes from a person wiser than oneself."

"You are making this up," I snarled.

He was the greatest magician of the greatest king in the land, and I was being disrespectful, but he laughed. "No, I'm not. You are here, in a place where sacred knowledge is revealed. And we are meeting. Make of it what you will."

"Maybe it's the other way around," I said. "Maybe *I* am the messenger and the gift."

I meant to challenge him, but he answered without hesitation. "That is entirely possible. Runes are mysterious. The meaning stays true. The interpretation varies according to the will of the Gods, human understanding, and the Norns of course."

He was referring to the Fates and I shivered. *Perhaps they mean for me to remain a beast forever.* "Alright Myrddin Emrys," I said, "I will go with you since, as you pointed out so rudely, I have nothing better to do."

We agreed to reconvene at the stone circle for the wolf moon. The wolf, another reminder of my dream. What I realized afterwards but kept to myself, was that for the entire time I was conversing with him, I forgot the wickedness of my appearance. We had been two people talking. That must be the spell he weaved upon me, to let me be a person again. In that way, he was a gift to me already, my messenger. But I would not reveal that to him as we prepared to embark on our travels. This knowledge was for me alone.

Chapter Eleven

January, the dead of winter, was a terrible time to travel in my estimation. But Myrddin Emrys disagreed. *Better to travel through snow than spring thaw.* What if it was unseasonably warm and we experienced the mud and sleet anyway? Weather changed fast in these lands. It must be the same or worse in Scotland and the Hebrides. We could find ourselves in the worst winter in a hundred years with constant snowstorms and freezing temperatures. What then? Where would we find shelter for our horses, for me? It seemed an impossible endeavor. I felt on the edge of a precipice, as if I would die if I didn't go, but would probably also die if I did. I must ask Hillel what he thought before I made up my mind to go on this journey, with the craziest druid I had ever met. Granted, he was the only one I knew, but still.

I went back to my little cabin to check on Espoir. He had grown a thick winter coat, and it kept him warm enough in the stable. He munched on hay left from the last batch Hillel had brought over. I asked Espoir if he wanted to go on an adventure. His brown jewel eyes seemed to say, *I'll go wherever you go.*

"Not much longer," I said to my four-legged friend. "A few things to organize and then we'll go on our grand adventure." I had made up my mind after all. I still wanted to let Hillel know what I was planning and couldn't wait till our next meeting.

I "borrowed" a boat from the pig farmer, moored nearest to the Gwynedd woods, more of a small scow, the kind with a flat bottom. I used a little tributary of the Glaslyn River not yet frozen, to row into the cave under our castle. It was faster than walking through the woods all the way back to Dinas Emrys. My animal body had a great deal more strength than I used to as a girl and I enjoyed the activity. The day was damp and foggy. No one was out except for a few little purple sandpipers and dunlins in the marshes. They watched me as I passed, with round eyes full of surprise. It was not every day they saw a beast rowing a boat.

I made it to the lake under the castle. I would have lingered longer in the cave, for it was an unearthly sight, full of magic. Frozen trees hung upside down from the ceiling, shedding stars into the lake. The cave walls shimmered, incrusted with purple stones, the ground was black onyx with white stripes and made a crystalline sound with each step I took, echoing throughout the place. I could well believe dragons had lived here.

I tied the scow with a bowline knot to a dock ring on the shore of the lake then changed my mind. I would walk back. I untied the scow and pushed it back toward the entrance of the lake. I watched it disappear into the darkness. Since I had been rowing upstream, I hoped it was a smart little scow and would find its way back to its owner. I didn't want to be branded a beast *and* a thief. I found the door in a recess of the rock wall. I pushed hard on it and it creeped open with a whine. Somer had described it all to me years ago. *It doesn't look like there is a door there because it's in a dark recess of the cave but if you look for the face of a bird in the cave wall next to the frozen falling water, you'll find its bill is pointing straight at the door below it.* I pretended not to believe him then, but I remembered every word. I was probably upset that he hadn't taken me along. It sounded like the best kind of adventure to share with my brother.

I walked through the tunnel blasted with dragon fire. Jutting out of the walls, jagged rocks of different size and shape made the most disconcerting shadows of beasts not unlike myself. But even though I was a beast, I was also still a girl and admittedly, not a very courageous one, and the dragon tunnel made me tremble, and my hackles rise. It was a cross between a dream and a nightmare. I didn't take another breath until I made it out, not far from the stables, heart thumping against my chest.

At first I headed toward Hillel's office behind the stables. But my feet took me to the top of the western hillock across from the castle instead. It was the site of my father's mausoleum. I had not returned since his interment. The gardens hid under the snow. No bird sang. A cold north wind rose and began to shake the trees that formed a protective grove around the gardens. The girl I was before the curse would be freezing by now but my animal body with its thicker skin and hair ran warmer. And my cozy Irish cloak with its thick layer of wool helped too.

A carving of my father's likeness had been created since the funeral and placed on top of the tomb. The artist had caught my father's inner smile exactly, the one that said, *I'm harder on myself than I am on you*. It was as if he could wake from his eternal slumber at any moment. I put my hand on the cold grey marble with its dark red veins and talked to my father as if he could hear me. "You were right. I liked Gawain. I was cursed on the night of my birthing day, in case you were not aware of it. Perhaps it was the same people who poisoned you. If you know who it is father, please tell me. I've not forgotten. I have learned terrible things about myself since the curse. I have so much rage and hunger in me. Sometimes I cannot control it at all. I want revenge against those who took my life away from me, and yours. Myrddin Emrys says there is a different future waiting for me if I can let go of the past, but I can't see it. I want my life back. Please help me father and I will avenge you. Please."

I slid down next to the tomb then, the manner of my father's death weighing on me as much as my own fate, like a double curse.

"Are you bargaining with the dead? You really think he's going to answer you?"

I looked up as my brother loomed near, footfall too soft in the fresh snow for me to hear.

"He never took the time to listen while he was alive. Why would he bother now that he's dead?" he said. "You were always so enamored of our father, as if he could do no wrong."

"And you always fought him as if he could do no right," I answered, my voice strangled with the emotions running through me. Grief, anger, surprise battling it out.

"Because his manners were a disguise to cover his false heart," said Somer. "You only knew what he wanted you to see, *the good father, the great man*. All lies."

"What are you doing here, in such weather, if you despise him so much?" I asked. "Are you ascertaining he's still dead? Are you afraid his ghost might haunt you?"

I said the last half in jest, but the look of horror on my brother's face halted the rest of the rant on my lips.

"You are the one who should be worried about ghosts," he said, grinding his teeth.

I didn't understand Somer's meaning, but even though he couldn't see me with my hood up, I wanted to hide from him, fade into the marble tomb. My brother was dressed all in black, which didn't suit his pale complexion nor his slender frame. His beautiful eyes looked troubled, huge in his face. They stared at me unblinking, almost unseeing, as if he was a man drunk, or about to attack me, like the wild boar that had me running for my life not long ago.

All the niceties were gone between us. There was no hello, no *Sutmae, little sister*. He went for the deadliest blow. "Do you want to know why Hengist betrayed us, after the Saxon gave his assurance that he would fight with Briton against the other tribes, after he was given half of Kent in return for his loyalty? Do you know why he turned on our father, the great Vortigern, turned on his new Welsh friends, the Night of the Long Knives?"

I knew Somer would tell me some dreadful thing. But I couldn't stop him, and I couldn't stop myself from listening. The wind abated around us as if to ensure I heard every word.

"Your mother's name is not *Rionach*. Our father gave her this name. It's not even like he tried. I could have come up with a better one. Everybody knew who she really was."

The savagery with which he spoke, the way he spit out his words reminded me of his fights with our father. I girded myself against what came next. I knew it wouldn't help.

"Your mother was Rowena, Hengist's daughter. Our father lusted after her. He was so self-important, he believed she fancied him too. He couldn't control his lust or bother to ask Hengist for permission to court her. He got drunk and he raped her. Such was his arrogance, it didn't occur to him that she'd wait until he fell asleep to go tell her father about it. Hengist's reprisal was swift. That very night he sent out his Berserkers. That's why all those lords were killed that night, *because of our father's lust*. And the only reason *he* survived was because of Lord Kay and his army's timely arrival. Hengist threw your mother out when he found out she was carrying Vortigern's child. The Saxon didn't want a half breed bastard in his family. She showed up at our castle one night, looking more like a beggar than a Saxon princess. Our father took her in and made up some lame story about her family being from a neighboring county. He supposedly married her on her death bed. She died of shame after you were born. She was the daughter of the Saxon beast. She was raped by a beast. And now, *you* are the beast."

Somer was telling the truth, or at least his version of it. I had no doubt. But the pain I felt on hearing it recounted with such brutality, every word dripping with so much hatred, left me speechless, groundless, and without a will to go on.

"You have no business here. Go back to your woods, *beast*," he said at last.

My brother walked away as quickly as the gusting winds allowed him, wrapped in his black cloak against the battering cold. I thought, *my brother has become the ghost he is afraid of.*

I sat by my father's tomb for a long time after that. The wind howled all around me, bringing with it snow flurries, and I began to disappear under the soft white cover. I wondered if I would get up again or let myself die here after all, save everyone the trouble of burying me.

But the beast in me refused to accept my choice of death. The promise to my father surged through the icy torpor invading my brain, then Myrddin Emrys's black eyes blazed into my mind's eye like stars in the night sky. I heard his voice say *this is no time to fall asleep. Wake up little dryw donn*. He called me little brown wren. *Dryw*, the same word for wren and druid. He sought my company, and I sought his knowledge of magic. And I was still and always desperately hungry. I shook off the snow from my cloak, fought my way back to the stables and walked around the back to Hillel's office. He must be there. It was too cold for any human to be out in that wind. Gusting icicles were flinging themselves over my face and body. I knocked. He opened right away. I turned my back to him so he wouldn't see me.

"Sutmae, Hillel. Can you follow me back to the stables. I can hide in one of the stalls while we talk."

"Please forgive me Lady Ragnell, but we will not do that today. You are coming in to sit by the fire. This old body of mine will turn to ice by the time I make it to the stables."

I didn't want Hillel to freeze to death because of me. I walked in, making sure to keep my face well hidden under my hood, and sat away from him.

"Do you have any food?" I asked, embarrassment flushing my cheeks, despite the cold.

"Yes, I do," he replied.

Before he had time to offer me anything, I saw the tray untouched on his desk with breakfast rolls and ham and cheese. I grabbed it all with my clawing hands and crammed it into my mouth. Bread, cheese, and ham were barely chewed and gone in an instant.

As soon as I was done, I felt remorse and shame for my gluttony and then rage about feeling shame. My whole body shook with the desire to rant and rave and hurt Hillel in some way for witnessing my shame, for not running out screaming about this uncontrollable beast in his office, devouring all his food. I squeezed my little dryw in the hidden pocket of my cloak and regained some control over the wild swings of my emotions.

I sounded almost human when I spoke. "I'm sorry. I ate all your breakfast."

"I can get another breakfast later," he replied.

"I apologize for my behavior," I grunted.

"It's not your fault, My Lady. And it's very cold out. You need more sustenance."

Hillel was a kind man. I let myself thaw out by the fire. Water droplets from my hair, nose, and hands made little puddles around me.

"I saw Somer at our father's mausoleum," I said. "Does he go there often?"

Hillel showed no surprise at my question. "I've seen him head that way before."

"It's as if he's going there to torture himself," I said.

"You may be right. His is a tormented soul," said Hillel.

"He told me about my mother." I said abruptly.

"Your mother?" asked Hillel.

"My *real* mother. Rowena, Hengist's daughter. Did you know who she was?" I asked.

"I did," he acknowledged. "And before you say anything, it wasn't my secret to tell."

"Am I even a legitimate child? Can you tell me that?" I asked.

"I don't know what information your brother gave you or how he described the events surrounding your birth."

"There was no love in it," I said.

"I can assure you, you are the legitimate heir of Gwynedd province," said Hillel.

"Is it true?" My throat was tight as I swallowed. "Did my father rape my mother?"

"I couldn't tell you," he replied. "I do know that war brings out the worst in men, greed, and lust and even the most honorable of men do horrific things in the heat of battle. Women, children, and the aged are always the ones who suffer most from men's wars. It is one of the most constant and tragic truths of the world men have created. I can also tell you that your father was very protective of Lady Rowena during her pregnancy, and she seemed to accept his care and love him back. Your father was more concerned with her health than marriage vows."

"Was it guilt?" I asked.

Hillel shook his head. "I don't know. But she was not well during that whole year so there was no wedding until it became evident that she might not rise from the birthing bed. I helped make the arrangements for a marriage ceremony which happened before your birth. I was one of the witnesses. Your brother was taken to Lord Kay at the time. Your father didn't want Somer to witness another death so soon after his own mother's."

"Then Somer wasn't present at my birth," I said, more to myself than Hillel.

"No. He wasn't," he replied.

Maybe Somer's truth was only a half truth, I thought.

“Did my mother know me before she died?” I asked, throat tight.

“She did,” said Hillel. “You were placed on her heart while it was still beating, and she was able to hold you. She wanted her heart to know yours and your heart to know hers. She made your father swear to love you and protect you.”

“I became a monster anyway,” I said. “Ironic, isn’t it?”

“Some may see you as a monster, but I know who you are, Lady Ragnell.”

Hillel might know who I was, but I didn’t. Not anymore.

“I do know one thing,” I said. “We must find out which doctor had a hand in my father’s death. Since my brother will not do this, will you help me?”

Hillel sighed and nodded. I knew I was placing a burden on him, but I was full of fury.

“Find out who it was. Make him confess. Make him drink some of his own poisons if need be,” I said, “Promise me.”

“It may take some time, My Lady, but I will, you can count on it,” he promised.

“That’s all right, Hillel,” I said. “I will be away for a while. I met with Myrddin Emrys. We’ll be traveling to the Isle of Skye.”

“It’s good you’re going together,” he said, as if he already knew of my travel plans.

“I’m not so sure. He’s a druid. They are hard to fathom,” I said.

“Yes, they are,” he agreed.

“You two are alike in some ways,” I mused.

He smiled. “I’ll take that as a compliment, My Lady.”

“He told me about the arranged betrothal to King Arthur’s nephew, to Gawain. It was supposed to be announced the night of the curse.”

“Your father mentioned it. He meant to announce it, but…”

“But he died,” I interrupted. “It doesn’t matter now, does it? I will take my leave. Is there any way you can keep me informed of your progress with the search while I’m gone?”

“Myrddin Emrys has a relationship with a clever crow. We have communicated messages through her before.” His tone was innocent enough but now I knew why he didn't seem surprised by my news. He'd already been informed.

"Have you?" I asked. "I didn't notice any crow when I met with the druid."

"She is unusual. She doesn't let herself be seen unless she means to," Hillel explained. "And she blends in quite easily in winter."

"How so?" I asked.

"She turns all white."

"I've never seen a white crow. It must be quite a sight," I reflected.

"It is, My Lady. Here, you might need these." Hillel handed me woolen mittens. I was about to refuse considering the current length and sharpness of my nails but realized he had cut off the ends to accommodate them. It was so thoughtful, I barely managed to thank him.

"Lavinia knitted them for you," he said.

Of course it was my dear Lavinia. "How is she faring?"

"Well enough, My Lady. Lady Amunet is exacting but appreciates Lavinia's work."

Hillel reached behind his desk and handed me two traveling packs. "I keep some extra food and grain ready for you."

"Thank you, Hillel." I put on the mittens and picked up the packs.

"Do you want my help?" he asked, "These are quite heavy."

I slung the packs over my shoulder, "They're not so heavy. Not anymore." The beast was stronger than the girl had been. It didn't make up for the horrid fate, but it helped a little.

He nodded with a knowing smile. "Safe travels, My Lady."

"You as well, Hillel. And may all our travels bear fruit."

I held back from touching him before I left, even though I craved arms around me, those simple gestures of human connection. I hurried back toward my cabin to get Espoir ready. The snow had stopped, and a pale sun struggled through the fog. I wondered again why I was going on this mad journey as I tacked Espoir with his hand tooled saddle and bridle. I had taken the bit out of the bridle long ago because I considered Espoir my friend, not my slave.

So many things could go wrong, some I could well imagine, like getting hunted and killed by villagers. And some I couldn't, like Myrddin

Emrys using me for his own dark ends. If it was my fate to die as a monster, and if I would travel with anyone to my demise, it would be with this half man, half devil of a druid. I didn't know that many people, but of anyone I knew, I felt certain he was most likely to understand what it was like to be a beast in a man's world.

Chapter Twelve

The path was hidden under the snow. It made it harder for Espoir to find his footing. He was high stepping like a tournament horse. My progress back to the stone circle was so slow, I became afraid that I wouldn't be able to find the place in time and miss my appointment with Myrddin Emrys. When I finally arrived, there was no one there. I was frantic, walking around the circle of stones, going nowhere, holding Espoir by the reins. I couldn't ride him in the woods in this weather. He was not his usual confident self, snorting, bobbing his head up and down, which added to my own disquiet.

I was about to give up when I saw her. The white crow. Thanks to Hillel, I knew right away she must belong to Myrddin Emrys. She was staring at us from a tree branch with her blue eyes, and her head cocked to one side. Then she took off and landed in front of us, unafraid, hopping a few steps. It was clear she meant for us to follow her.

After a while, Espoir and I got used to her appearing and disappearing from view. When she stood still, I would lose sight of her but then she'd take off again and we followed. From branch to branch, from tree to tree, she led us all the way to the main road, just outside Caernarfon and left us. I stopped at the edge of the road, in the hedgerows, not wanting to be seen, and foraged for food while we waited.

The sun was setting when Myrddin Emrys came down the path on his dapple-grey mare. Espoir immediately took notice of her, nostrils flaring, ears forward, and nickered, pleased with what he saw. The druid was dressed for travel, with a heavy cloak and thick boots, a pack laced with leather ties behind his saddle.

I had a complaint ready about how late it was and how tired I was when he said, "I'm glad *Eira* found you. And you found her. She can be a little difficult to spot sometimes. I apologize for my tardiness. I was arranging our lodgings for the night. Follow me."

The druid took the wind right out of my sails. The rant I was about to give snuffed out by his apology. Instead, I said, "Eira is the perfect name for your crow."

"Yes, Snow. But she is not *my* crow. She is my friend," he corrected.

"I understand. Like Espoir is my friend." I got back on my horse, and we trotted after them, Espoir with his tail high in the air, frisky all of a sudden.

"What are you so happy about?" I asked Espoir.

He shook his head, snorting, and pointed ahead at the mare's long swishing tail and hips.

"That grey mare is beautiful, I'll grant you. But be careful whom you follow. It might lead you somewhere you don't want to be."

I should have minded my own words, because Myrddin Emrys led us straight to the Roman Keep of Caernarfon, *Caer Rufeinig Segontiwm*. It was held by one of the chieftains, Segon Fawr. I definitely did *not* want to be there. The man had a fierce reputation as a warrior.

I tried to maneuver toward the stables, but Espoir wouldn't leave the mare's side. We rode right up to the main entrance. The gates opened without even a question as to who we were and in we walked.

I had not been around strangers in a very long time. I wanted to bolt and run away as fast as I could, but Espoir was keeping so close to the mare, I couldn't move my leg to spur him on. I wondered if the mare was so enticing or if Myrddin had spelled my palfrey. I looked over at the druid. I didn't trust the mild expression on his face at all. Not a good beginning to our travels.

Myrddin Emrys got off his mare and told the young squire, whom I was about to kick in the stomach for trying to help me dismount, that I preferred to be left alone. I quickly got off Espoir. The druid asked that our two horses be kept together. I was grateful for that. I didn't want Espoir left alone in a strange stable.

Segon Fawr planted himself at the entrance to welcome us. He was as wide as he was tall. I might be a beast, but he was a bear.

"Myrddin Emrys, *Croeso nol*. What will you ask of me this time?"

Welcome back? I suppose the druid must travel a lot on the king's business.

"We are just passing through," said Myrddin Emrys.

"And you happen to arrive exactly when I am meeting with the lords from all our kingdoms?" said the Bear. That's how I thought of him.

"A little bird told me you might need some help," said the druid.

A little bird. That's funny. He must mean his white crow.

The man snorted then turned his gaze on me, his hands on his hips. I kept my hood up and my face down, but I could feel my muscles tensing, getting ready to run or to attack. It was instinctive and beyond my control.

"And who have you brought to my door, Myrddin Emrys?" asked the Bear.

I thought Myrddin would make up a story, *this is my helper, prefers to stay outside, prefers horses to humans.* To my horror, he said, "This is the Lady of Gwynedd."

Segon Fawr took a step back. Most of the neighboring nobility knew of my curse since a good half of them had been invited to my birthing day feast and many had stayed the night. It was no surprise that the Lord of the Keep in Caernarfon knew. What surprised me was his response.

"You've brought the Cursed Lady to my house?" he bellowed to cover his fear.

"Do I need to make other arrangements?" asked the druid.

I saw the struggle on the man's face. The multiple consequences of turning away Myrddin Emrys, King Arthur's Magician, the most powerful druid of his time. Then I saw him resign himself to navigating an awkward situation with his other guests.

"No, of course not," said the Bear. "I will make sure the lady has her own lodgings."

He meant to put me in some tower, as far from anyone as possible. Fine with me.

"No need," said Myrddin. "We'll share whatever accommodations you've prepared for me. She may be cursed but she has wisdom beyond her years. And we'll not stay long."

I couldn't believe my ears. The druid credited me with *wisdom*. Maybe this journey was not such a terrible idea after all.

The place looked old and dusty, and I suspected nothing much had changed since the Romans had abandoned Segontiwm. But Segon Fawr strode through the mostly bare halls like an emperor.

"The meeting is about to start," said the Bear. "Your timing is uncanny."

"Time is an old friend," answered Myrddin Emrys.

"Is it now?" The Bear chuckled as he led the way to the receiving room where the heads of the other principalities of Powys, Dyfed, and Seisyllwg, were seated at the table.

It occurred to me that Myrddin had planned for me to represent Gwynedd instead of my brother. And he must be representing the interests of King Arthur. The lord of Penrhyn Castle, Marchudd ap Cynan, a neighbor of our host, was also sitting there. Some of these Lords had been present at my birthing day feast, the night of the curse. I stood next to Myrddin, hiding myself as best I could, furious with the druid for putting me, and them, in this position. Despite the cold, I was sweating and, certainly, smelled foul as a pig.

Segon Fawr introduced us, "My Lords, Myrddin Emrys and his traveling companion… The Lady of Gwynedd."

He wasn't sure what to call me. I understood his difficulty. I was a beast, and my brother had taken over as Lord of Dinas Emrys and Gwynedd.

The lords nodded at the druid. They took one look at me, hidden beneath my cloak and hood and turned their faces away. They had to tolerate my presence because of the druid, but they would not acknowledge it.

This was no round table. There was a pecking order, and our host was at the head of the table. Myrddin Emrys stood by Lord Marchudd ap Cynan who was seated facing Segon Fawr at the other head of the table. If it was a test of wills, the Lord of Penrhyn was sure to lose. The moment he looked up at Myrddin Emrys, he turned pale and got up from his seat. I knew the potency of the druid's eyes, and no one could resist the magnitude of the love therein. It made one feel as vulnerable as a newborn babe in a cradle. The druid gestured for me to sit on his right and the lord of Penrhyn sat himself across the table from me with a scowl. The lord of Dyfed and his cousin from Seisyllwg were sitting on either side of Segon Fawr.

"I hope you have all come here today to resolve your differences and support your king?" It was more a statement than a question. Myrddin Emrys was taking control of the meeting before any of them had a chance to start bickering. "We must present a united front to keep Wales free from any more Saxon attacks. *A fo ben, bid bont.*"

"Yes, *He who wants to be a leader must be a bridge*," said the Bear. "And, we must protect our own lands and people first and foremost. Wouldn't you agree, Myrddin Emrys?"

The Penrhyn Lord interrupted. "Arthur is not my king. He doesn't care about us. He wants to keep control, and you do too, druid. My concern is the new Christian faith."

The Lord of Penrhyn didn't mince his words. He was so rude to Myrddin, it made my teeth ache. I wanted to bite into his flesh until the blood flowed. A soft growl escaped me. Penrhyn shifted his body away from me. Myrddin kept his equanimity.

"I agree, Marchudd ap Cynan, the Christians scare me more than the Saxons. But the Saxons want to steal our lands right now and we have to stop them."

Lord Powys spoke up. "And what do the Christians want?"

Myrddin replied forthwith, "The Christians, Lord Powys, want to destroy our way of life, convince us that we are sinners, and that our reverence for Nature comes from the devil, and a few other things."

Everyone was quiet after that. I remembered the priest in Beddgelert, I remembered the lashes on my body, I remembered his words, also like lashes, on my soul, and the animal of my body started to tremble of its own accord. Myrddin put his hand on my arm. It was a reassuring gesture that helped bring me back to our present surroundings. I was in Caernarfon with Myrddin, not in Beddgelert.I took a breath and squeezed the little wooden wren in my pocket.

"The attacks will keep coming regardless. And if not them, someone else," said the Bear.

"That is correct Segon Fawr, which is why it's important to come together and present a united front. We are all *Cymri* here. Personal gain will only bring loss for all in the end. Retreating behind your own walls will not keep you safe," said the druid.

"What makes you so sure?"

It was the first time the Lord of Dyfed spoke. I was about to throw myself all over the *pice ar y maen,* our traditional Welsh cakes. They had just been brought to our table along with some refreshments and were still warm. The smell of dried fruit and spices on top of the cakes was torturing me so much I was salivating, and a grunt of desire escaped my lips. I couldn't help it. The Lord of Penrhyn jumped back in his seat. I was thoroughly ashamed of myself.

When Lord Dyfed asked his question, it drew my attention away from the cakes, and I was grateful for that. He had a strong handsome face, with dark reddish hair and eyes the color of the wild hyacinth, or fairy flower as it was called in these parts, that carpeted all the pathways, woodlands, and gardens of Wales in spring. His square jaw belonged to a man certain his authority would not be contravened. And yet there was a melancholy, an ache etched in the lines around his eyes and on his brow, as if he had lost something precious.

His presence was undeniable though he barely spoke five words. I could tell that he and the Lord of Seisyllwg spoke with one mind. They were cousins. Dyfed was the elder of the two and it was clear Seisyllwg looked to his cousin to take the lead.

All the lords looked at Myrddin, waiting for his answer.

"I have seen it," he said. "My Lords, the Saxons are closer than you think. War is coming to your door. We will not survive unless we *all* work together."

There wasn't much these lords could say to that. They all knew Myrddin Emrys was a renowned seer.

Then I had to open my big mouth. "Even in defeat, together we can claim a better peace than if we are divided."

They all turned to me. They were trying their best to ignore me and here I was, like a fool, reminding them that a monster was seated in their midst.I wanted to hide or eat the whole plate of cakes or both.

Myrddin Emrys came to my rescue. "Quite right, My Lady."

The Bear chimed in, "Yes, something to keep in mind, My Lady. Although we all hope it won't come to that." Then he said something totally unexpected. "Did you know the only reason I inherited this place from the Romans is because of your brother's grandmother?"

It was odd to hear him mention Somer under the circumstances. I wondered what point he was trying to make.

"Magnus Maximus, The Emperor of Rome, came here to Caernarfon and fell in love with Elen, my uncle's daughter, and he built three castles in her honor including this one. He took her back to Rome but granted sovereignty over Briton to our family."

"I thought the *Cymri* refer to him as *Macsen Wledig* here."

"We do, we certainly do, My Lady."

Then he said what he really meant to say, "I was going to invite your brother, Sir Gromer Somer, but our friend here told me not to bother. I understand why now."

He was being courteous in his address but meanwhile, letting me know that Myrddin Emrys had planned this. And it was odd to hear my brother mentioned by his full name.

"Is that what my brother calls himself now?" I asked.

"Indeed," the Bear replied. "It is what he prefers."

"Does he think it more dignified?" I asked.

"I have no opinion on the matter. It is his full name. Isn't it?" he probed.

"Yes," I said. "But unused until now."

I made up my mind to ask the Bear the one question I believed mattered. "Since you referred to the sovereignty of your family over Briton granted by the Roman Emperor, I was curious about one thing. Do you still consider your claim to the throne legitimate, or have you sworn fealty to King Arthur?"

That really got his attention. I refrained from looking at the druid in case he disapproved. Everyone waited for the Bear to answer as it would determine the outcome of Myrddin's visit, and what position the other lords would take in the future. They all knew it. I was berating myself for speaking up. I guess I was tired of all this talk not getting anywhere. It was as if he had baited me, telling me about my brother.

Segon Fawr rose from the table to his full height, looking every inch the Bear, and all the lords followed suit. My heart was beating fast in my chest, and the feelings of running away or attacking rose again, fighting each other inside of me.

"I swore fealty to King Arthur after your father's funeral," he said. "Your brother didn't."

They all breathed a sigh of relief. I wondered if he swore fealty because my brother didn't or because our father died. In either case it must have been as a way to restore the balance of power somehow. *And why on earth did my brother refrain from swearing his allegiance to the king. Does his dislike of King Arthur run that deep? Was it a way of getting back at our father, even after his death? Was Hillel right?*

The Bear pounded his fists on the table, looked around at his guests and said, "Our business is concluded, I think. For now. Shall we adjourn to the dining hall?"

I went from relief to panic. I knew I wouldn't be able to contain my appetite once I started eating. I whispered to Myrddin, "Please, I cannot. I must not. My hunger is too wicked."

Myrddin nodded and whispered back, "That question was quite the gamble. You forced him to declare his allegiance. Well done."

Coming from Myrddin Emrys, that was high praise. He turned to Segon Fawr and asked if someone could send food to our rooms as *the lady is too tired to join us in the dining hall.*

The Bear was as relieved as I was. "Of course."

He immediately sent two valets to fetch food for me to eat in our rooms and someone else to accompany me there straight away.

My escort was a very young and very scared squire who kept well ahead of me at a brisk pace. I could not find a way to ease his worries, so I kept quiet, but the silence made him more nervous. He kept turning his head back to make sure I wasn't going to pounce on him. I had to try something. Perhaps if I asked him for help, it would shift the nature of our relationship.

"Would you mind checking on my horse after you deliver me to my rooms?"

He stumbled, turned around and gawked at me or rather at my hood since I was careful to keep it lowered over my face. It was the shock of hearing the *Cursed Lady of the Gwynedd Woods* talk like a human being. My brother had worn the same stunned expression.

The squire, who couldn't have been more than nine or ten years old, recovered his wits enough to answer, "Yes, My Lady. Is your horse the one called Espoir?"

"Yes he is," I nodded.

"I saw you and the King's Magician arrive," said the squire.

"Oh." *He is the one I almost kicked in the stomach.* "I think Espoir is in love with the Magician's mare," I said.

The boy giggled, "She is very fine to look at."

"And she knows it," I said.

We both giggled this time, though, in my case, it was more of a silent snort. It worked. Talking about horses had eased the boy's mind. I was glad of it. I felt terrible about such a young lad being scared of me. I wondered if his imagination was worse than the reality of my appearance. I wasn't about to test him when his pace was less hurried and his demeanor more comfortable, but a part of me was tempted.

"What is your name, squire?" I asked.

"Daniel, My Lady," he answered.

"That's a very Christian name, isn't it?" I said.

"We were all baptized last week. My entire family. But my real name is *Osian*."

I smiled under my hood, "Little Deer. How beautiful. Keep it close to your heart."

I loved that he still believed *Osian* to be his real name and that he trusted me with it.

"Thank you, My Lady. I will."

The place was cavernous and full of marble, marble columns, marble floors, imported from Rome no doubt. It was chipped and ill-maintained, but the effect was imposing, nonetheless. There were sconces with giant torches illuminating our path and an abundance of deer hunting scenes on all the tapestries I saw. Segon Fawr must be fond of deer hunting.

Osian brought me to my door. "I will check on Espoir straight away, My Lady. I'm sure the food will get here shortly."

"Thank you, Osian. No need to return if all is well."

He bowed and left.

Our accommodations consisted of three rooms: a sitting room with a fireplace and two bedchambers across from each other, also with fireplaces, all of them lit. After looking through the other rooms, I came upon one more with a sunken bath in the middle of it, in the Roman style. The tile floor was heated from below. For all its dilapidated air, and sparse furniture, the Bear had kept up the best of the Roman luxuries, a warm bath. I hadn't had a bath like this in three years. Well, I had *never* had a bath quite like this. I occasionally bathed briefly in cold streams in the Gwynedd woods. It was very tempting. I caught myself whimpering with eagerness like a puppy. I was still trying to make up my mind when I heard a knock on the door. In my excitement about the bath, I had forgotten about food. A first for me since the curse. They brought two trays laden with enough food for four people. The druid had warned them of my appetite. They deposited the trays on the only table in the main room, bowed briefly and left quickly. It looked delicious, there was fowl with gravy and potatoes and dried fruit, cheeses and bread. I was salivating. I knew if I started I wouldn't stop and would be too full to move afterwards, so I decided to take a bath first.

I ran into the back room, took off my cloak and the shreds of clothing I wore underneath and plunged into the bath. It was blissful. I grunted and splashed and howled without a care for who might hear me, for a good long time. Then I just let myself sink to the bottom, for a moment. And Rowena, my mother, came to mind unbidden. At first, I was back in her womb. Then I *was* her, walking away with nothing but her present and future shame, from the only family she had ever known, in the dark of night, with no one to hold her sore back, no one asking her to stay, a hand on her growing belly, wretchedly tired from the beatings she had received, and from the begging she had done, like a supplicant, on her knees, the apologies she had made to anyone and everyone, and from the fear and worry mingling like a dark brew in her blood. How desperate, how alone she felt, rejected by her own family. What courage to reach out to the man who had… I couldn't say the word, even in the silence of my own mind. I couldn't imagine my father doing such a thing, raping a woman against her will. *Even the most honorable man*, Hillel had said. I couldn't abide the thought and threw myself out of the bath. I wrapped myself in the cloth sitting near the edge of the pool. The water was dark with dirt and other things, probably lice and fleas and even twigs. No one else would be able to use this water again tonight.

I looked down at my body for the first time in a very long time. My legs were dark with a hairlike covering of soft fur, my toes harbored big strong nails that looked more like claws, just like the nails on my fingers. I stopped there. I couldn't bear to look at anymore. I was filled with rage when I put my rags back on, and my cloak, and the hood up to cover my face. I told myself I was being careful and considerate, protecting others from my ugliness, the servants who would pick up the trays, or the Lords, or Myrddin Emrys. But I was hiding from myself most of all.

I was ready to bolt again. I made for the door, but the food stopped me. I was too hungry to leave right then and so I devoured whatever they had brought in with my hands, tearing through the meat, soaking the bread in the gravy, adding chunks of cheese with it, until there was hardly anything left, and I was panting from eating so much, so fast.

The shame began to invade me then, I wanted to howl my fury against it and tear the room apart. The wild beast in me took over, and my nails began to scratch the skin of my arms and my face, as they sometimes did of their own accord. Myrddin Emrys walked in right then. He took one look at me and wrapped my thrashing body into his arms so fiercely, so tightly, I could barely breathe. I fought him and I howled and screamed until we were both exhausted. He slowly let go of me. I slumped down by the fire. He joined me. It took me a while to get my breath back.

I was hoarse when I spoke. "You didn't have to hold me. My bestial skin heals quite fast. It only takes a day and I'm as good as new." I couldn't leave the sarcasm completely out of my voice.

There was none in his when he said, "That's no excuse to tear yourself apart." His scolding was far too gentle for the monster I was.

"I didn't think you'd be able to hold on to me like this. You have a great deal of strength, Myrddin Emrys."

"You tested its limits," he answered. "Tell me what happened."

"Nothing happened. I'm a beast," I said.

"I already know that part," he replied. "What brought this on?"

"I took a bath," I said.

"Ah yes. Segontiwm's famous Roman baths," said the druid.

"The water is filthy now," I said. "Sorry."

"I can have one prepared in the morning," he said.

"I took a bath and thought about my mother, my real mother."

"Rowena," said the druid.

"Yes. You know?" *Of course he knows. He is Myrddin Emrys.* "I thought about how desperate and alone she must have been. I thought about my father, what he may have done to her. Then I *was* her, feeling what she felt. Her anguish, her loneliness. I got out of the bath and looked at my body. Something I usually avoid entirely. And I wanted to run but then I saw the food and my hunger took over. After I finished eating, I felt so much shame I wanted to scream and to tear things and scratch my face and my body. And then you arrived."

"Why the shame?" he asked.

"Because I eat like a beast," I hollered.

"Considering you are a beast, I find it quite normal," he said.

I wavered between getting mad at him for calling me a beast to my face or laughing.

"Since this is what you are now, why not accept it?" he argued.

"Accept my curse? Are you mad?" I asked, bewildered.

"There are some who think I am," he acquiesced. "Until your curse is broken, *if* it can be broken, and it's a big *if*, you are a beast with unhinged hunger. So why not accept it? Better than be filled with shame and rage for something you can't change and have little power over."

I was speechless for a while, considering this unusual idea.

"We should both get some sleep. We have a long journey ahead of us," he said.

I followed him until we reached our bedchambers across the hallway from each other.

"*Nos da* little Dryw donn." Myrddin Emrys was saying good night to the little brown wren, to me, not the beast. No one had said *goodnight* to me in a very long time.

"*Nos da* Myrddin Emrys," I sighed. I made myself comfortable on the carpet, with its ubiquitous design of deer hunting, by the fireplace. I would not sleep in a bed again.

Chapter Thirteen

Segon Fawr met us at the stables to say his goodbyes soon after dawn. Myrddin Emrys was in a good mood after his morning ablutions in the Roman bath. And so was I. I'd left some breakfast for the druid, even though I'd followed his suggestion to eat like the beast I was.

The Bear still kept his distance, but his manners took a gentler turn toward me. "I can see why Myrddin Emrys chose to bring you along. Your wisdom was valuable to us all. And may the gods see fit to lift your curse."

That he was addressing the curse straight on instead of avoiding it, was the kindest thing he could have done. It was the first time someone wished it lifted from me. "I am honored by your hospitality and your good wishes, My Lord. May the Gods heed your request."

"If Myrddin Emrys has anything to do with it, I wager they will," he said, giving the druid a friendly slap on his shoulder, which would have knocked out a lesser man. "Safe travels to you both, my friends." The Bear looked up at the iron-grey sky and sniffed the air. "Snow is on the way. I can smell it." He turned around and strode back up the steps into his home, looking every inch a king himself.

My new friend Osian, in attendance at the stables, assisted me onto Espoir. I didn't kick the lad for helping. Myrddin Emrys observed the exchange, his black eyes locked on me.

"*Hwyl Fawr,* My Lady," said the squire.

"*Hwyl Fawr* to you, Osian. May we meet again."

It was going to be a long ride. Myrddin intended to go all the way to Cambria. A weeklong ordeal, at the very least. I had no idea how we would manage but he insisted that we needed to be there in three days. An impossibility. Though he didn't mention it, I assumed it must be for another important meeting. We'd be late for that one. I worried about exhausting our horses. And what about having enough to eat on the way? I shared none of my concerns because I had a feeling he knew them all already.

We traveled slowly due to the snow falling off and on, as our host had predicted. Myrddin Emrys didn't seem to mind. Espoir and Rhian were happy, with coverlets to protect them and each other for company. The white dusting on the path didn't hamper our progress too badly for now.

"You know my palfrey is in love with your mare," I said. "Tell me the truth. Did you spell him?"

"I didn't," replied Myrddin. "He simply has good taste. *Rhian* is beyond compare."

"And she knows it," I scoffed, thinking of young Osian.

Hours passed with snow turning into flurries then dying off then starting again. Myrddin's rhythm was unhurried and steady, like his horse. They were completely attuned to each other. He held the reins loosely and I noticed no spurs on his boots and no bit in Rhian's mouth. I was glad to know Myrddin, and I felt the same way about putting a bit in a horse's mouth. I never wore spurs. I didn't need to, my horse was a mover, and very fast if need be.

Myrddin Emrys was so deeply silent, so still, all I could hear was the squeaky crunch of Rhian's and Espoir's steps in fresh snow. The intensity of the quiet made me uncomfortable. Not because I wasn't used to silence but because I wasn't used to it while in the company of another person. He seemed to be bending his ear to the trees, a rowan, a hawthorn, or a holly, as we passed by. A particular rowan tree caught his attention, and he stopped in front of it. He said it must be close to two hundred years old and that druids wrote their runes on its bark.

He dismounted and went right up to it, touching the bark, and almost cooing to it in the old Futhark language, the language of the runes. When he was done, he cut a long thin branch which gave in easily into his hand, returned to Rhian, and attached the piece of wood to his pack.

We crossed paths with the occasional bird, a nuthatch, with its compact body, blue-gray back and stark white cheeks, or a siskin, the small lively finch with its streaky yellow-green body and black crown. We even saw a whole flock of redwings hurrying toward the coast. But none were as entrancing as Myrddin's white crow. Eira would appear and disappear. I tried to keep track of her for a while, but she could hide better than I ever did as a child, playing hide and seek with my brother. At one point, she sat on Myrddin's shoulder and bent her head toward him then she took off again on some errand. I could swear they were talking without words. He nodded, frowning with concern by whatever she had communicated to him.

I began to fear that Myrddin would never stop. The sun was setting. I was nervous about finding a place to bed down for the night, and I was ravenous, having eaten through the contents of my pack hours ago. It was as if he knew I was getting ready to grumble about the lateness of the hour because he made a sudden right turn off the path, straight toward the setting sun and through the trees which lined both sides of the road. I followed, full of unease, and more concerned by the second. The snow had stopped, and the moon, almost full, was rising. We were heading toward some hills, though it was hard to see through the thickness of the forest. We came upon a rock formation that took some space around a clearing. I could hear the sound of water, what must be a stream hidden beneath the snow. Myrddin Emrys dismounted, and I followed suit. He led his mare straight toward the rocks. I thought he had lost his mind unless he could walk through rock, which on second thought may be possible for a druid. It was deceptive: there was an imperceptible fold in the rock face that hid an entrance. From a distance, it was completely invisible.

We walked inside. There was room for all of us, horses and riders. We took our packs off our mounts, untacked them and gave them some grain. Myrddin made a fire. I saw the magician at work for the first time. We gathered a few branches wet from snow. I thought it pointless to try and light a fire. But Myrddin sat in front of those wet pieces of wood and spoke to them in the old language, as if he was speaking to a good friend in need of reassurance. Among the words, I could only distinguish two which stood out as he uttered them, *Fehu* and *Kano*. They were runes. The rest was beyond my comprehension.

Heat rose from his body, his arms. I saw it, I felt it. And all at once the wood burst into flames so high, so excitedly, I had to jump back to avoid getting burnt. He didn't just speak the runes. They came to life and acted through him, through his body. I never would have believed it if I hadn't been a witness myself.

He took out a small cauldron which we filled with melted snow, dropped in a few root vegetables, some dried herbs and made soup over the fire. It was not nearly enough food for me. He must have sensed my misery because he took out a chunk of cheese from his pack and handed it to me. I devoured it in seconds. I was still hungry when I was done. I got up and looked out of the cave, contemplating going out to hunt but the weather was worsening by the minute.

"Get curious about something else," he suggested.

I turned back toward Myrddin. He was carving into the branch of rowan tree he had picked earlier.

"What are you doing?" I asked.

"Carving runes into the rowan," he answered.

"What for?" I asked.

"For you," he answered.

That sparked my interest, and I sat next to him, by the fire.

"I'm carving the first rune for now," he said.

"You mean *my* first rune, *Ansuz*."

"You haven't forgotten," he said.

"How could I?" I retorted. "A rune given by Myrddin Emrys is a treasure."

He chuckled. "Treasure or trouble."

"Maybe both!" I replied. I bared my teeth into a smile before I remembered I was a beast, and that my attempt at smiling must look at best, like a grimace, or more likely, a snarling wild dog. My hands flew up to cover my mouth.

"Is that a cheeky grin I see under that hood of yours?" said Myrddin, smiling back at me.

My hands came down. *He knew I meant to smile. He wasn't appalled. He smiled back at me*. I could've hugged him.

He handed me the piece of rowan wood. The rune carved in it looked back at me, as if we belonged to each other. It glowed in the firelight. There was room for more.

"When will you carve the others?" I asked.

"They will arrive in due course, when it's time," he said.

"And then?" Patience was never my strong suit.

"Then the rowan will be yours. A beginning," he said.

"A beginning?" I frowned.

"The beginning of your new life," he answered.

I didn't want to know if he meant a new life as I was now, as a beast. He wouldn't tell me more anyway, so I asked about the runes he used to light the fire.

"I heard you speak the words *Fehu* and *Kano*. They are runes, aren't they?" I asked.

"They are," he said.

"Which one is the word for fire?" I asked.

"They both are," he replied.

"Doesn't it complicate things?" I asked.

"No," said the druid. "There is the spirit of fire and how it moves through each of us and ignites our passion, and there is the reality of fire and how we borrow its power in our daily life."

I pondered his answer in the crackling silence. The idea that there was more than one fire was intriguing. Perhaps everything was thus two-fold, the spirit of a thing and the reality of it. Perhaps I had the same two-fold nature, perhaps I was a twin, spirit and reality, and my spirit was a fire, and my essence could never be quelled by the monster

I had become. Or perhaps the monster was somehow part of that fire too. I stopped myself, frightened by my own thinking. Myrddin served soup, and we ate. Fire crackling within and snow flurries without.

The next two days were more or less a repeat of the first after we left Caernarfon. Myrddin followed his own path, and I followed him. I had no idea where we were or even which direction we were heading. Everything was white. The path, the ground, the sky. Bare branches of trees stood out starkly against all this white and so did the few huts and farms we passed on the way. After Caernarfon, we stayed clear of towns and castles.

We happened upon an abandoned village. Cottages with their thatched roofs burned to the ground, gardens turned to rubble, filled with stones from adjoining garden walls. I glanced at Myrddin and saw a grim look on his face. I remembered his words about the Saxon threat being close. He was right. We were no longer among the Cymry, our fellow countrymen, in Wales. We had crossed into Briton proper, and there were signs of war all around us. I hurried my pace to catch up to him and stay close. I didn't want to be left behind in these parts.

Myrddin knew all the caves and all the abandoned huts in the area, at least he never failed to find us a place to bed down for the night. What all these places had in common was their practical improbability. They shouldn't even exist and yet appeared at the very last moment in the most unexpected spots, around the corner from a rock, near a large hawthorn, behind a waterfall. I wondered if Myrddin conjured them on the spot. He assured me he didn't, that these were very old, and well known among the druids. And that they were a secret. A well-kept secret. No one else would have been able to find them.

On the fourth day, we approached Cambria. The weather cleared up. No wind or snowfalls. A blanket of snow covered the countryside, the continuous crunch of hooves stepping through it, a comforting sound. We had progressed much further than I anticipated but I *was* traveling with Myrddin Emrys.

We began to climb up a hill. The air was cooler than it had been. I could see our horses' breath, a steaming fog coming out of their nostrils. They were straining with the ascent. We kept going up and up until we reached a plateau, a vast expanse surrounded by mountains on all sides. The clouds, like agitated angels torn from their beds, swept across an upside-down bowl of sky, close above our heads. Hillel had shared many secrets about the sky with me, including its color. Blue was a secret only the Egyptians knew long before the rest of the world. To identify a thing by its true name was precious knowledge. It meant you could see it. Looking to the north, I could see Skiddaw and Blencathra, to the south, High Rigg and Helvellyn, to the west, the Derwent Fells, and to the east through a gap, the Northern Pennines.

I had only ever been to Snowdon Mountain in Gwynedd, but I knew about these from conversations with Hillel and my father. Hillel had described the smooth top of Helvellyn, a plateau itself, the soaring ridges of Derwent Fells with its stunning views of the lakes, the Northern Pennines with their open heather moors and tumbling upland rivers, and the ridge of Skiddaw continuing northward toward the Whitewater Dash waterfall, an exhilarating place where you could feel dizzy and free at the same time. Whoever had designed this was a great artist and if any landscape could take your breath away this was surely it.

The sight of all these mountains was amazing enough, but the stone circle on the plateau was the jewel at its center. I could see everything around me *ad infinitum*, no matter where I turned. The circle was made of forty-two standing stones. I counted or at least I tried. The number kept changing every time I counted. The stones looked ten feet tall and instead of being covered with lichen and moss like the ones in Gwynedd, these were smooth and stark white. The two tallest formed the pillars of the entrance. I stood there with Espoir and could not move. The magic of the place leaked everywhere around us. Myrddin Emrys had already dismounted.

I got off Espoir and followed Myrddin Emrys inside the circle. I didn't speak, for fear I would disturb the peace of the circle. Anything could happen here. Myrddin Emrys headed toward a smaller circle in the east I had not immediately identified. As I counted ten more stones, I realized it was a square. It reminded me of my dream, although it had been a circle inside a square. This was its opposite.

Myrddin Emrys spoke for the first time since we arrived on the plateau, "This is Castlerigg. And this square circle of stones is called the Sanctuary."

It was an odd wording, but Myrddin had named something which reflected what I felt: that even though the "Sanctuary" was a square, it seemed right to call it a circle. Perhaps because it was part of the circle of stones. He made all of us, including Rhian and Espoir stand inside it.

"Sanctuary?" I asked.

"To keep us safe," he answered.

Safe from what, I wondered. There was nothing here. Only us, the stones and the mountains. We waited for what seemed like hours. I kept fidgeting, scratching my neck, glancing over at Myrddin as he stood, wrapped in the stillness of the stones. Sunset had come and gone. I couldn't take the silence anymore, "Are we spending the night here?"

"If need be." His words were slow. His voice deep.

Annoyed and frightened, I asked, "Any particular reason?"

"Until I get an answer."

"An answer to what?" I asked.

"An answer to what's next," he replied.

"Are you saying you don't know where to go next?" I thought a great druid like Myrddin Emrys always knew what to do. I pressed him, "Are you telling me that you won't move from here until you get some message as to what comes next? What if it takes days?"

"So be it," he said.

"This is insane," I said with a great deal of vehemence. "Who lives like this?"

"I do," replied the druid.

"And why this place?" I asked, even though the moment I did, I knew how foolish it was.

"Do you not have eyes to see and ears to listen, little Dryw donn?" he asked. "Do you not understand where we are? This is the most sacred place of all druid lore. Answers come here. The runes are strong here. Listen. Even your horse knows it."

I looked up at Espoir and he was rock still. Not frightened but alert, taking his cue from Rhian. I was so entranced by the landscape, the mountain range surrounding us, the vastness of the circle itself with its white standing stones, it hadn't occurred to me to listen. I closed my eyes and instantly heard a low hum. It was so startling, I opened my eyes against its power. I tried again and this time it was even stronger, and there was more than one hum, like the stones were humming in a harmony only they understood.

Myrddin Emrys was watching me. "All stones can sing but few can do so in such harmony."

I remembered Snowdon Mountain and the exhilaration I felt as a child when we reached the top. It was one of those rare occasions when we had been together as a family, Father, Somer and me, allowed to join them as long as I did not complain and kept up. I had done both with all the fervor of an eight-year-old.

Hillel had accompanied us as well and needed to rest more than once on the way up. Our father was more solicitous of Hillel than of anyone I knew and always agreed to a pause for his sake. Looking back, Hillel had undoubtedly exaggerated his tiredness for my sake. The memory of it pierced me with melancholy. I believed I could be a mountain fairy then, a *gwyllion*, and fly, so buoyed was I by the place.

On that night of bleakest despair, driven back to Snowdon Mountain, running all the way, propelled by the new strength of my bestial limbs, Yr Wyddfa's song had called me in the dark, appeasing the devastation in my heart. The song was so vast and resonant I thought I'd never hear its like again and yet it didn't compare with what was now touching my skin and vibrating my skull, raising all the hair on my body. This was a choir of giants. A call and response began between the standing stones of Castlerigg circle and the mountain range all around us. The moonrise poured its own strength into the song.

I thought the power of the song would turn *me* into a stone. No wonder Espoir was standing so rigidly. It's hard to explain what I saw that night. All of it being more a dream than anything, like the time I managed to join my dear Lavinia during the solstice, in Dinas Emrys, even though I didn't leave my room.

Considering I awoke in a completely different setting and miles away from Castlerigg the next morning, it made it even more dreamlike. A thick fog emerged out of the stones on each side of them and linked them together. The fog spread over the entire circle after that, without reaching the Sanctuary. I kept looking over at Myrddin Emrys, but he was as a stone himself. There wasn't a word to be gotten out of him. I'm not sure my tongue worked to call out to him in any case. It was dry and stuck to the roof of my mouth. Then I saw the runes come to light on Myrddin's body. He was fire, lit from within. It must be excruciatingly painful like the time they inscribed themselves on his body. I could see the tension in him and the concentration too. Beads of sweat started to pour down his face even though it was cold so high up on the plateau. His breath came shorter and faster, as if he was running. He kept blowing it out periodically. He started to speak the names of the runes, and then he called her name, *Rhiannon, Sovereign Goddess, Night Queen, mother of moon and mercy, of the underworld and rebirth, Goddess of horses*.

I thought it was a terrible idea to call the Goddess, any Goddess, in this place. The full moon hit her zenith over the center of the circle, sitting like a crown between the two pillars of the entrance. The fog receded to the outer perimeter. I remember holding my breath, then breathing fast, panting, like a dog. And then I saw a white horse for a moment by the light of the moon. I blinked and the horse was gone and then I opened my eyes again and saw the Goddess dressed in gold on her white horse, a white bird sitting on her shoulder. She looked into Myrddin's eyes and called him *Myrddin Wyllt*, Myrddin of the Wilds. He bowed to her and told her we were heading to the Isle of Skye and asked for assistance with our travels. That I could understand them even though I didn't know the old language was baffling. A part of me was more than a little annoyed with Myrddin. Why not ask for something more important, like reversing my curse?

She must have heard my thoughts because she turned her gaze on me and in her eyes I saw the world, rivers and forests and mountains. I saw the twins of darkness and light, *Efnisien* and *Nisien*. I saw terrible grief, and wrenching pain and wondered how it was possible for a Goddess to experience such suffering. I saw so much I thought I would die. I trembled like the animal I was but could not move. I was glad she didn't come any closer, that the Sanctuary offered us some protection from all this power, all this magic.

The inside of my wrist began to burn. It was so intense I thought surely there must be a raging fire burning my flesh, but when I looked down at it, there was nothing I could see, until a sign revealed itself from beneath onto the skin, slowly. This was the first rune I ever received, *Ansuz*, engraved on my skin, embodied from within by the power of the Goddess Rhiannon. The rune Myrddin Emrys had written down in the snow at the stone circle of the Gwynedd woods, then carved on a branch of the sacred rowan tree. The rune was fire and ice on my skin and shone like gold in the darkness. I was mindful that the space taken up by the rune was free of the curse. That spot of skin was human, not leathery or covered with bestial fur.

The last thing I remember from that night was the Goddess sending off her white bird who flew straight at Myrddin Emrys. He offered the bird his fist to land then placed her on his shoulder. It was Eira, his white crow. Our horses bent their heads in recognition of the sacred horse and the Goddess riding him. My wrist was a flame, my body ice, my eyes had taken in more than they could bear, and the world turned black as I fainted.

Chapter Fourteen

Lying on a rug in front of a fireplace, I thought I was back at Caernarfon. Except the deer motif favored by Segon Fawr had been replaced by thistles which had a distinctive Scottish flavor. I couldn't imagine how we'd arrived in Scotland when we had been in Cambria the night before, if indeed this was the next day. Thankfully no one had undressed me. I was wrapped in my cloak still.

I looked out from under my hood to take in my surroundings. My eyes went to my wrist first. The rune was still there. I was convinced *Ansuz* was the rune for Myrddin Emrys, that *he* was my guide, my messenger. So why was the rune inscribed in my flesh? I couldn't make sense of what happened in Castlerigg. And what place was this?

The chamber with its large canopy bed, round oak table and chair, and tapestries hanging on the stone walls, did remind me of Caernarfon. The fire was down to embers in the fireplace which reassured me that no one had been here to replenish the wood or stoke the fire while I slept. A tapestry on the wall above the fireplace caught my attention. It depicted a warrior on his rearing horse at the top of a hill, overlooking a field of battle, brandishing a flag. The lord seemed to be declaring victory. The title of the work written below said *Dunvegan Caisteal Am Bratach Sith.* I knew where I was then, Dunvegan Castle, on the Isle of Skye, and there was the laird of the MacLeod Clan brandishing the fairy flag, *Am Bratach Sith.* I knew *Sith* meant fairy or fairy hill and pronounced *Shee* in the Gaelic. But that was all I knew.

I felt so disoriented, so dizzy, if I had not already been on the ground, I would have fallen over. I remembered Myrddin Emrys asking the Goddess for help with our travels. I wondered if that is what he had in mind. I could not imagine it and yet here we were. I was debating what to do next when I heard a knock on the door.

"Come in," I said, staggering upright and ascertaining that my cloak and hood were fully concealing my bestial self.

Myrddin Emrys walked in. "How are you faring this morning?" he asked.

The casualness of his question made me mad. "What morning is it? What happened exactly? Why do I have this rune etched on my wrist? Explain!" I demanded.

He chuckled, which annoyed me even more. I started to growl.

"No need to be a beast with me, little Dryw donn," he said. "I will tell you everything I can. I brought you some freshly made *pice bach.*"

He put down the plate he was holding on the round oak table and took off the towel protecting the baked goods. The sweet yeasty smell filled the room. They looked just like the ones I never got to taste at the meeting in Caernarfon. I couldn't resist. I grabbed one and the doughy, crispy, sweet bun melted in my mouth. It was so delicious I groaned with delight. I stared at Myrddin, and with a mouth full of cake, I mumbled, "These are *pice ar y maen.* The baker *mmm* must be from North Wales. I still *mmm* want *mmm* an explanation."

"You are right," he said. "The baker is from Anglesey Island."

I immediately wolfed down a second one and a third. They were on the small side as cakes go. Myrddin Emrys sat down and waited till I was done. I licked my fingers carefully one by one. There was a pitcher of water on the table, I seized it between my hands, long nails clicking against the ceramic, gulped down half of it before slamming it back on the table, wiped my mouth with my sleeve and said, "I'm listening."

"What do you want to know?" he asked.

"Everything!" I said. "Are we where I think we are?"

"Yes. We are," he answered.

"How do you know what I'm thinking?" I asked.

"Dunvegan Castle on the Isle of Skye?" he offered.

"Yes," I conceded. "But how did we get here? What about our horses? Are they safe? And what day is it?"

"The day is today or tomorrow's yesterday," he answered.

"You are toying with me," I said.

"No, I'm not. Time is my friend. It works with me."

Myrddin Emrys said something similar to Segon Fawr.

"And we had divine assistance," he said. "It got us and our horses here safely through the portal of the Sanctuary, though it was a bit disconcerting for the horses."

Of course it was. How could it not be? But I was relieved to hear our horses were safe. My own head was spinning.

"Are you saying there is another kind of sanctuary door that opened to us here in this place," I asked.

"As a matter of fact, there are several on the Isle of Skye," he said. "But we came through the Fairy Garden of the castle."

"The *Fairy Garden*?" I wasn't sure I even believed in fairies. They were more of a childhood tale.

"Yes," he confirmed.

"Let's say I believe you," I said. "How did we get through it in one piece. How did our horses?"

"With the help of the Goddess Rhiannon," he answered. "She is not only the Goddess of sovereignty and rebirth but also the Goddess of horses. Do you think she would let anything happen to them?"

"I know your mare is named for her," I said. "But did you really summon a Goddess just for help with the horses?"

"No," he answered. "The Saxons were planning an attack right by Castlerigg. It was unsafe to travel by road."

"The Saxons?" My body grew rigid with fear at the mention of the word.

"Eira warned me about them," he said.

I tried to remember if I saw anything on our way up to Castlerigg. Except for following Myrddin's purposeful steps this way and that, I didn't remember seeing anything. Of course I wasn't really looking either. But I didn't smell anything or sense any unusual movements, and the animal of my body had strong senses these days.

"I didn't smell anything," I said.

"I shielded us," he explained. "But it's near impossible to shield horses. They don't take to enchantment so easily. I couldn't have kept it up for the four days it would have taken us to cross that stretch of road up to Scotland."

"Why is it so hard to work magic on horses?" I asked.

"Because they can't be fooled. Not easily," he answered. "They know what's real. I would have to make what is unreal more real than what is real. It's very hard work and demands too much of my attention."

I didn't hear the druid's answer. I was thinking about the fact that half of me was Saxon, and that Saxons were the enemy. It was an uncomfortable realization. I tried to shake it off, but the thought was sticking to me like a rabid dog until what Myrddin said next jolted me out of it.

"Rhiannon came mostly because of you," he said. "Don't you know who she is? The ordeal she has gone through?"

A Goddess came for a cursed eighteen-year-old? That sounded implausible at best and dangerous at worst. And I didn't really know the Gods of my own country well. "My tutors taught me more about Greek and Roman Gods than about our Welsh Gods," I grumbled.

"That's a shame," he said. "Rhiannon fell in love with a human and married him. Generally, marriage between Gods and humans don't work out well for humans but in this case it was the opposite: She was the one to suffer. You met him in Caernarfon, Lord Pwyll of Dyfed."

"The one with the strong jaw and eyes like wild hyacinth?"

"Yes."

"What happened?" I asked.

"They met and fell in love. She was promised to Gwawl, a knight with a surly disposition. But Rhiannon helped Pwyll win her from Gwawl in a tournament. Gwawl didn't believe he lost fairly because he was the greater warrior. When she gave birth to her son, Pryderi, Gwawl took his revenge by abducting him with the help of her lady maids. Rhiannon was found guilty of killing and eating her baby boy. Her own husband refused to believe in her innocence. She was made to wear a yoke like a beast of burden and pull a carriage."

I couldn't believe people would do that to a Goddess. But then I thought what greater vengeance could there be for a man than to humiliate a Goddess?

"How could she let that happen to her?" I asked. "A Goddess."

"She relinquished some of her divinity in order to be with Pwyll," he explained.

"I didn't know Gods could do that," I said.

"I don't think she knew either," said Myrddin Emrys.

"She must have loved him very much," I pondered.

"Yes," he answered. "The boy was found. She was proved innocent in the end. But she couldn't stay with Pwyll after his betrayal, even though he begged her to."

"Did you have anything to do with this?" I asked.

"Yes," he said. "I found and returned the boy."

"No wonder. It must be nice to have the friendship of a Goddess," I mused.

"Depends on the God," he said. "Rhiannon isn't like most Gods. She has endured unjust punishment. She knows suffering."

"What does that have to do with me?" I fretted.

"She has chosen you to be her messenger," he said.

I looked down at the rune inscribed in my flesh. "I thought *you* were my guide. I'm nobody's messenger or guide. I'm a beast. I'm a cursed monster."

"Exactly," said Myrddin Emrys.

"Not *exactly* at all. She is *your* friend. Not mine."

"She chose you *because* of your curse, *because* of your suffering, *because of who you are*. Remember the meaning of your name."

"Ragnell?"

"Yes."

I looked at him blankly. I had never thought about it.

He answered for me, "It means *the Power of the Goddess*."

"Can she reverse my curse?" I asked.

"That's not the point," he said.

"Then it's point*less* to me," I snapped.

"This is not personal," he explained. "It's part of a greater canvas, for the future."

"I don't care about your canvas or her canvas," I growled. "I'm suffering *now*. It's been three long years."

I was so mad, before I could stop myself, I cleared the plates off the oak table with one sweep of my arm. They shattered on the stone floor, regrettably, with the rest of the cakes. The gesture was so reminiscent of my father, of his temper, I staggered into silence. I was awash in images from the past: my brother and my father ready for a fight. Neither one backing down. Me, feeling helpless to stop it. The aftermath, being left alone at the table in the dining hall. How lost I felt; how small I was. Feet dangling from the chair. Then grabbing my sweet Daffodil, the only one brave enough to stay, and pressing her warm little body to my chest to stop the shaking in my own.

I got hold of myself as best I could. I was here to find out who'd weaved the wretched thing and turned it into the curse I'd been living with for the last three years. Myrddin's schemes did not interest me. "I don't know about you but I'm here to find the weaver," I said.

"We are. Absolutely," said Myrddin Emrys. "Let me take you to meet our host. He will help us proceed."

It hadn't occurred to me that Myrddin could be working for a Goddess as well as a king. Finding the weaver must also be part of Myrddin's scheme. I wished I could talk to Hillel or Lavinia. I missed them. Then I remembered that Hillel mentioned exchanging messages with Myrddin through his white crow.

"Where is your white crow?" I asked.

"Eira is nearby," he answered.

"Unless she is not yours, unless she is Rhiannon's bird. Is she?" I questioned.

"No. She is with me," he answered. "Rhiannon has her own magical birds. But Eira is a crow and can cross worlds. She has helped me communicate with the Goddess before."

"That's convenient. Well, I'd like to communicate with Hillel, if you don't mind." I was short tempered and not very reverential with my asking for help. Eira was his crow after all. But my back was up with all this scheming of Gods and druids I couldn't fully grasp. And I was still trying to find my bearings after our unearthly crossing. All too much for one little beast to bear.

Myrddin Emrys didn't scold me. He had such command over his emotions, he wouldn't let anyone disrupt his peace of mind. It was profoundly annoying.

"Certainly," said the druid. "I will arrange it after we meet with our host. I don't want to keep him waiting any longer."

Myrddin Emrys led the way through the corridors of yet another castle, sure footed and at ease. The halls were adorned with many ancient weapons on display, from sword and lances to daggers in all sizes and shapes, as well as suits of armor, chain mail and the like. The tapestries hanging on the wall all depicted one kind of a battle or another. This *Laird* must love war. I followed, hidden beneath my cloak, wondering what I had gotten myself into that required the involvement of a Goddess, if not to lift my curse.

I remembered Myrddin Emrys explaining that in order for the curse to be lifted even partially, it would require a man being willing to marry me as I was now. The idea that anyone would want a beast for a wife made me snort. I could not imagine any circumstance under which such a thing was possible. Myrddin looked at me askance as we entered another great hall.

At the far end of the hall, stood a giant of man. I had never seen the like. He must have been close to seven feet tall. A different breed altogether. Blond hair hanging down around his shoulders and a beard to match. His smile was as large as he was. I was no more than a twig compared to him. My hackles rose as we approached. He opened his arms wide in greeting. He must be one of those Norsemen I'd heard about. As wild a beast as I could ever be. Wilder.

"You didn't tell me he was a Norseman," I whispered to the druid.

The giant covered the distance between us in a couple of strides. He spoke, his voice deep and surprisingly gentle, lighthearted even.

"Druid, well met. What do you have to say for yourself? How is the king? Still on his throne? When will I get a seat at that round table?"

The man laughed as if it was all spoken in jest, but I couldn't tell for sure.

Myrddin Emrys answered, "There is always a seat for you, Magnus MacLeod Olafsson, but we both know you would never want to leave this place."

"That is true, my friend. My heart is forever here. But if the Saxons dare attack the king, my men are his."

The laird didn't beat about the bush.

"Thank you MacLeod," said Myrddin Emrys. "If you are with us, nothing can defeat us."

The laird turned quickly, his eyes searching boldly into the darkness of my hood, "And what manner of creature do we have here?"

"This is my traveling companion, the Lady of Gwynedd."

"Ah. The Cursed Lady of the Gwynedd Woods," said the Norseman.

Did *everyone* know who I was? I looked over at Myrddin Emrys who glanced at me with that mild look of his I still distrusted.

"You're welcome here, *Changeling*," said the Norseman.

This man was not afraid of me. He didn't react like Segon Fawr. He didn't step away. He called me Changeling, as if my true human form, my true self, had been abducted by a supernatural being and replaced with a beast. I didn't know how or why, but he knew something about magic, or curses. Myrddin was right. The Norseman could help us locate the weaver.

"Lady Ragnell, may I present our gracious host Magnus MacLeod Olafsson, Laird of Dunvegan Castle," said Myrddin Emrys.

After such a formal introduction I felt obliged to curtsy. It was awkward and ridiculous in my present condition. I was mad at myself for doing it and mad at the druid for forcing me into it. I barely stifled a growl from escaping my lips.

"And it is my pleasure to welcome you," said the laird. "Please come close to the fire. It's too cold to stand on ceremony."

His accent was pleasing in its musicality, though it took some getting used to. We followed him to a standing fireplace surrounded by chairs large enough to fit two of me. Above it was the only tapestry so far which didn't represent war in some way. It was a woman holding a baby. Her beauty appeared so ethereal, surely the artist made her up to represent an ideal.

I turned my gaze back toward our host and realized he was observing me. I perceived it like a blow to my body. I was not used to being observed without my knowledge. I was the one spying on people usually. For being such a giant, this man had the ability to be still and quiet. And yet he was full of life at the same time, with such vibrant energy, I could have sworn heat rose up from his flesh. I doubt he ever got cold. He had a particular way of attracting all eyes on him. I watched the servants follow his every move, trying to anticipate his needs, bringing some extra tartans for warmth, mead for drink. They loved him. And he loved them back, addressed them with a respect that reminded me of my father's relationship with Hillel.

We sat down and were brought more refreshments and enough food for a banquet of twenty. My ungainly appetite was upon me. I made no excuse for it this time. And if the laird noticed, he said nothing. He was quite a big eater himself, and I took it as permission to eat my fill. It was a relief not to feel so ashamed of my wanton hunger. I tried mead for the first time and found it sickly sweet, made as it was, from fermented honey and spices.

Our host raised his glass for the traditional toast, "*Slainte Mhath*!"

Myrddin took it up, "*Slainte Mhath*, MacLeod."

I felt obliged to follow and finished my drink in the process, which the laird promptly replenished. After the second glass, the mead grew on me. And then I had a third. I had never been drunk in my life, but I must have imbibed more than I can recall that night because at some point it all became quite blurry, and I saw thrice as many people as were present.

I repeated more than my fair share of *Slainte Mhath*! as the night unraveled and undoubtedly snorted and burped and generally made a spectacle of myself. But neither Myrddin nor the laird remarked on it then or later. I don't remember exactly what was said that night except for a lot of talk about Fairy Folk.

The laird asked us how we managed to get here in the middle of winter with no boats crossing due to the inclement weather. Myrddin

Emrys answered that we came through the Fairy Garden. The laird nodded as if it was perfectly normal.

I slurred my way to a protest, "Don't tell me you believe in fairies, Laird MacLeod."

To which he said, "I most certainly do, considering I was married to one. The Fairy Garden is her creation, as are the Fairy Bridge and the Fairy Glen."

I snorted, "You what?"

He repeated sweetly, "I married one."

My limbs started to feel tingly and loose, with a mind of their own. I pointed a leathery finger at him, sharp with claw, "Right! And she made the waterfalls and the pools too."

He smiled, "She did. How did you know?"

I squinted at him, trying to keep him singular but he kept splitting himself into two.

I looked up at the tapestry I had dismissed as mere fantasy earlier. Following my gaze, he pointed at it, cup in hand, "My wife with our baby boy. She went back to her people mere weeks after it was finished."

I blurted out, "She was your wife! How could you let her go like that?"

"I didn't have a choice, Changeling. Fairies should never be held against their will. Their nature is freedom. It is a blessing when they come into our lives."

"She never came back?" I asked. "What about her son? How could she leave her son? Rhiannon didn't give up on her son."

To my horror, I started sniveling. I was incredibly upset. I didn't know why.

"Calm yourself, Changeling," said the laird. "She did come back, once, a year later. Our boy was crying in his little bed, having been left alone by his nurse. And though she was far away, she heard her son's cries and came to tend to him."

"I knew she had to come back. She loved her son. She loved *you*," I exclaimed. "What happened next? Did you stay together?"

Eyes fixed on his cup, the laird struggled with his memories.

I pushed him, in my drunken state, with no care for his feelings. "Come on. You'll feel better if you tell the rest of the story. Your secret is safe with me. Who am I going to tell? The foxes in the Gwynedd Woods?"

"It's no secret," said the laird. "I sensed something and rushed up the stairs, leaving my guests to wonder what happened. I walked into the room. She was putting a silk scarf on our son's little bed. I stood, undone by her beauty as always. She told me to hold up the scarf as a banner during difficult times in battle and it would protect me and my people. That was the last time I ever saw her. Sometimes I can feel the nearness of her, in the brush of the breeze by the Glen, or in her garden. I could swear my little son can see her where I cannot. The silk scarf rings with a beautiful melody when it is unfurled. It's been three years. But I think about her every day."

"And have you used the scarf as a banner?" I asked.

"Yes, I have. I unfurled it and held it high for all to see, and it worked. It turned the tide of the battle in our favor. Ask Myrddin Emrys. He's the one who suggested we use it."

I turned to Myrddin and scoffed, "Myrddin Emrys, you have the most uncanny way of being everywhere you're needed all at once. Time must be your friend indeed."

The druid chuckled. "Don't you think it's time you went to bed? And you can stop calling me *Myrddin the Immortal*. Myrddin is enough."

I grunted and turned my full attention back to our host, "Laird MacLeod, you are a *goood* man, an *honovarble* man and I am very *sooorry* your *fffairy wwwiiife* left you." (I was having trouble with my words by then.) "I would fight under your banner anytime, anyplace. I am your man," I slurred. Whereupon I stood up, the world swaying all around me, opened my arms wide, throwing my cloak back, and faced him in all my monstrous glory. We stared at each other for a brief moment, the laird with an air of bemusement on his face, me with horror dawning amidst the drunken fumes of mead clouding my brain. I promptly passed out. I don't know if it was on the floor or in someone's arms. If it was, I dearly hoped it was in Myrddin's.

How I made it back to our rooms remains a mystery. I woke up the next morning with star fire exploding in my head at the merest sound and a tongue like a thick piece of tweed was stuck to it. Where was my cloak? I looked all around the room for it, got on all fours, and finally found it, neatly folded on the back of a chair. I looked in all the pockets until I got my hand around my little Auseklis, Gawain's gift. I was so relieved, I squeezed it in my fist and sat down on the floor right there. I didn't trust myself to get up again. I felt as if my head was full of needles prickling my scalp. I reinserted my little wren in its safe place.

I was trying to put my cloak back on and groaning in the process, when Myrddin Emrys walked in. There was a look of deep commiseration written on his face. It made my headache worse. "Mead can be deceptive. It goes down so sweetly, one forgets its potency."

I held on to the oak table with one hand as I endeavored to get myself up, my other hand on my forehead, trying and failing to hold back a headache that could crush a monster. "I don't understand. I only had a couple of cups."

"You've never had fermented drink before, and I stopped counting at four," he said. "Have some food. I brought you some of those *pice ar y maen* you like so much."

For the first time since the curse had descended upon me, I couldn't bear the sight of food. And these were my favorite. I thought I was about to vomit when Myrddin offered me a small piece of a root I didn't know.

"Here, chew on this first. It will help settle your body. And drink some water."

I was too sick to my stomach to argue with him or question the nature of the root. I took it from him and started to chew. It had a strong and sweet tangy taste, and I found it helped.

"No need to swallow," he said. "Keep chewing on it for a while."

"What is it?" I asked when I started to feel more like myself.

"It's ginger root. It comes from the East," he explained.

Only Myrddin Emrys would have such a root handy.

I got hold of the pitcher and drank most of the water in it. I must have felt better because the cakes started looking good to me again.

"Myrddin Emrys, was the laird really married to a Fairy or did I dream it?"

"You didn't. He was. And *Myrddin* is enough."

"Yes. Right." The evening was coming back to me in bits and pieces, most of them embarrassing. "Rhiannon called you by a different name. Didn't she?"

He smiled, "Yes. A previous lifetime."

I didn't know if I should take this literally or not. I was too tired to think about it. Instead, I looked up at the tapestry in our room, the one where the laird was brandishing the fairy flag, the one that said, *Dunvegan Caisteal Am Bratach Sith.* I knew about the flag that brought good luck to the MacLeod clan as a fairy story from my childhood. I had no idea the flag was real or where it came from until last night.

When I felt recovered enough I asked Myrddin if we could speak to the laird about finding the weaver. And I also reminded him about getting Hillel a message.

He answered, "I already spoke with Laird MacLeod, and he will take us to the weavers. And Eira is on her way to Hillel as we speak."

"But I didn't get to write my message," I protested.

"I wrote that you needed his advice. Was I right?" he asked.

"Yes," I said. "But I would have been more detailed."

"You can't write a long account on a message. Eira is unable to carry a full parchment."

I chastised myself for not having thought of it. But I wished I could have seen her fly away myself. And I thought it was presumptuous of Myrddin to send Eira without consulting me first. I had expected some reluctance on Myrddin's part about using his crow for my personal needs. Unless he needed some information from Hillel himself which was entirely possible.

I almost regretted seeking Hillel's counsel now, but the rune inscribed on my wrist was like a flame and I felt unprepared, as if anything could happen. And it had. After three years of struggling alone in the Gwynedd Woods, everything was new and exciting. New stories and fancy lords and meeting a Goddess. It was nothing short of miraculous for a beast such as I. One thing troubled me. It was bad enough being chosen by a Goddess to be her messenger for who knows what, but the druid was King Arthur's Magician. Did he see me as some political pawn to be used for his own aim? There was no guarantee my curse could ever be reversed. What if it was to his advantage that I remain as I was? My hackles went up as I considered how far I could trust the druid.

Chapter Fifteen

We met with the laird outside the stables. I did my best to avoid him, keeping myself wrapped in my cloak, and my hood pulled close over most of my face as I walked toward my palfrey. Espoir whinnied the moment he saw me. He must have recognized my cloak. My appearance still frightened him, so I did my best to talk to him and stroke him first and stay well hidden. Rhian and he looked rested, groomed to a nice shine, and well fed.

"Glad to see you're standing on your own two feet this morning, Changeling," said the laird with a grin as wide as his face.

I coughed to hide my embarrassment and got busy with Espoir's bridle. I couldn't think of anything to say that wouldn't add to my growing discomfiture, humiliation, mortification; you name it, I felt them all.

I heard nothing but kindness in his voice as he said, "I do hope you feel well enough to ride with us. Mead can be treacherous."

I muttered, "I'm well enough. Thank you for your concern, Laird MacLeod."

Right at that moment, my mind decided to reproduce the image of me declaring my devotion to the laird by shouting, *I'm your man!* and ripping off my cloak. I began to wonder how I could do myself in without bringing further shame to the laird or to Myrddin. Fortunately for me, he interrupted the noxious progression of my foolish thoughts.

"I will guide you to where the weavers work. It's up to them if they think you can meet Mary Ferguson or not. Even for you, Myrddin, I won't force them. They are her gatekeepers. They keep intruders at bay."

Myrddin nodded. I wanted to argue that our business was important but changed my mind and decided to take my cue from the druid instead and keep quiet.

"Mary is the only linen weaver on the island," said MacLeod. "Everyone else weaves wool. She lives in a secluded area, not far from the Fairy Folk who help her out. And they don't like to be disturbed."

Myrddin nodded as if it made perfect sense to him. I still couldn't quite believe it even though I had just met a Goddess. I don't know why it seemed more unlikely for Fairy Folk to exist than for a Goddess but in my mind, one was acceptable, and the other was not. Granted, it was a strange distinction to make, but there it was. My brother never believed in them.

The laird got on his destrier, and we followed. I was glad to be riding Espoir again. I gave him his head, and he took off at a gallop. The two men surged on each side of me, as they exhorted their mounts to follow. We climbed a hill and went down into a valley and back up again, jumped across streams, followed a trail between trees and headed toward a small hamlet set against a hillock. It was as if Espoir and I knew which way to go. And then I heard it, the music in the air, flute and fiddle playing off of each other, and people singing and stomping their feet. Some kind of celebration was going on. I wasn't as afraid as I would have been before. Between the druid and the laird, I felt safe enough.

We got off our horses, let them drink their fill at a water trough, and tied them to a rail nearby. I could hear a lead singer and then the call and response taken up by the other women.

"You're hearing the waulking song," explained the laird. "It's the last step once the cloth is woven. The shearing is done earlier in the season after the lambs have grown a bit. After shearing, the fleece is scoured in the stream and then dyed in large pans over the fire with our local plants and roots. Then the fleece is hand-carded to sort the fibers, spun into yarn on a spinning wheel, then wound onto cones ready for weaving. The women weave the cloth on large wooden floor looms and the men then wash it in the stream. What you are seeing now is *Òrain Luaidh* or *Luathadh,* the waulking of the cloth. It's part of the finishing process. The women sit around a table and thump the soaked tweed to shrink and soften the fabric. It's hard work which is why they do it with song to help them keep the rhythm going."

"You know a lot about weaving then, Laird MacLeod?" I asked.

There was pride in his voice as he answered. "I know the process. These are my people. I know how hard they work."

As we approached, I noticed the lead singer was an old woman with white hair. She sat at the head of the table. Her eyes were almost closed as she sang. The other women, twelve of them, all younger, took up her song in response. The men were sitting around drinking. Children were playing, screaming, as children do, too joyous of the day to contain their emotions, feeling safe amidst their parents and neighbors, running about or joining in song when the refrain came around again.

"This is the last of it. After today they are done for the year until next spring. Then the process starts all over again. It's unusual for any *Luathadh* to be done this late in the winter. But we had an unusual season this year," said the laird.

"How so?" asked Myrddin. The hint of concern in his voice made sense to me since he was first and foremost a Priest of Nature.

"Nature has been at odds with us for the last three years in a row," said the laird. "We had quite a few lambs die. The lambs that survived were born very late this year. Summer was too hot. It was hard to work. Harvest was difficult with too much rain and early snowfall. The weaving began late. But today could be spring."

The laird was right. The weather had turned surprisingly mild for midwinter. Perhaps Nature was trying to trick us into thinking winter was over.

"The women take turn with the *Luathadh*," he said. "Every few hours or so. As soon as any of these women get up others come to take their place. But the old woman never moves. She is the leader. And the one you need to ingratiate, Changeling. If you want to find out where Mary Ferguson lives. Mary is her niece."

I wondered how we would accomplish this, especially if the old woman was going to sit all day, leading everyone in song. The laird and Myrddin walked over to join the men and got some mead. They offered me to join them.

"I want *no part* of that supernatural brew," I answered emphatically.

The men laughed and continued on their way. I stayed away for other reasons as well. My Scottish Gaelic was limited, and I was who I was. And I wanted to avoid any temptation to drink.

I stood there, awkward and conspicuous in my cloak, listening to the songs, the Luathadh as the laird referred to the practice. Two songs, two melodies stuck out. One was slower and the second one picked up the pace. The women alternated between the two. They were simple songs with a contagious refrain. Occasionally, a woman got up, and another took her place at the table. It was seamless. No one stopped. They kept slapping, squeezing and turning the soaked tweed in rhythm, back and forth, between them. The songs helped lighten the work which was hard and required strength. Only women sat at the table. I was humming, my body swaying to the rhythm when a voice behind me said, "This song talks about the sadness of Sundays. It's mostly nonsense words to keep the rhythm going."

Ddomhnaich agabh mi uil'e
Na hi ri hu, hi ri hua
He o challa ni hi ri hu bha hu bha

I turned and saw a young woman with deep sea green eyes and black hair. I didn't know if she could see into the darkness of my hood, but she didn't jump back in fear. Instead, she walked over to the old woman sitting at the head of the table and spoke into her ear. The old woman nodded. Meanwhile the second, more rousing song started again.

The young woman came back to stand next to me and translated: "This is the famous wedding of black-haired Morag. Her hair is black this year and every year."

'Si Morag, 'Si Morag
A rinn a' bhanais ainmeil

Bha i dubh an uiridh
Agus tha i dubh am bliadhna

'Si Morag, 'Si Morag
A rinn a' bhanais ainmeil

'S bha i dubh a h-uile latha
Chunnaic mise riamh i

'Si Morag, 'Si Morag
A rinn a' bhanais ainmeil

She was singing along while I listened. I could pick out a few words. The name *Morag* and *dubh* meaning dark. I knew the word *bhanais* meant wedding. We stood there for a while.

"*Yae* can go take *yaer* place at the table if *yae* want. *Yae*'re welcome," she said.

I didn't know how to respond. Didn't she see who I was? Didn't she know?

"Go on. It's time for a change," she urged on.

I looked over and while the song was still going, one of the women, who was sitting next to the old lady, stood up.

"Go on. Go replace her," said the woman with the sea green eyes.

"But I don't belong," I said haltingly. "I don't know the songs."

"Easy enough to follow the rhythm," she said.

"My nails are too long." I was getting desperate. I didn't want to sit with these women. They would be repulsed by whatever they saw. I would disrupt their work. As a last resort, I showed her my ugly beastie hands with claws for nails.

"I've seen worse," she said. "Make sure yae use the palms of yaer hands. Hard work is what's called for here. Yae look strong to mee."

I *was* strong, and I was running out of excuses. I glanced despairingly at Myrddin and MacLeod, but they were deep in conversation, and drink, with some of the local folk and paid no attention to me.

She pushed me forward and, reluctantly, I came to stand at the waulking table next to the old lady who called out the songs. She nodded for me to sit down. I did. I sat there for a while before I dared show my leathery hairy hands and thick black curvy nails and help with the thumping and kneading of the tweed. No one screamed. No one got up and left. And after a while I joined in, and by the end of the day, I had more or less picked up the words and was even singing along. It was a day I would never forget, being welcomed back into the human community as I was, still a beast. It slipped my mind to even ask the old woman if I could meet the linen weaver.

Eventually, the work was done, the tweed shrunk and tightened. All the women got up to leave. I was at a loss. The old woman looked at me sideways instead of straight on. Her head tilted toward me. I realized then she was blind. She wore it lightly. It was part of her but wasn't all she was. She was the leader of the women. A singer and a weaver.

"Good work, Changeling," she said. "Now, how can I help yae?" The old woman smiled.

This is easier than I thought. I introduced myself, "I come from Wales. My name is Ragnell. I was cursed three years ago. I need to find the linen weaver and ask her about a linen gown she weaved for my birthday. Her name is Mary Ferguson. I believe she is your niece?"

"I'm Mary Ferguson," replied the old woman. "And aye, Morag is my niece."

Her answer left me wondering which Mary Ferguson I needed to talk to.

"She's also called Mary by birth, but we call her Morag in these parts so as not to confuse the matter," the old woman explained.

"Like the song," I said.

"Aye *M'eudail*, like the song."

"*May doll*?" I repeated, uncertain.

"*M'eudail* is like saying my dear or sweetheart in the Gaelic. That's what we grannies call all the yun' ones like yae."

"Oh." I was dumbstruck. The old woman was calling me sweetheart, me, the beast of the Gwynedd woods was this granny's sweetheart. My eyes filled. I thought I would burst into tears. She came to my rescue describing where her niece lived. "Best to wait until morning for such meetings. The lads can accompany yae, but the meeting is for yae alone."

I wondered which *lads* she was referring to until she tilted her head in their direction, and it became clear she was talking about Myrddin Emrys and Laird MacLeod. I went from wanting to burst into tears to almost bursting out laughing.

When Myrddin and the laird approached, ready to return to the castle, I couldn't help myself, "Well, hello *lads*, granny here told me where her niece lives. We'll be going in the morning."

They were gracious about it, but I could tell they were more than a little surprised by my casual address. I was delighted to see the look on their faces as I, the eighteen-year-old demon, called them, the Great Seer, and the Laird of Dunvegan, *lads.*

The morning saw us back on our horses, heading into what Laird MacLeod called *Shidhe* or Fairy Country and particularly toward, *Sìdhean Dubh,* 'Black Fairy Hill.' The day was still mild as if winter had stayed its cold arms for a while longer and let the sun come forth. It was a pale orb, and barely made it above the horizon, but I couldn't help seeing it as a hopeful sign.

We approached the hill by mid-afternoon. The laird and Myrddin got off their horses. I followed suit. There it was, the Fairy Glen, a wonder of rock, mossy hills and valley that belonged in the story books. Rain and sun played hide and seek creating a double rainbow over the glen the moment we dismounted. We were standing in a dream. We stayed transfixed for a while, until Laird Macleod broke the silence and explained that the Fairy Glen was situated between the villages of Sheader we had just passed through and the village of Balnacnoc on the other side.

"The rest is up to you, Changeling," said the Laird. "Mary Ferguson's cottage is over yonder on the path toward Balnacnoc. Follow the trail. You can't miss it. It stands alone behind a low wall of old rocks. Not too many sheep out and about this time of year to get in your way. You're lucky."

I thanked him and was about to get back on my horse when the laird stopped me. "Best leave Espoir with us, Changeling. We'll take good care of him."

"If you think it's best," I said, reluctant to part with him.

"I do," said the laird. "Mary doesn't have a horse. If she takes you to the Fairy Pools, you'll be walking."

Espoir snuffled into my chest. And I handed the reins to Myrddin.

"We'll be here when you return," said Myrddin.

"If you say so," I grumbled. I was feeling rather unsure of myself. I had not been alone since I began my journey with the druid. I had grown accustomed to his presence and to the companionship it afforded me. And I had no idea what I would find at the end of that trail.

I started off dragging my feet. I kept looking back to see if they were still watching for me. They were, for quite a while, and I was grateful for that. I could well imagine them talking about me as they observed my slow pace down the trail. *For being a monster, that Changeling is such a scaredy cat. One would think she'd know she is the scary one by now.* Their imaginary conversation in my head raised my hackles, and I hastened my pace. When I looked back and realized they were gone, I almost quit right then. I wanted to run after them, back to Dunvegan Castle, forget the whole thing. I swallowed, mouth dry, while putting one foot in front of the other and silently repeating, *I want to know the truth. I want to find out what happened.* Part of me hoped the weaver would talk to me and part of me hoped she wouldn't. I was going on, back and forth in my head, when the cottage appeared in view. Like the laird said, there was an old stonewall along the trail and the little house behind the wall, far enough away to avoid unintentional encounters with passersby; its own short lane leading up to the front door. I took a deep breath and walked off the trail, through the opening in the wall and down the lane to the dark green front door. I languished there for a long while and couldn't bring myself to knock when the door opened.

"Yae're supposed to knock, or don't yae do that where yae're from? Wales, is it?"

My mouth opened. The woman standing in front of me had black hair and sea-green eyes. It was the same lass who had been at my side and told me to go take my place at the table for the waulking of the tweed.

"It's you? We met yesterday."

"Yes, I'm Morag Ferguson."

"Why didn't you tell who you were?" I asked.

"Yae didn't ask. Come on in. Did the son of Ljod accompany yae?"

"The son of who?"

"The laird, that great big son of the Viking."

I could tell she liked him by the way she emphasized *that great big son of the Viking.* He *was* quite the specimen.

"Yes, he did. Both he and Myrddin Emrys."

"I'm sure they'll be back to fetch yea in three days' time."

"Three days?" I asked, wondering what on earth would take three days to say.

“I’ll be takin’ yae to the Fairy Pools and that’s a lang day’s walk from here.”

“Do we need to go to the fairy pools?”

“Aye. There is one who wants to meet yae there. But not tonight. Yae can rest. And I’ll tell yae everythin’ I know but it’s not very much I’m afraid.”

I went from fearing the answers to being disappointed I wouldn’t get them. Changeling indeed!

Morag told me to make myself at home and showed me where I could sleep later, in front of the fire. There was a pile of tartans and cushions by the fireplace. I nodded. She had some soup, bread and cheese ready. I did my best to restrain my ungainly appetite.

While we ate, Morag noticed the rune on my wrist, “I see yae have the blessin’ of Rhiannon on yae.”

“How do you know it was Rhiannon?” I asked. I heard my voice rising in genuine surprise as I contemplated it for a moment, still unsure of how I felt about such an honor, if that was indeed what it was.

“It’s her way. Rhiannon likes to have her messengers be special people like yae.”

“You mean cursed,” I said.

“Well, people who know betrayal and sufferin’.”

When she brought out some *cranachan*, the sweet dessert made with oatmeal, honey and cream, I couldn’t hold back any longer and ate the whole thing in great big mouthfuls.

“If I’d known yae liked my cranachan so much, I would have made more.”

“Sorry. I apologize for my appetite.”

“Not at all. I’m glad it’s pleasin’ to yea. I have some shortbread left over from yesterday if yae’d like. We could have it with some sweet broth,” she offered.

“That would be grand. Thank you.”

While Morag made her sweet broth, I looked around her home. It was plain but full of colors with the MacLeod tartans, yellow background and the red and black stripes, and full of mouthwatering and interesting flavors, from baking and from collected plants and herbs. There was another tartan I didn't recognize, with a soft purple and green base and shades of green and brown. I pointed to it.

"What's that tartan? I don't know it."

"That's because it's not from a clan exactly," said Morag. "It's the tartan of the Isle of Skye."

"I didn't know an island could have its own tartan colors."

"Well, I don't know about anywhere else but here we have our own colors. Yae can wear them if yae'd like."

"Thank you," I said. "But I don't think so."

"Better than those shreds of clothing yae wear under that cloak of yaers. They'll last longer too," said Morag.

I didn't expect that. I didn't know what to do with Morag's generosity. And I was afraid of showing any more of my beastlike nature. I didn't want to witness the horror on her face.

"Winter is coming back in full force in the next few days. Even with the heat in yaer animal blood, yae'll need more than yaer Irish cloak. Yae'll need some good Scottish tartan wool."

She knew what she was about, and she knew what I was and didn't make a fuss about it. These Scottish people were like no one I had ever met before. I capitulated and reluctantly unwrapped myself out of the cloak and rags I was wearing. I stood in front of Morag in all my animal monstrosity, for the first time since the curse. One look at them and she threw the rags in the fire before I could object. They did look muddy and torn and mostly unwearable. She proceeded to demonstrate how to wear a tartan, the different ways it could be tied and used, and how generally practical it was since it could also serve as a blanket.

She said nothing about my appearance. Not once. I was burning with shame in the beginning. My limbs trembled with the desire to run away and hide. When she was done, she took a step back and said, "There yae go. The tartan looks good on yae. Fits yae perfect."

"I'm sorry? How so?"

Morag kept surprising me.

"Most Scotsmen are beasts. And *yae* are a pretty beast, Changelin'. No doubt about it. Whoever changed yae into a monster failed to make yae ugly. Anyway, no one could be truly ugly who has the mark of Rhiannon on them."

My mouth dropped open again. It was such a surprise to hear, I couldn't speak for a good five minutes. But I couldn't bring myself to believe her. I'd spent my life, since the curse, hiding from people. When I recovered my wits, I said, "I *am* ugly. I frighten people. I frighten myself. Even my horse is frightened of me. I'm a monster."

"If yae say so," she answered, her voice airy as a songbird. "To me, yae just look different, an interesting interpretation of the human animal creation. Yae look like no one else really. But then again, I work with Fairy Folk. What do I know? *Oidhche Mhath.*"

I didn't attempt to repeat that. I just said good night back to her. She walked into her bedroom and closed the door, leaving me to contemplate her last words. I couldn't reconcile the monster I had become with Morag's idea that it didn't necessarily make me ugly, just different. It sounded ridiculous to my ears. A monster was a monster. And yet I couldn't stop thinking about it all night long. I sat by the fire and stared at my monstrous hands, all leathery with nails like claws. How could there be any beauty in that? They were well made and efficient. I had survived three years in the woods because of these hands and these claws. I turned them over to look at my palms and they surprised me. I had never noticed before that the inside was so smooth and pink, like real human skin, or what I could remember of it. I brought them up to my face. I touched my forehead and cheeks and found no fur. I knew my face was dark and looked more like an animal's than a human one, especially because of my teeth. But it didn't feel as leathery as the back of my hands. I brought my hands down to my legs. They were the most furry part of my body, but they still looked like legs, well formed, stronger than before. I liked their strength. I relied on it. Like my feet, with soles thick enough to walk barefoot in the woods without dreading that with every step I would get splinters from wood or cuts from rocks. My hair was a nest of brambles. There was nothing I could do about that. I went to sleep still trying to see myself through Morag's eyes. It was an invitation to reconsider a view of myself I couldn't wholly dismiss but neither could I accept it fully.

ᛖ

EHWAZ

Chapter Sixteen

Morag placed a pile of shortbread and a couple of shots of whiskey on the table. I didn't touch the whiskey but shoved one piece of shortbread after another in my mouth, wondering how to broach the subject of the cursed linen gown.

"This is how yae eat shortbread in these parts," said Morag. She proceeded to dunk a piece in the whiskey. She didn't just dunk it. She soaked it in there for a full minute. "Go ahead. Try it. See if yae like it."

I didn't want to be rude, so I tried it. It was heavenly. These Scottish people knew how to do things. But I remembered the mead and stopped after my second soaked shortbread. I wondered if Morag was trying to get me drunk. I made up my mind to ask her about the linen, see if she would reveal something helpful or if I could catch her in a lie.

"Tell me, Morag, how do you make the linen?"

She took a sip of whiskey, "Same way as the tweed. I weave it." She pointed at the loom in a corner of the room. It was fashioned out of some dark wood.

"This one was made from a pine that comes from the black wood of Rannoch. It was a gift from Laird MacLeod. A good man, that one, like one of our oak trees, certainly almost as tall." She laughed.

"Yes, a good man." I didn't want to think about the laird right now but there he was in my mind, as clear as the winter morning. His pride as he talked about his people, about the weavers. His enormous smile that held nothing back. How tall he was. How long and wavy his blond hair, like wheat floating in the summer wind. How fierce and fundamentally kind. Accepting of what was different.

I had to bring my mind back to the task at hand. I wanted to catch her out, find out if she had a hand in tempering with the linen gown.

"What happens after you finish the weaving?" I asked.

"It gets a good soak at the Fairy Pools. Like the shortbread in the whiskey." She winked, soaking a second piece into her glass. "One more. To keep warm on our journey."

"And how does that work?" I could feel my temper rising like a squall again.

"Yae'll find out soon enough. Come now. We need to make sure yae're properly dressed for the Fairy Pools. It will get mighty cold even for one such as yaerself, with the extra bits of fur and all. I recommend two pairs of socks before the boots go on. And mee tartan of course."

I couldn't take it anymore, "I don't want to be half an animal. I want to be whole, to be human again. I'm here to find out who cursed the linen gown and why, so I can make them reverse the curse."

Morag stared at me, wide eyed. "Nobody *cursed* anything here. I weave the linen and send it on its way. It was pristine when it left."

I was so disappointed by her answer, I started to howl. "Who did?!"

"I don't know, *M'eudail.* What I do know is that yaer father, Lord Vortigern, ordered it for yaer birthin' day and when it was ready, our messenger delivered it."

"My *father*?" I couldn't make sense of her answer at first. "My *father* ordered it? No, you're mistaken. It was my *brother*, Somer."

My head was spinning. It took any suspicion away from my brother, which was a great relief, but I couldn't bear the thought of my father being involved in my curse at all.

"Do you trust the messenger who delivered it?" I asked, grasping at straws.

"The messenger is my cousin. I trust him with my work which is to say I trust him with my life. He delivers the linen all over Briton. Yaer father ordered the linen many moons before yaer birthin' day. He wanted it to be a special surprise for yae."

She patted me on the shoulder, "I'm taking yae to the Fairy Pools this morning. Yae may get more answers there. That's where the final cleansing process of the linen takes place; that's where it receives its purity and protection. Yae'll see."

I couldn't hear any of what Morag was telling me. My mind was churning. I tried to hold on to myself, hold back the beast I was. *My father ordered the gown. My father, not my brother. He must have done so before he became ill. But why curse the gown when he planned to deliver Dinas Emrys into my hands. Or did he intend to get rid of me all along? Could that be true?*

It was devastating to contemplate. I looked at Morag without seeing her, eyes wide with fear, claws out to strike at anything that came my way, legs quivering, ready to run.

"Calm yaerself, Changelin'," she cooed.

I blinked. This time seeing what she saw, the wildness of the beast upon me. I could see it in her eyes. I took a breath and said, "I cannot fathom it. I cannot."

I wanted to tear at myself the way I usually did but managed to restrain myself in front of Morag. "But it must be so. Who else? There is no one else," I moaned.

"Do not worry so, yae'll get more answers at the Fairy Pools."

What did I care about Fairy Pools? "I'm not sure I want any more answers." I sighed, slumping on the floor, and said out loud what I could barely admit to myself. "I'm afraid."

"No need for it. Yae'll be all right. Yae'll see."

I appreciated Morag's kindness, but I hated feeling so weak.

"I'll be with yae the whole time," she said.

Fear was a reminder of how powerless I felt on that church floor.

The rage grabbed me again, "He knew. Myrddin Emrys knew it all along. *The weaver not the giver*. What rubbish! Why bother to give me hope, bring me all the way here? What for?"

"Yae best ask him that yaerself. I don't know the druid's reasons. I doubt anybody knows what goes on in his head. Maybe the one yae meet tonight will know."

I was so disconcerted and flustered, I gave up arguing about the usefulness of a trip to those bloody Fairy Pools. I didn't even bother to ask who we were meeting or complain about why I should go there in the first place. I got ready under Morag's close supervision, as she encouraged me to put on at least two pairs of socks and a scarf long enough to circle around my neck three times. She did the same.

I followed her down a new trail, away from the house to the other side of the glen and back up toward the snow-covered mountains.

It took us most of the day to get to the Fairy Pools, like Morag warned me it would.

"The trail may be icy in parts around here. Please watch yaerself," she said.

Morag was right and I tripped and almost fell more than once, so lost was I in my own thoughts. I didn't really notice my surroundings, how beautiful the northern slopes of the *Black Cuillin* mountain range were, until we arrived at the Fairy Pools. And whether you believe in fairies or not, these rock pools of translucent mountain spring waters were aptly named. It was a new melody of otherworldly inspiration to add to the ones I had experienced with Yr Wyddfa and with the white stone circle at Castlerigg. It combined the earth power of the mountain with the gold otherness of the Goddess, but different, like being wrapped in a sweet taste of spring in the middle of an icy winter spell. I felt bewitched, unsteady on my feet, drawn by a new force so mysterious and so desirable, my instincts told me I needed to be held by this limpid pool of liquid silver. I would have fallen into the water if Morag hadn't pulled me back.

Morag took advantage of my slack expression and unsteady body to sit me down and explain where we were. "The pools are fed by many tributaries of the river Brittle." She seemed intent on explaining the practical geography of the place while being completely unaffected by its beauty. I couldn't imagine anyone being that indifferent, even with years of familiarity.

I nodded, still caught in the melody of the rock pools and the resonance bouncing all around us, off of the mountain range and smack into my body. It dawned on me that Morag was trying to help me return to myself, to this moment in time and space.

"This here," she said, pointing to a stream snaking down the hillside, "is the *Allt Coire a' Mhadaidh*. It goes from *Coire na Creiche* into *Glen Brittle* where it becomes the river."

"Now I understand why this is where you come to clean the linen." The uncanny marvel of the place kept my voice to a murmur.

"Oh, I don't do the cleaning. The *Daoine Sith* do, or *Tylwyth Teg* in your language," said Morag, pointing at the nearest pool.

A part of me was still resisting all the Fairy talk. I rolled my eyes. I didn't mean to do that, but Morag caught it and arched her black eyebrow at me.

"We need to sit and wait for them. See if they'll come. The moonrise might bring them out. Fairy Folk are the blessin' of the Mothers." Morag looked up at the mountains above us and the darkening sky. "Not too long, I wager."

The sun was going down behind the mountain range, rays piercing through gathering clouds, and illuminating the whole mountain glory with purples, pinks and red hues worthy of the greatest painter, an Egyptian, if Hillel was to be believed.

I looked back down and noticed the clear pools turning dark. "The water must be freezing, especially at night."

"Aye, it is. But it doesn't bother them. These fairies are a bunch of cold fish, bless them."

I guffawed, shocked by her irreverent assessment of the creatures.

"They *are*," she protested. "And I love them. But they can be ruthless, the lot of them."

Even if I wasn't entirely convinced of their existence, except for MacLeod's wife of course, it was something else to hear Morag refer to them that way. After all, they worked together. "Maybe they're trying to protect themselves from those who would hurt them," I said.

Morag looked at me with a critical eye, "For someone who doesn't believe in the Fairy Folk, yae do a grand job of defending them."

I felt the heat rise in my cheeks, "I never said I didn't."

Morag put up her hand to interrupt me, "No need to make up some story. I think you care and maybe even understand them."

She could be right. I often felt protective of other non-human creatures. I had rescued enough foxes from traps during my time in the Gwynedd Woods. But Fairy Folk? That was another *kettle of fish* altogether. Half a chuckle escaped my lips at the thought.

Morag raised her mighty eyebrow. I shook my head. "Nothing."

We settled into a companionable silence, waiting for the moonrise. She offered me food from her traveling pack. I gratefully accepted and ate with my usual voraciousness.

Soon enough, the moon rose over the pools and the waterfalls that gave birth to them. Despite the noise of the water, it was quiet. I was grateful for the tartan Morag had offered me otherwise my limbs would have turned to ice from the cold. Behind the waterfalls, the snowcapped mountains rose out of the darkness. They watched in stony silence, like the grandmothers of time, the moon shining upon their eternity.

The water started to churn, and I woke up. I didn't know I had fallen asleep. I looked for Morag and spotted her kneeling at the edge of the pool, whispering, "*Daoine Sith, tha caraidean an seo. Tha caraidean an seo, mas e ur toil e trobhad.*" She kept repeating it, like a rondeau.

I crawled next to Morag. "What are you saying?" I murmured.

"I'm saying, *friends are here. Please come here.*"

She continued to repeat it through the night, for hours. It was a song of water and darkness.

"Do they need so much convincing?" I asked, wondering how long Morag and I would need to keep on our knees by the shore of the freezing pool.

"Only someone who cares will keep asking them to come, for as long as it takes. Others will tire and give up too quickly. And yae were right about them, they *are* trying to protect themselves. There are those who would hunt them and keep them as prisoners to do their biddin'. They are curious creatures by nature, but they have grown weary of humans. Although yae should pique their interest, being of two worlds as yae are."

"You have a particular relationship with them, why would they hide from you?" I asked.

"They know I'm not alone."

"They know I'm here, with you?" I asked, in disbelief.

"Aye. This is their home," said Morag. "Anything that disturbs the land, they feel."

The night turned deepest black, and I grew weary. I couldn't imagine Morag having to do this every time she came with her weaving. My eyes closed despite myself.

Then, I don't know how long it had been, I heard Morag say something different.

"*Halo a ghraidh.*"

She was greeting someone. My eyes flew open, and I saw a creature tall and thin half out of the pool with wings or fins; they could be both. Tiny silver scales covered her entire body, including her arms and legs. I thought she looked beautiful and strange, like a mixture of human, butterfly, and fish.

"Do you know her? Is she your friend?" I whispered.

"She is not a *she*. *She* is a *them*," said Morag.

"Can I talk to her, *them*?" I asked, correcting myself.

"They'll talk to yae if they wont to. But yae are on good terms with Rhiannon, and she is known as the Goddess of Fairies around here."

I was engaged in some kind of staring contest with the creature, but I had to look away. Their eyes burned with moonlight that spilled into mine like drops of quicksilver. Their voice filled my head with an elemental stream full of storms and something infinite. It reminded me of the darkest depths in a well of love, akin to what I had experienced in Myrddin's eyes.

"Welcome Changeling," they said. "I cleanse all of Morag's linen. It comes out of this pool a spotless blessing. Those who tempered with your gift and made a curse of it, were greedy human folk. None of us here would ever do that. It is not our nature."

No, it wasn't. The goosebumps on my skin told me so. My entire body trembled with it. Their nature was a remembrance of life itself, created out of boundless generosity and I believed them. But it left me bereft, with no idea where to go from here.

"Go home, Changeling, and be strong for your folk. I will always be grateful to your people for letting me go free."

I squinted at the creature, not understanding, and my eyes grew wide as their appearance began to stretch and transform. They became as white as the moon and as tall as the mountain, shrinking all the space around us. I was beholding the white dragon of the legends. The dragon of Dinas Emrys, of my home. I forgot myself, my needs and even my fears. I beheld the perfect beauty of this creature made of water and timeless time and the brilliance of silver scales reflecting moonlight.

The voice felt cold like the north wind. I heard it only inside my body. It was the song of many. "You are a creature of two worlds, and it is helpful to the future of this land. Myrddin Emrys knows it; the Goddess Rhiannon knows it; you must know it too. The magician thinks he can use it to his advantage, change the future." The dragon chuckled and my body was rocked by a tempest. "You must come to know who you are as a blessing."

"I must come to know my curse as a blessing?" I asked, unable to repress a growl, forgetting for a moment that I was in the presence of a dragon.

"May I share myself with you so you can understand me better?" they asked.

It was an odd request. They already overwhelmed my senses. I was afraid it would be too much, that it would kill me.

"I will not hurt you," they said.

I stood in the moonlight with this creature of power beyond human imagination and thought, *I will never get this opportunity again.* I heard Morag's voice, faintly, from somewhere behind me say, *this never happens.* I bowed my head to them, acquiescing.

I was filled with their essence. I was Dragon. I was silver water and moon, I was bird, light as air and I was fish, dissolving into water like rain. I was the multiplicity of creation. I was a moment, suspended in eternity. I was the beginning of things and the end of things. It came to me then, a sudden revelation, being as I was, in such an intimate state with them, *the dragon was dying.* Not for a while yet but they were coming to the end of themselves and would vanish from this place forever. Tears welled up in my eyes at the loss of this magic, this singular expression of love. I felt their breath within me and around me. I was surrounded by blue fire and the blue fire was me. I was the cursed one, and I was the blessing. *The curse was the cure.* I didn't know how that was possible but the moment I knew it was true Dragon separated themselves from me, and I was myself again. I staggered, an insignificant little beast once more. I almost fell into the water again. I stayed on my hands and knees for a while, panting.

"When you truly know who you are, your value, and what you really want, you will be able to use your curse to cure yourself and protect the king."

"Do not give me riddles. Please help me," I begged.

The dragon's voice reached a higher pitch. They were using at least three different tones at the same time. They hit my mind, my heart and my gut separately and together, building upon the new harmony in my body. "I give you the truth. You know it. You felt it. It is no riddle. Do not hide yourself from it again. Accept both your natures and it will be your path to healing. You must go home now."

The dragon was growing less substantial in the greying pre-dawn light. My eyesight was failing me. I couldn't follow them into the more subtle realm of the Tylwyth Teg. My body was already yearning for a reunion with them.

"Come back when you're finished with the world of men."

I wanted to say I was finished with the world of men the moment I was cursed. But there was little point in arguing with a dragon. I felt disappointed, cheated and exhausted. And how in the world was I supposed to protect the king? Wasn't that the druid's job? A new burden was being placed upon me instead of getting relief from mine. It was all so unfair.

It was as if Dragon heard my complaints and my fears. "Here is my gift to you, Dryw donn. It will give you strength to continue with your journey. Close your eyes."

The dragon called me as Myrddin did. I remembered that they knew each other and perhaps saw me in a similar fashion.

I was lost in my thoughts and speculations once again when the dragon hit me with their blue fire. It was sharp, precise, like a lightning bolt, but still cold, like the Fairy pool. I kept my eyes tightly shut against the sheer force and brightness of it, and I knew without having to look. Below the first rune, seared into my wrist, there was a new symbol: *Ehwaz*, carved into my skin by the blue fire of the dragon. It was their parting gift.

"This didn't hurt as much as when the Goddess inscribed the first rune," I said, staring at the symbol on the new smooth patch of skin.

"Hers is the fire of earth. My blue fire belongs to the deep waters and to the stars reflected in them. She will probably be angry with us."

"Why?" I didn't want to be caught on the wrong side of the Goddess by association.

"Because *Ehwaz* is the sign of the horse. And the horse belongs to Rhiannon."

I knew next to nothing about the significance of the rune. I only remembered the name. I needed to talk to Myrddin.

Morag whispered, "You should thank them. This is a rare gift."

"Thank you," I said, blushing, in spite the cold, at my horrible manners and glaring oversight. In my defense, I was unsure of how grateful I was in that moment.

The silver dragon dissipated in the first rays of the morning sun like a waking dream.

Chapter Seventeen

We didn't make it back to Morag's cottage until after nightfall. I threw myself down like a ragdoll on the blankets by the fireplace and fell asleep. I kept dreaming of Dragon all night. Their fiery blue breath upon me. I woke up wondering what two-fold nature they were talking about. There was the two-fold nature of spirit and reality that Myrddin had introduced me to and there was my own two-fold nature of being human and beast. Was that what Dragon was referring to? There was something else. Something I couldn't put my finger on right then, but it was whirring at me.

Morag walked out the door with me, after we had our final breakfast together. "*Mar sin leibh an-drasta*, Changelin'," she said.

"What does that mean?" I asked.

"It means, *until we meet again*."

I repeated as best I could, "*Mar sin leibh an-drasta*."

She squeezed me into her arms before I could object. I walked down the lane and back up the trail toward the Fairy Glen. I turned around once, and she waved. I waved back. She walked into her cottage and closed the door. I followed her inside with my mind. I could see myself sitting with her, among her things, making broth, weaving the linen, chatting by the fire.

Sure enough, when I got to the top of *Sìdhean Dubh,* the black fairy hill, MacLeod and Myrddin Emrys were waiting for me with Espoir in tow. They didn't ask me any questions. They let me be. It irked me that they were being so thoughtful. I wanted to be mad at them for putting me through all this. I missed Dragon. I wondered if I'd ever see them again.

I was taciturn through the whole ride home, through dinner. I ate like a banshee, and I didn't care what anyone thought of me. But they didn't seem to care either. We were back in our chambers when the druid finally asked, "Would you like to talk about your experience at the Fairy Pools, Dryw donn?"

"Why? Do you want to hear it?" I asked, full of belligerence.

"Of course," he said. "It's up to you. But it might be helpful to discuss it."

"I'll tell you about it if you tell me the truth," I said. "You knew my father was involved, right from the start and yet you reassured me that it could be *the weaver not the giver*. Why did you do that?"

"We still don't know how the curse came about," he said.

"Stop trying to make me feel better."

"Would you have believed me if I'd told you the curse was your father's fault?" he asked.

I fell back as if he had hit me.

"You see, even now you can scarcely hear it."

He was right, I could hear no more, so I talked about something else. "I'm tired of not having all the facts. That's why I asked Hillel to find out if our father was poisoned, and which doctor was involved."

The words were ash in my mouth. Why should I care to find out about my father's death, when he was the one responsible for my curse.

Myrddin's eyes were upon me, scrutinizing me. "Do you still want to pursue this? Find out who poisoned your father?"

"Yes. I do." It startled me to hear myself say so, but something in me kept insisting on it. That it was a key to unlocking more mysteries.

"Good."

Myrddin's approval surprised me, but it reassured me. He must think as I did, that it was worth investigating. Still, I wondered what his motives were and thought it must have to do with his king and kingdom which were paramount for Myrddin. "What part would you have me play in your scheme, Druid?" I asked.

Meeting Dragon had changed something inside of me. There was a new fierceness in my voice, not only anger but a confidence that wasn't there before. The new rune burned into my skin was a tangible reminder of it, the token of a shared mystery, like a wedding ring. Despite their declining strength, Dragon had chosen to impart some of their own life to me. Their generosity reminded me of the night sky filled with stars, which brought me such a feeling of wonder and awe as a child, I wanted to live in them. Dragon was dying. I couldn't get it out of my mind. That such a magical creature, who had lived a thousand years or more, could disappear forever, was unimaginable, an unbearable loss, compared to my little life. Who was I to complain about my fate? But I did anyway.

"Because you are who you are," said Myrddin, interrupting my thoughts.

"What? What does that even mean?"

Instead of listening to his answer, I continued with my questions, so anxious was I about the answers. "And how on earth am I supposed to protect the king? How has *that* become *my* job suddenly?"

"Is that what the white dragon told you?" asked Myrddin.

"Yes, among other things," I answered.

"Then it must be true," he said.

"But how and why?" I complained.

"I don't know," he said. "Dragon can see things beyond my abilities, even though I *am* a pretty good seer."

"What about my question," I said.

"Which question?" he asked.

"What does it mean, '*Because you are who you are?*'"

"Because you are the Lady of Dinas Emrys with everything that it represents, all the power and lands. You represent what the future could look like beyond war."

I laughed, "A monster?"

"No. The marriage of two nations, Saxon and Welsh in one body."

I had been holding my body tightly in my arms and I felt the rage surge through my limbs and up my throat. "How dare you bring up the circumstances of my birth. You of all of people."

Myrddin continued, ignoring my feelings, "You are the embodiment of what can save Briton. Make her stronger. It's who you were born to become. We are being overrun by Christians, who would kill our gods, and steal our sacred places. We are being overrun by Saxons who would kill us and take our lands, and soon it will be the Normans' turn. We cannot stand alone. Who you are, the Lady of Dinas Emrys, Saxon and Welsh both, will show the people that our strength will come from our alliance with the Saxons, instead of staying enemies and destroying each other."

This was not for me to hear. It belonged to lords and kings, not for the likes of me, an eighteen-year-old demon. I couldn't listen anymore. "Stop!" I shouted. "First of all, that will never happen. Secondly, I'm not even my own person. My fate is out of my control. And no one in their right mind will ever listen to me anyway. You have chosen wrong, Druid."

"I have not. The white dragon sees it as I do. She belonged to the Saxons until I freed her. She loved the red dragon, our dragon."

"I didn't know that," I said, shaken up.

"Everyone believed the dragons were fighting."

"She says she is a *them*."

"She is whatever she chooses to be. Fairy Folk are more mutable than we are."

It pleased me to hear the druid confirm my thinking: Dragon was Fairy Folk.

"That's nice," I said, dripping with surliness. "*I*, on the other hand, have no choice at all."

"But you do," he said. "Haven't you noticed during our journey here, how people respond to you? It really depends on how you hold yourself, and what you think of yourself. Your own fear is what gives wings to theirs."

"No. I disagree. It depends on the people and how they see me. Here, on the Isle of Skye, for some reason, they accept me. They call me Changeling. They are not afraid of me. So, I'm not as afraid of myself here. But it's the only place so far."

"Not so, Dryw donn. People anywhere can change their minds about you, given a chance. And they have. It happened in Caernarfon."

"I'm done with this conversation," I growled, claws itching to strike. Myrddin could be so irritating.

"If you wish," he acquiesced.

As I walked away from Myrddin (not something I did often) and into my chamber, I knew he was not being respectful of how I felt but rather, conciliatory, for the moment. He was far from done with me or I, with him. He was right about one thing. I wasn't in as much dread about people's reactions to my appearance as I had been at the onset of our travels.

At breakfast, I felt more settled. I kept staring at Myrddin while I ate, trying to gauge his mood. I wanted to know more about Dragon's gift. I couldn't catch his eye, so I thrust my wrist under his nose.

"Tell me about the new rune. I know it's the sign of the horse. But what does it mean?"

Myrddin took hold of my wrist and examined it closely. "I've never received a rune from a dragon. What is it like?"

"Dragon's blue fire is like a winter storm," I said. "Not blistering hot like Goddess fire."

"Sounds about right." He let go of my wrist.

"You didn't answer my question."

"It will give you strength to continue on your journey," he said.

"That's exactly what Dragon said. It doesn't explain anything."

"Runes are not *explained*. They are *experienced*, Dryw donn."

I hated that answer. I'd heard it before.

My temper was beginning to flare when he said, "Eira has returned. She came while you were at the Fairy Pools."

My blood turned to ice. My voice weakened, "Any news?"

"Yes. She carries news from home, from Hillel."

I waited for him to say more, heart beating too loud in my chest.

Myrddin studied my face as he spoke. "He says he found the doctor. You know what that means?"

I nodded, not trusting myself to speak.

"He confirms poison was used," he added.

I forgot about my own pain, my father's betrayal. His agony rose up in my memory. His death. My helplessness. I began to pace back and forth, then stopped and faced Myrddin, "Did he say more? Was someone else involved?"

"No. Nothing else."

"Could I see the message for myself?" I asked.

"Yes," he said. "Let me take you to Eira. It's time you were formerly introduced. Come."

I followed Myrddin. He knew the castle well, rushing along corridors, climbing staircases up a tower I had not been in. I didn't know what a formal introduction to a crow entailed but I wanted to see the message with my own eyes. All this talk of great canvas, and future plans, made me nervous. Myrddin was speaking in terms irrelevant to my situation and yet I had some part to play in this future scheme. I felt at a distinct disadvantage. I started to scratch my neck. It was unseemly, but I couldn't help myself. Definitely not something a courtly lady would be caught doing. I tried to picture myself at Arthur's court and failed. It was absurd to contemplate.

We went to the top of the tower. Myrddin opened the door, and we were in what could be called a bird haven. Eira had her own apartments. It seemed grand for just one bird. But Eira was the druid's own magical bird. There were carved stone basins of water. One for bathing and one for drinking, according to Myrddin. And all kinds of food. Seeds. Nuts. Fruit. Even a special dish full of worms in a closed box that somehow the crow knew how to open. There were four openings around the tower for a crow to take off in each direction, wide enough for her wingspan. There was a brazier running quite hot in one corner of the room.

Eira cawed once and hopped on Myrddin's shoulder the moment we walked in. She cuddled up to him, bending her head into the curve of his neck. It was unexpected to watch a bird do that, like Daffodil would do with me. They clearly had a loving bond. She stared at me with her blue eye, unblinking.

I had never talked to a crow before, so I decided it was best to keep it simple. "Hello, Eira. I'm pleased to meet you,"

Eira shifted her head in my direction, giving me her side eye. It was unnerving.

"She acknowledges your hello," said Myrddin.

I believed him.

Myrddin walked over to a small pinewood cabinet that stood on long skinny legs like a crane. There were several open drawers. I peered over his shoulder. One contained the tiniest rolls of paper I had ever seen and equally small cylinders in another drawer next to it. The paper was made from the bark of birch tree, spirit of new beginnings and protection, Myrddin explained.

"Is all this for Eira's benefit?" I asked.

"No," he answered. "The Laird has his own birds. They are off somewhere else right now."

"Do they get along, when they are altogether?"

"They respect one another. Eira gets first bid on any food or drink when she is visiting. She is the only female. The other two are males."

"Also crows?" I asked.

"Yes," he said. "Crows don't get along with other avian species. They hunt smaller birds."

I would remember that. Eira was a hunter. Better to stay on her good side. I waited for Myrddin to show me the missive. He handed me one of those tiny little scrolls. I used one of my long nails to unfurl it carefully. The bark was so delicate, I didn't want to tear it. It read as Myrddin had stated: *Found doctor. Poison was used.* There was something else Myrddin didn't mention. *More cannot be said.* Which meant there was more. But what? Too much for such a tiny scroll? Or too abhorrent to write down?

I confronted Myrddin about it, "There's something else on the scroll. Why not say so?"

"Because it says nothing important," he replied. "Enough for you to fret. And I know how you can agonize over the smallest things."

"This is no small thing," I argued. "It means there is more."

"Are you going to worry about it all the way home?" he asked.

"No, I won't," I answered, more to convince myself than him. "You should have given me the whole message. Now I think maybe there is more that you're not telling me. Is there?"

"There's a second scroll," he admitted. "But it's for my eyes only. Hillel and I have a long-standing conversation."

"Hmm. Does it involve my family?" I asked.

"Not directly," he acknowledged.

"Indirectly then?" I pressed on.

"Stop fishing, Dryw donn. I will tell you no more now. There is no point in it."

I eyed the drawer with the other scrolls, wondering if I could find my way back here.

"Do not even think about trying to come back here," he said, following my gaze. "The door is locked at night."

I acted offended. "I wouldn't dream of it."

He scoffed. He didn't believe me. *I* didn't believe me.

"We're heading back in the morning," he said.

"Already?" It came as a surprise even though it shouldn't have. It made sense but I didn't feel ready to leave. I liked this place. I liked the people. They were odd, like me. They were on friendly terms with Fairy Folk, with dragons. I could belong here.

Myrddin accompanied me back to our chambers. He said he had to discuss some things with the laird before our departure and asked if I wanted to come along. I said no, that I would rather stay in our chambers.

If Myrddin was surprised that I declined the invitation, he showed no sign of it. All he said was, "You might as well get some good rest before we set off. Our travels will be harder. Winter has returned."

"Shall I go ahead and eat supper in our rooms then?" I asked, eyeing the food someone had obligingly laid out for us.

"By all means. I can have supper with the laird."

"Good," I said. "Because I'm not leaving you anything to eat."

He smiled and wished me goodnight, "Nos da, Dryw donn. No need for you to wait up."

"Nos da, Myrddin Emrys. I won't."

I wouldn't. I was determined to steal back into the bird room and examine those other scrolls for myself. I ate then waited. I ate some more. Then waited until I felt sure he was in the company of the laird. I was nervous and excited in the same way I used to be as a child when Somer and I were about to play hide and seek or prank each other, back home in Dinas Emrys. This place was unknown to me. I took a candle with me then thought better of it and put it back. My bestial eyes could see well enough in the dark. And I needed the shadows to hide.

I was tentative about finding my way back to that tower. I got lost trying to avoid running into any of the servants. There were too many servants in this castle all running here and there, doing who knows what at this time of night. I kept having to retreat into alcoves, hiding under my cloak and hood. Missed a change of the guards by a hair's breadth. It was uncanny. As if they knew I was roaming around. I hid behind tapestries, cursing my beastly feet for sticking out. My smell almost gave me away. Some soldiers made a rude comment about rotten meat.

Eventually, after a few errors down corridors resulting in dead ends, I made it to the bird haven tower and climbed up the long spiraling staircase to the top. Myrddin hadn't lied. The door was locked. But I had sharp nails, and I was going to put them to good use. I introduced my longest nail into the lock and slowly started to turn the spring inside the lock. It was simple enough. It should have worked. It didn't. The key was on the other side. Eira had the key on her side of the door, inside the lock. And if I wanted to come in, she would have to open the door. This was shocking: a bird with so much power over their own lives. I got so upset I stomped my foot on the stone floor hard enough to break it, my foot, not the floor. I didn't, but I bruised it badly. I refused to give up. I put my eye to the keyhole and clearly saw the key stuck in it. I crouched down to the sliver of space under the door and begged.

"Please Eira, open the door. I need to know what's on those scrolls."

No response.

"Please Eira, most venerable of all crows. Please help me."

Nothing.

"Winter Snow beauty. Oh Eira, respectfully. Please let me in."

Silence.

I began to think Eira was enjoying this and taking me for a fool.

"That's enough foolishness," I scolded. "Open this door now!"

"That *is* enough foolishness!"

I was so preoccupied with convincing Eira to open the door, I didn't hear any footsteps. I slowly got up and turned, finding myself face to face with Myrddin Emrys and Laird MacLeod. Myrddin looked very stern, but MacLeod was attempting to hide the grin on his face. They had caught me on all fours, begging a crow to open the door.

"You shouldn't go around after dark in someone else's castle. My guards could have mistaken you for an intruder and run you through," said the laird. The smile he couldn't quite conceal from his lips gave the lie to his furrowed brow.

I struggled to regain my composure. "Yes, my Laird, you are right. I apologize."

Myrddin lost his stern exterior and smiled at me, eyes full of mischief, "MacLeod and I had a wager as to how long it would take you to get up here."

"You knew I would try and still let me make a fool of myself?" I said, offended.

"Yes," he answered. "You were much too agreeable about staying in our rooms for dinner."

"That is so..." I couldn't think of a satisfactory word. "So mean."

They both laughed outright. Then MacLeod struggled to speak in between bursts of laughter. "I summoned all the servants and urged them to roam the castle and act very busy."

"You enrolled the servants into this prank of yours?" I asked, remembering all the servants going hither and thither as I tried to make my way to the tower.

"Yes!"

"And the guards too?"

MacLeod nodded, unable to speak. Their laughter redoubled in hilarity. They had to hold their stomach. I swear, there were tears streaming down Macleod's cheeks.

It *was* pretty comical, so I joined in, eventually. I couldn't stay mad at them. I laughed and laughed, so hard. I snorted and howled, laughing at myself, the lengths I would go to in order to get my way. It was the best thing in the world. I had almost forgotten how.

I never got to take a look at those scrolls. The laughter was worth it though. And I trusted Myrddin, more or less, to tell me what I needed to know in due course.

Chapter Eighteen

Morning brought a fresh blanket of snow and a uniformly white sky. I was determined to stay awake for our passage back to Castlerigg through the Fairy portal. We broke our fast in Laird MacLeod's company. He was cheerful. His mind still intent on recalling my escapades of the previous night. I did my best to rein in my appetite, which was difficult, because he ate with such relish. Eventually, I gave up trying and joined in.

He rewarded me with a wink. "My compliments, Changeling. I don't know many people who can keep up with a Norseman's appetite."

We were just about done with breakfast when he put down his knife, looked at me squarely and said, "I like you, Changeling. I like your honesty and your passion. If you ever decide to come back to our little island, Dunvegan Castle will welcome you with open arms."

"I like you too, Laird MacLeod." I felt bold answering, but his jovial countenance gave me permission.

"Then it's settled. You must visit with us again."

"It is a place worth visiting many times over," I said. "And I hope you will visit us in North Wales."

"I may do so unless you come here first," he answered. "Please call me Magnus."

"Magnus," I stammered, feeling shy.

Myrddin stood up. "Time to saddle up before the weather turns."

"Your horses should be ready," said the laird. "I sent my squire to the stables earlier this morning."

We walked to the stables. I was a little ashamed of my neglect of Espoir, but we were barely within sight of the barn when he greeted me with a whinny that erased all my fears. He had made up his mind to love me as I was, beast ugly, forgetful, selfish.

"Thank you MacLeod," said Myrddin, embracing the laird warmly before he got on Rhian. These two were close friends or good conspirators.

Then MacLeod did the most extraordinary thing. Before I had time to retreat, he took hold of my furry leathery hand with the long nails and kissed it like I was a beautiful maiden. He then bowed and said, "My Lady. Safe travels. Until we meet again."

I was left dumbstruck, completely at a loss for words except for, "Umm. Yes."

He held the stirrup to my saddle so I could more easily get on Espoir. And I did so without another word passing my lips.

Once seated, I said, "Thank you," in a simpering voice I barely recognized as my own.

We rode away and MacLeod waved goodbye. I kept looking back.

"You're going to hurt your neck if you keep twisting it like this," said Myrddin.

I ignored the druid's remark. "Laird MacLeod is a very special man, isn't he?"

"There are none like him. And very smart too. Not the brute most people assume he is."

"Oh, I don't think he is a brute," I said. "I think he's quite handsome."

Myrddin took note of my foolish remark with a raised eyebrow. I chastised myself, *you need to stop thinking out loud in front of Myrddin. It won't do at all.*

We reached the Fairy Garden which turned out to be quite a distance from the castle.

"I thought this place would be closer," I said.

"No," he answered. "It's a gateway to the Fairy Kingdom and other realms. It cannot be in close proximity to any human dwelling. It would create too much chaos."

I didn't understand what he meant. "Too much chaos?"

"The pull of such magic would exert too much power over the human realm. It needs to be in a safe place for both sides. The Fairy Queen made a wise choice with this location."

Of course she is a queen. Beautiful enough to be one. For the laird to marry her. I felt an odd squeeze in my heart. I was so young still, I didn't understand myself. And being a beast, I couldn't let myself follow those inclinations.

I looked around to take my mind off the laird and his Fairy Queen and noticed we had reached a secluded valley surrounded by hills and populated with trees. It was covered in snow so I couldn't say if it looked like a garden. But the snow sparkled with soft light like a smooth pearl and the weather was its own thing in the valley. There was no bite to the cold here.

Myrddin dismounted and I followed suit. He turned to me and said, "Go find the gate. I'll wait here."

I didn't think I heard him right. "What?"

"Go find the gate to the other realm," he repeated.

"That's your job, isn't it?" I said.

"Not today," he replied.

I had no idea how to do this. I kept staring at him like he was the madman I always suspected he was.

"That's ridiculous," I grunted.

"Listen for it. The gate has no malice in it," he answered. "It's welcoming."

"That may well be the case, but I have no idea how to find this gate," I said.

"Better start listening," said Myrddin.

"What if I cannot find it?" I asked.

"We'll remain here until you do," he said.

I was getting mad, snorting and growling, frightening my poor Espoir. "That's absurd. I demand that you do your job, Druid."

"Be still!" His voice resonated in the space as if we were in a cavern. "It's time you learned how to do this. Use your senses, Dryw donn."

I got quiet then. The druid had made up his mind. And there was no convincing him otherwise. I grudgingly handed him Espoir's reins to hold and walked ahead into the valley which didn't seem so small anymore. He said to listen. I sat myself down in the middle of what looked like a snow field and opened myself to all the sensations and feelings around me.

The whole valley resonated with the song of winter winds and snow. It was like a mad ring dance. I couldn't distinguish anything. I closed my eyes against the too-muchness of it. After a while I forgot to listen and became essentially part of the landscape, like another tree. It was as if I was growing roots into the earth and branches into the sky. My eyes opened and noticed a pattern I hadn't seen before. There were a few rowan trees scattered here and there on the valley floor. They seemed to be standing randomly when I first looked at them but now my eyes could draw a straight line from one to the next into the shape of a star. At the intersection of all the lines there was a slight depression in the snow-covered earth. I got up and walked over to it. The air vibrated with Fairy magic. I had found the gate. I looked up at Myrddin, feeling rather smug. He walked over with our horses in tow.

Part of me expected praise from him. I received none but a nod and then he said, "Good. Now that you found the gate, call upon the runes, so you can get us back to Castlerigg."

"You want me to do what?"

"You heard me, Dryw donn. Get on with it," said Myrddin, calm as can be.

"You've truly gone mad! I cannot," I protested. "That's what you are here for. You are the druid with magical powers. Not me. Isn't it enough I found your bloody gate?"

"Quite right," he agreed. "This tells me you're ready."

"To get us lost between realms!" I shouted.

Myrddin chuckled. I really hated it when he did that.

"Not if you connect with your runes," he said. "You have everything you need. As her messenger, Ansuz is your direct connection to Rhiannon. And Ehwaz is your spirit horse, the one who moves through hidden places and gets you where you need to go. As long as you keep where you're going in mind."

"Is that all?" I was being sarcastic, but the druid smiled.

"And of course you need to keep all of us in mind as well, so we don't get left behind."

That was the last straw. "Stop fooling, Myrddin. It's insulting."

"Far from me to insult you, Dryw donn. I'm quite serious."

And I was *seriously* considering walking back to Dunvegan Castle and waiting until spring thaw. I looked over at Espoir. Myrddin still had a firm grip on my horse's reins.

"Why don't you try. See if I'm right about you," he said.

I couldn't think of anything pithy to respond to that. I was afraid of the consequences if I failed, of what could happen to Myrddin and Espoir and Rhian. I couldn't bear the thought of any of them getting hurt because I didn't know what I was doing, *because that devil of a druid let me do something I shouldn't.*

"What's so important about me doing this anyway?" I asked.

"To trust the unknowable, go past your idea of yourself," he answered.

"That's a druid's answer for you," I snorted. *To trust the unknowable. Utterly absurd.*

He kept waiting. His dark eyes, trained on me, were full of the very same unknowable mystery, this fierce love that could turn to rubble the fortress I had constructed around my heart since the curse. I felt the weight of his stare on me, inescapable. I surrendered.

"Fine," I said. "But you have to promise you won't let anything bad happen to my horse. Or my shade will haunt you for eternity. I swear it."

"If you keep your connection to the Goddess foremost in your mind, any promise I make will be irrelevant," he answered.

"Nevertheless, I need your promise," I demanded.

"I promise," he said.

I took a breath and felt slightly more at ease. "Thank you. What do I need to do again?"

"You listen to the runes, one at a time," he answered. "Don't try to get to both at once. It would be too much. Ansuz first. Its song will attract you to the Goddess, and her to you. When you are filled with that melody then turn your attention to the second rune, without losing your relationship to the first. It's pretty simple. You know where you're going. That's half the battle. Like I said. Simple."

"Simple?" I shook my head.

We stood all together within the circle of the Fairy gate, and I began to focus my attention on the first rune I had received, Ansuz. Soon enough, the burning sensation pierced through the skin on my wrist. Snow flurries began to rise around us in swirls. It was distracting. I lost my connection with Ansuz. This was not so *simple.* My frustration caused me to growl. The horses became agitated, pawing the snowy ground. Myrddin spoke in dulcet tones to restore them to a calmer state. I tried again. I slowed my breathing and called to the power of Ansuz once more. The burning sensation returned, and with it, the image of the Goddess Rhiannon dressed in gold, set, like a jewel, in velvet darkness. I could barely hold myself up as I was confronted with her formidable presence, even though she was only an apparition from the underworld, not her full self.

"You have the Goddess in mind." Myrddin knew the exact moment I connected with her. "Now hold on to that and connect with Ehwaz."

Myrddin's voice sounded indistinct, faint, and vaguely reassuring. I knew what I was supposed to do. I didn't know if I could do it. Not because of any difficulty in keeping Rhiannon's image in mind. Rather, the vision of the Goddess was so strong, I didn't think I could call on anything else.

I couldn't do it. I tried but felt no connection at all with Ehwaz. I kept trying, feeling inept and scared. I wanted to give up when the white dragon appeared, unsought, in my mind, and with it, the lightning breath of their blue fire. Dragon's blue fire was my key to Ehwaz. It rose up from me and intertwined itself with the red fire of the Goddess, expanding into a double spiral. We were enveloped in the twin flames, and I could see nothing at all anymore.

Instead of the whole world turning black, we were surrounded by whiteness. I thought I'd gone blind, but no, we were in the middle of a snowstorm.

"Your protégé has the stink of the lizard all over her."

"Yes. She was at the Fairy Pools, with the weaver."

"That explains it."

I couldn't orient myself in all this whiteness. And the furious hum of the snowstorm was deafening. In spite of it, I clearly heard Myrddin speak with a woman. Her way of referring to Dragon as *the lizard* offended me. *Who does that woman think she is,* I thought. I felt it like a personal insult.

"How could you let the lizard gift her with *Ehwaz?* What right do they have to do that? *Ehwaz* is mine. *I* am the Goddess of horses. How could you let that happen, their *pawprint* on *my* messenger?"

Rhiannon. He was speaking with the Goddess. I was impressed by Myrddin's calm when he answered, "I wasn't there."

"You should've been," said the Goddess. Her disapproval was unequivocal.

I thought it wise of the druid not to respond to Rhiannon's last quip. I was still unsure if I had actually managed to get us all to Castlerigg or if we were in some transitional unearthly place. I was still questioning my newfound skills when the storm began to dissipate, and giant stones emerged out of the white fog. I felt such relief and pride, I let out a small *Whoop*!

My pride was short lived as the Goddess fixed her eye on me. I couldn't hold her gaze. I stared at the ground instead. *How does Myrddin manage to look her in the eye so easily?* I was filled with renewed admiration for him, while cowering under her scrutiny.

"You. Beast girl. Come over here. Show me Ehwaz."

She stared at me in all her golden glory, on her white horse, with her eyes of infinite power and suffering. I swallowed hard. Where was the sanctuary when you needed it? On the far side of the circle, that's where. I turned to Myrddin for support. He gave me a nod of encouragement which didn't reassure me in the least.

Rhiannon was sitting erect on her white horse, and I had to raise my arm up to her. She grabbed my wrist, and I felt the burn of her red power. I couldn't help but whimper.

"Now, that can't hurt as much as what that lizard did to you, can it?"

"It does, Rhiannon. I'm just a puny thing. You are a great Goddess," I said.

She scoffed at my answer, but I saw a little smile appear on her perfect face.

I didn't say what I really wanted to say: that her fire was much worse than Dragon's silvery touch. She had no love for them, and I wasn't about to antagonize her any more than I already had.

She sniffed the quicksilver lightning of Dragon's sign on me, then let go of my wrist as if she didn't care one bit. I wasn't fooled. She was as curious as Myrddin had been and wanted to see Dragon's mark for herself.

"Dragon take liberties, don't they? Not your fault, Changeling," she said more gently.

I didn't think she expected me to answer, so I kept quiet.

"You have a long road ahead of you. And there is strife. Avoid human dwellings between here and Wales." said Rhiannon.

And with these words, her white horse reared, the earth cracked open, and they raced into the underworld. The ground closed upon itself as soon as they were gone.

Myrddin turned to me. "That's a Goddess for you."

"Very impressive," I said. "I wish I could crack open the earth at will."

"Not that," he explained. "I meant how possessive she is sometimes. That *pawprint* business."

"It's more than a pawprint. They shared their essence with me." I regretted mentioning it the moment the words passed my lips. Myrddin looked stunned for the first time I can remember.

"Well. That *is* something. Isn't it?" he said.

"What?" I asked.

"The love of a dragon," he answered.

I had not thought of it that way. I hadn't given it a name at all. It thrilled me a little.

"No telling what that will do," he said.

I wanted to ask *do what*, but he interrupted my thoughts. "Rhiannon is right, we have a long journey home," he said. "We best be going." He didn't move though. The druid kept scrutinizing me. It was getting uncomfortable. "You're not tired, are you?"

He didn't sound concerned. It was a rhetorical question.

"No," I answered.

"Good," he said. "You're strong."

That was all the acknowledgment I was going to get for successfully using the runes for the first time to transport us through the Fairy World to Castlerigg, horses included.

Chapter Nineteen

The smoke of destruction was visible from far away. It rose above the human dwellings despite heavy snowstorms and glacial temperatures once the sun disappeared. We had to wrap our horses' heads, ears and noses included, in bits of wool to keep them from freezing at night. It was as Rhiannon warned us. We couldn't stay anywhere near the villages due to the Saxon raids.

Even Myrddin's magic had trouble keeping us warm in this kind of weather. His fire was no match for the freezing air in the dank caves we slept in. I kept giving thanks for my thick leathery skin and my fur and especially Morag's tartans. Even then I was bitterly cold. It reminded me of my night at the Fairy Pools, except that this was lasting for days on end. I longed to be back at Dunvegan Castle. And I missed Dragon.

The weather had been mild by comparison on our journey north to the Isle of Skye. But every step toward home was a drudgery, a hardship for all of us, including the horses. Rhian and Espoir constantly stumbled in the deep snow which hid all kinds of treacheries, rocks, fallen branches, and holes. I loved winter as a child, but it was from the inside of our castle in Dinas Emrys, by a cozy fire, wrapped to my chin in blankets, listening to our father talk about the crops with Hillel after supper or to Somer recite his latest poetic masterpiece. This was a white hell.

One night, Myrddin dropped another wet log on the fire, and attempted to work the magic of the runes. He tried and tried but the result was pitiful. Nothing like the roaring fire he had been able to cast before. I could tell he was getting frustrated.

"That's it. I've had enough. You must get hold of yourself, Dryw donn." He was glaring at me.

I looked up at the druid, wide eyed. I wasn't doing anything.

"You're making our travels near impossible," he said.

"Are you saying this weather is my fault?" I asked.

"Yes, it is!" he said. "It's interfering with my ability to work with the runes."

"Your difficulty with the runes is *my* fault too?" I couldn't believe my ears.

"It can't be helped," he said. "We are related in magic since you received your runes."

I denied his accusations. "I've never heard of such a thing. And I don't have that kind of power. You have it wrong, Druid."

"I'm *not* wrong," he said. "You proved your mettle when you got us through the Fairy gate back to Castlerigg. I didn't think you could manage it, not yet, but you did."

"What? You didn't think I could do it, and you let me do it anyway?" I was incensed. I did notice that as my resentment toward Myrddin increased, the blistering wind outside our cave redoubled in strength almost instantly. I could hear it whistling about my ears.

"Calm yourself," he urged. "Can't you see what's happening around us since we left Dunvegan Castle?"

Grudgingly, I recognized that the weather had been uncanny in its intensity for some time, but I had no idea what I was doing to affect it in such a way. And I admit, part of me was pleased I managed to disrupt Myrddin's habitual serenity.

Battered by the snowy wind that crept inside, I stood near the entrance of the cave like an insolent beast with my arms crossed. "Perhaps if you explained to me how this could be happening, I might be able to *do* something about it," I said.

He sighed. It was his customary response to my petulance. He tried to put two more logs on the miniscule fire. It helped not at all. "You have received two of the runes that make up the primary cycle of druidic initiation." He had to raise his voice over the wind to make himself heard. Something he never did or needed to do. I doubted he even *liked* speaking.

He kicked our meager fire, and the sparks flew like fireflies into the cave for a moment before dying down. He shouted over the howling wind, "Your connection to them was awakened when we traveled through the land of the Fairy Folk back to Castlerigg. Your creature self already has an instinctual relationship with the powers of Nature. So, when you add the magic of the runes to your own, not to mention Dragon magic, there you have it."

He stopped to catch his breath. I almost felt bad for him.

"The elemental forces are responding to your inner storm."

The wind echoed Myrddin's words, shrieking into the cave, blowing our cloaks about. The horses whinnied, frightened out of their wits. I heard him then. I was the mad winter wind and yet I couldn't give voice to it. I couldn't articulate the words. I wanted to *be* ice so I wouldn't have to feel anything anymore. I wanted the whole world to turn to ice rather than say what was on my mind or feel the terror in my heart. Myrddin didn't turn away from me as the glacial wind raged outside. And I raged back at it, with it. I had no evidence that what I thought was even true. It *felt* true and I hated myself for it.

"You must get hold of yourself, or we'll never make it home," he said. "Perhaps that *is* the point. Isn't it, Dryw donn?" Myrddin wasn't mad at me. He was worried about me.

I just fell on the ground in a heap, legs like *pwdin Eryri*, our famous Snowdon steamed pudding and howled back at the wind. I didn't even know I wanted to howl. All at once, a rush of feelings came over me, confusion, shame and terrible sadness.

In the midst of this wintery madness, I heard Myrddin's words in my heart: "What are you so afraid of?"

I didn't know what would come out until I uttered the words, "I can't go home. I'm afraid of what Hillel will tell me. As long as I don't hear any of it, it won't be true."

"Now, now, little Dryw donn." Myrddin took me into his arms and rocked me. "Even if the worst you can imagine turns out to be true, you will survive. You are strong and you have strong allies. As a matter of fact, you are the strongest person I know."

"I'm not a person," I said between hiccups.

"Alright, the strongest *Changeling* then."

I heard the smile in his words as he said them. I was flooded with memories of Laird MacLeod, and Morag Ferguson and Dragon. It helped me settle down. Then Espoir came over and snuffled his breath on top of my head, as if to give me encouragement.

Myrddin asked again, softly, "What are you so afraid of?"

I took a shaky breath in and whispered, "That my brother is responsible for my father's death."

"Is that worse than your father cursing you?" he asked.

My mind was on fire with his question. "Yes. No. I don't know."

"Don't you?"

I felt suspended between worlds for a moment.

"I would rather my father cursed me than for my brother to have poisoned him."

My answer struck me as a defeat, but it was the truth as I knew it in that moment. As soon as I said the words, the wind died down. Everything became eerily quiet and still. And the fire Myrddin had been trying to coax for hours, roared into life.

The rest of our travels was more manageable. Still hard but not impossible as it had been. Being more conscious of my connection to Ansuz and Ehwaz, I could be more responsible and was able to assist Myrddin. I could find the way forward, see a path where there was none and even lend my help to the lighting of the fire when we rested in other caves along the way. We avoided the villages and towns. Sounds of skirmishes reached us, even deep in the woods as we were. I never heard full on battles, but raids were on the rise. I didn't feel equipped to help anyone, but I thought Myrddin should interfere and wondered why he didn't.

I will never get that night out of my mind. It started near sunset. We had settled for the evening. We were close to Llanymynech, the border town between Wales and Briton. We heard screams, people pleading for their life as it was being snuffed out. It felt close, as if they were dying next to us. I smelled the iron scent of spilled blood. I could taste it on my tongue. It overwhelmed me and excited me at the same time. I wanted to do something. I grimaced, holding my face between my hands, then abruptly stood up, having made my decision. I was about to run outside when Myrddin reached up and grabbed my arm.

"Settle down Dryw donn. This is not your fight. Not yet."

I yanked my arm out of the druid's hand. "But it is. These are human beings. And the Saxons are slaughtering them."

"War is chaos," he said. "It breeds chaos. Runes become unpredictable in such a setting. You might not be able to keep them in check. You have no idea what's happening out there. There will come a time when you must act but this is not it."

I heard the wisdom in his words. I could feel the heat of the runes coursing through my body, eager to ride the wings of my passion. I could see the red and blue fires begin to rise from my wrist in a double spiral. I was far from any mastery over them, if that was even possible.

"Why don't *you* do something then?" There was bitterness in my voice, tinged with defiance. As if our friendship gave me permission to speak to him this way.

"This is not my war," he said. "I fight for the future of this land in my own way, you know that. Make alliances where they can make a difference. I do not interfere in such battles."

I was adamant that something must be done. "The future begins *here,* with *these people*, *this village*." And relentless, when he didn't respond, "You cannot leave them to be slaughtered. You can't. It's wrong, Myrddin. You know it. I know it. You have to *do* something, or I will."

Myrddin stared at me and sighed, "You are not going to let this go, are you?"

"No. You know I'm right."

"Magic takes a lot of strength, Dryw donn," he said. "It's important to use it wisely. Otherwise, you'll exhaust yourself and won't have it when you really need it."

I didn't understand what he meant. Not yet. But I nodded, willing to agree with anything he said as long as he helped these people.

He got up, brushed himself off, and said, "Don't follow me unless I ask for your help. I need to assess the situation."

"How will I know if you do?" I asked.

"Your runes will start burning and you may hear me or see my name in your mind."

I began to wonder if I was putting Myrddin in serious danger by asking him to use his magic in such a way, to interfere in a battle. Never mind risking his life, being wounded or killed by a spear or a sword. If there was an end to Dragon, surely, there must be an end to Myrddin Emrys. I didn't want to be the cause of it. I was getting nervous, about to tell him I had a change of heart and to forget the whole idea.

"One more thing," he said. "My magic is in service of Nature, first and foremost. It works *with* Nature. If Nature wants to help, then she'll do so. But I cannot go against her, or I will lose her good will. I'll be trying to direct the runes as it is."

I didn't know what that meant but I could tell it was serious. Something else to worry about if it all went wrong.

"You don't want me to come with you?" I asked, feeling more like sheep than beast.

"No. Please listen, Dryw donn. Just this once. I will call on you if I need your help."

I nodded and let him go out into the wintery dusk. Night was fast approaching yet Myrddin used no torch to light his way. His eyes could see in the dark as mine did.

I opened my senses to the growing darkness, hoping to keep track of the druid as he moved closer to the fray. He was going straight into the battleground because of me, betraying his own rules. I listened to every sound, trying to discern what was happening. I listened for his voice. I heard nothing unusual for quite a while, except for the screams and cries and grunts, the clash of metal of the continuing battle. The smell of fire and blood was everywhere.

I sensed a rumbling, different from the sounds of battle. The ground began to shake, gently at first. Then a ripple, undulating under my feet. It got bigger and bigger until it turned into a series of continuous waves of gigantic proportions, as if the ground had turned to water. I heard the earth scream, like a thousand boulders crashing down from Yr Wyddfa. I fell down on all fours. No one could stay upright with the earth moving like a storm at sea.

The runes burned my wrist. The red fire jumped out first, shaped like the Goddess on her horse, and galloped into the night, followed by the silver blue fire in the shape of Dragon. They soon became entwined, weaving in and out into the darkness, searching for their sisters. My mind followed them. My runes locked into Myrddin's magic and became one with it. I didn't mean to do it. They had their own will and took over, like a river running through the village and into the battlefield. They wanted to merge with his power. Myrddin's body was a vessel, consumed by the light of the runes. Only the fire of the runes, only the power of magic, there was nothing else left of him.

Saxons, Britons and Welsh alike, frightened out of their wits, dropped their weapons and attempted to run in all directions. The earth moving under their feet made it impossible to take more than a few steps without stumbling and falling over. They went down on their knees, screaming in fear. The fighting ceased. The torched abodes continued to send flames into the smoky black sky until they petered out with nothing but ash left to burn.

All was quiet except for the whimpering of the fearful and the plaintive cries of the wounded. Even the bravest warriors were reduced to stunned silence. The battle had ended. My body felt Myrddin's collapse on the earth as the runes' power receded. When Ansuz and Ehwaz vanished, I was left weak as a lamb and bereft from their sudden departure. I understood now what Myrddin meant when he said that magic took strength and could leave you exhausted.

I hadn't really thought through how to stop a battle without hurting the people you meant to save, the amount of power that would need to be summoned. It didn't dawn on me till after the fact that it was a huge undertaking, of a magnitude only someone like Myrddin Emrys could attempt and even then, at great personal cost.

He didn't make a fuss, but he was even more quiet than usual. I could see he had trouble walking for more than a few miles each day and would collapse into deep sleep as soon as we stopped for the night. I did everything I could to help with finding food and lodging. Going out to hunt while he rested in our next temporary refuge. He needed my help to locate our new shelters. I wanted to make up for what I had gotten Myrddin into with my foolish demands. Ehwaz came in handy, my spirit horse, the finder of hidden places. And perhaps for the first time, being of service to Myrddin, I was glad for the gift of my runes.

That night of the battle, I had only assisted with the runes, unwittingly at that. Myrddin had done the bulk of the work and so I was able to recover more quickly. This, I saw now, was how a druid could come to the end of themselves, being consumed by their magic.

Eira must have sensed something was wrong because she stayed by Myrddin's side for several nights in a row. She was agitated at first, cawing and flapping her wings. There was nothing I could do to help her. She did settle down on her own after a while. I saw it as a good sign when she finally left his side and took flight again. Myrddin never spoke to her in words but the way they stared into each other's eyes, I knew they were communicating. It took a week for him to be back to himself, able to light a fire easily and walk steadily for miles.

"I want to talk to you about your use of the runes on the night of the battle," he said.

I thought he might have forgotten about that. Or chosen not to speak about it. But Myrddin was too thorough for that kind of forgetfulness.

"I'm sorry Myrddin. Please forgive me," I said, penitent. "I wanted to keep track of you without getting in the way, but I couldn't do it. The runes took over as you said they would. I should have listened."

"What you did was exactly right. And with perfect timing," he said. "Of course, you'll need to practice aligning your instincts with the runes on purpose in the future."

I was quite prepared to grovel some more. Myrddin's weakened state had frightened me. I was completely *un*prepared for the praise. My mouth was agape, my eyes round with astonishment until an intense sense of relief burst through me, something I hadn't felt for quite a while. I hadn't made a mess of things. I had done something right, helped Myrddin, my mentor, my friend. I wanted to hug him. I had a renewed buoyancy in my step as we proceeded with the last leg of our journey home.

We did not stop at Caernarfon. Instead, Myrddin took us through the deepest part of the forest. I wondered why.

"Our work there is already done," said Myrddin. "And there are too many visitors."

When I heard him mention visitors, Hillel's face instantly came into my mind's eye. "Does this have anything to do with the missive you received from Hillel?" I asked.

"It does, Dryw donn," he replied.

"Do you think these visitors are trying to make a bid for a different alliance? One without King Arthur, perchance?" I asked.

Myrddin's eyebrow shot up in surprise. I had guessed the truth.

"That may very well be the case," he said. "But I don't believe it will sway Segon Fawr. Whatever his faults, at his core, he's very loyal. And he takes pride in it."

"You're counting on his pride to keep faith with Arthur?" I asked.

"I am," he replied.

I wondered about that. What pride could do to a man, for good or ill. Pride in one's character or position. Hurt pride and its consequences. From where I stood, there was no room for pride in my life. Not only because I was a beast, but I didn't think there was any room for pride in women's lives. Except perhaps for pride in one's appearance before marriage and then pride in one's children who were never really your own but your husband's.

"Here we are," said Myrddin.

I looked up from the snowy trail we had been following for some time, expecting to see another cave but we were still deep in the forest. I was about to ask where was *here*, when I took a more careful glance and noticed the path looked familiar. We soon reached a clearing and there indeed, we were, back at our original meeting place, Myrddin's circle of stones. It looked insignificant compared to Castlerigg but beautiful to my eyes. Instead of giant bare white stones, these stones were all mossy and glistening with lichen, more welcoming. They held the friendliness of home. I dismounted and began to jump up and down with excitement. We had made it back to the Gwynedd Woods and Dinas Emrys was close by.

My joy was short-lived as I pondered what awaited me. Myrddin Emrys would certainly return to his service at King Arthur's court, telling his king about the meeting in Caernarfon. I would be alone once more, surviving as a beast in the woods, like nothing had changed.

"You're leaving me, aren't you?" I said. "Going back to court."

Myrddin must have noticed the glum look on my face after I abruptly stopped jumping up and down. "I'm not leaving quite yet. Come now, Dryw donn, this is not the end of things. It is the beginning of a new chapter in our story."

"In *your* story maybe," I grumbled. "I'm going back to being the Cursed Lady of the Gwynedd Woods, the beast who frightens children in their dreams and peasants who can't find the way home because they drank too much at the fair in Beddgelert."

"You may soon frighten kings as well."

"Not likely. Besides, I would never subject myself to such ridicule," I said empathically.

"It's time for you to meet with Hillel. He's waiting for you," said the druid.

"That's what I'm afraid of," I said.

"I asked Eira to inform him of our return," he added.

"I'm sure you did," I scoffed.

It was hard to say goodbye to Myrddin. He had come into my life when I thought the beast would engulf all of my humanity and I wanted to die. My association with him had changed me, probably as much as meeting Dragon, maybe more. But it made it harder to return to my previous existence, merely surviving in the woods. I didn't want that for myself anymore, but I couldn't see another way forward, not even with Ehwaz. I stood there, planted like a tree.

"Go on, little Dryw donn. It'll be alright. You'll see," he said.

"I *can't* see it," I replied. "I'm not like you. I'm not a great seer."

"Don't underestimate yourself, Dryw donn. That would be a grave error." He smiled. "Unworthy of my *protégé*."

My heart swelled as he said the word. It was his parting gift to me.

As we started on our separate ways, our horses refused to budge. They didn't want to leave each other. I had to bribe Espoir with apple chunks and convince him that all would be well even though I didn't believe it myself. There was a deep dark moat between Myrddin's trust in my abilities, and my own faith in myself which vacillated between tenuous and nonexistent.

Chapter Twenty

The weather grew fierce again as I made my way back to Dinas Emrys. It was annoying because now I wondered if it was just weather or if my anxious mind and reluctant gait were contributing to it. It was my tendency to assume that whatever was going on was somehow my fault. I scolded myself, kept my feet moving, and chose to talk to Espoir instead.

"We are almost home, Espoir. We'll go directly to Hillel's office and talk with him first. You remember where it is, don't you? In the back of your old stable. And after that, we'll go back to the hunter's cabin in the woods. You'll have your own private little stable back. And Hillel will bring your favorite treats, like oats and *Afal Enlli,* the apples from Bardsey Island. Do you know the secret name of that place? I bet you do. It's *Afalon.* Not a place for Fairy Folk like the Isle of Skye, but a place for bandrui where they go when they are tired of the world of men. Some druids are allowed too."

Espoir snorted and shook his head. He was missing Rhian and didn't care for my babbling. He had been sharing his hay and his bed with the beautiful grey mare for weeks now. Going back to his own stable to be alone didn't seem like something to look forward to. I completely understood and commiserated with him.

It was too cold to leave Espoir tied outside, so I put him in his old stall. There were no grooms about, thankfully. He was not happy to be back, snorting and pawing the ground. He didn't like the company which consisted of my brother's fancy horse and another mare, not half as pretty as Rhian, who probably belonged to Lady Amunet. There was another horse I hadn't seen before, stocky like a Percheron. The kind my brother would take to war.

I kissed Espoir's silky nose. "I won't leave you alone too long."

Whoever took care of the horses now would be surprised to find an extra mouth to feed upon their return. I hoped they wouldn't raise a fuss. I proceeded to Hillel's door and knocked. I was shaking but I wasn't so certain it was from the cold.

Hillel opened the door immediately. He always knew when I was near. I suspected his communications with Myrddin via Eira had been going on for a very long time. I made a mental note to ask him about it. He looked older than I remembered. More bent, and more lines around his eyes. The groove between his brows had deepened. His hair was all grey. Did I see rightly? Had he changed so much in just a few weeks? Or was he reflecting the changes in me? I still didn't fit in, but I experienced more annoyance than despair about it now.

"Welcome back, My Lady. Do come in."

He sounded genuinely pleased to see me. I obeyed, walking in. He closed the door behind me with care. There were still piles of parchment on the desk, and many more rolled up in the shelves against the wall behind it.

"Have a seat. I'll bring the broth." He walked over to the kettle singing softly on the tiny stove, which Hillel had built himself. "You seem well."

"I'm still a beast," I quipped, sitting on the stool near the fireplace.

"You don't seem as burdened by it. Am I wrong?" he asked, squinting an eye at me.

I hesitated before answering, "You are not wrong, Hillel."

He carried the pot and a cup for the three steps it took to cross the room. He handed me the cup and poured the dark herbal broth.

I blew on it then took a sip. I didn't recognize the taste at first. Then it dawned on me, "This is not broth at all, it's cider!" I took another sip to confirm my discovery, smacked my lips, and sighed, delighted with the festive aroma and the frothy tart sweetness.

Hillel gave me his best crinkly smile. "I received a big batch of apples from Bardsey Island a few months ago. I decided to make cider from it. I'm glad you like it."

"It's delicious. Much better than boring old broth."

Hillel moved his chair from behind the desk to sit closer to me. I didn't shift away from him. I didn't try to hide.

"I left Espoir in his old stall in the stables. Will it be a problem?" I asked.

"No," he replied. "Caden is still the marshal. He will know Espoir. Not to worry. Old Caden is no gossip."

"I remember him," I said. "A good man."

Hillel nodded. A man of few words, like Myrddin. No wonder these two got along.

The light tone of our conversation got to the beast I was. My claws began to scratch the surface of the table. I managed to stop and plunge into the heart of the matter before the wood was ruined. "I received your missive."

"Yes," he said.

"There is so much to ask." My limbs trembled with anticipation.

"I will try my best to address all your concerns," he replied.

"You found the doctor?" My mind was swarming with questions pushing past each other to get out first and whether I'd be able to live with the answers.

"I did," he acquiesced. "It wasn't hard. I had the list of doctors who had seen your father. There were seven of them. Most of them were scattered throughout the county so I sent people out to find out if anything unusual had happened recently with any of these doctors. One of them had come into possession of a new domain with sizable lands right after your father's death. He had no property beforehand to trade. No fortune of any kind. He lived in a cramped thatched cottage with his aging mother. I had him brought here and I spoke with him."

"Did you have to torture him?" I asked. Part of me hoped the man was tortured. I wanted him to suffer as my father had suffered. I still loved my father even though he had ordered the cursed linen gown.

I needed to talk with Hillel, not only about the poison and the poisoner but also about my father. I was desperate to understand his motives.

"I threatened to poke his eyes out if he didn't tell me the truth," said Hillel. "But he was more afraid of the person who ordered him to poison Lord Vortigern."

"I knew there must be someone else involved. Why would a doctor put their reputation on the line by poisoning my father?"

"People are unpredictable," said Hillel. "This man sold his soul for money, and a nicer home, but he was so frightened, he almost drank poison himself rather than talk. I was able to stop him and take the vial from him. I examined it myself. As I thought, a lethal combination of several poisons. It is a testament to your father's strength that he lasted as long as he did."

The specter of my father's awful death rose before me. "So, who was the doctor so afraid of?" I asked, wondering if I could bear the answer.

"The Lady of the House is what he told me," said Hillel.

"The Lady of the House?" I frowned.

"The *other* Lady of the House." Hillel watched for my reaction as it began to sink in.

"You mean Lady Amunet," I said. I swallowed hard.

Hillel nodded, "Lady Amunet has particular knowledge of plants, given the family business. She would know the lethal dosage of such remedies."

It was so outlandish to be talking like this, almost nonchalantly, about my father's murderer. But when I conjured her image in my mind, I found I could believe it. That Lady Amunet could be this ruthless and determined in her destruction of other people's lives if it served a higher purpose, like *family*. She had the will for it. At the same time, I was still trying to come to terms with the idea that my father was involved in my curse. I couldn't believe it and yet I felt undone by it. I couldn't hold all the pieces of this mad puzzle together in my mind. I had to ask Hillel.

"Did you know my father was the one who ordered the linen gown for my birthing day celebration?"

"I did," he replied.

I was shocked. I shouldn't have been. Hillel knew everything that happened in Dinas Emrys. He answered like it was the most normal thing in the world.

"Are you saying you knew he was involved in cursing me?" I asked, my voice harsh.

"I didn't say that, My Lady," he replied.

"But he ordered it," I said, insisting.

"He ordered the linen. That's all. He never got to see the gown made, and he never got to present it to you. Your brother, Lord Gromer Somer, did that."

Morag's words came back to me, how the linen had left the Isle of Skye pristine. *She never stitched the gown.* "The gown was sewn here then. And my father was already ill when the linen arrived?"

"Correct, My Lady." Hillel was staring at me, as if he was still expecting me to resolve the puzzle I should understand but didn't.

"Who took care of the package when it arrived?" I asked.

"I was there. And Lady Amunet with Lavinia. Lady Amunet took charge when you devoted your time to care for your father."

"Who took the linen?" I pressed on.

"Lady Amunet thought it best if the linen was kept safe in her chambers until it was to be sewn." Hillel was speaking slowly as if he wasn't sure I could understand him.

My heart was beating fast and loud in my chest. I was beginning to hear a strong hiss in my ears. Hillel's voice was receding, becoming indistinct. I asked another question. My words came out slowly as well. My lips felt numb.

"Do you know who sewed the linen into a gown for my birthing day feast?" I asked.

"I do," he replied. "It was your ancilla, Lavinia."

I heard a loud crack. Something must have broken. I vanished from myself. I was floating above the room, close to the ceiling, looking down at my prone form, next to a broken stool and Hillel was on his knees, yelling something at me, except I couldn't hear the words. It was comforting to be separated from my beastly body. I was myself again. I felt safe. There was no pain, no feeling, a benign disinterest in what was happening to me. I don't know how long it lasted. At one point I began to hear again.

"Lady Ragnell! Wake up!" he shouted.

I didn't want to wake up. I didn't want to return to this terrible world, where people got poisoned or turned into beasts and parents hurt their children and brothers abandoned their sisters. A fiery sensation burned my cheek. Hillel had slapped me, hard.

"That hurt," I growled, still groggy.

Hillel helped me get up and took me to his chair.

"I apologize for the slap, My Lady, but it was necessary. You fainted dead away. You were stone cold, not waking up. I feared for your life."

I could have died. Perhaps I did die, momentarily. If that's what happened, it wasn't so bad. Compared to the earthly miseries I was dealing with, it wasn't the worst thing.

What did Hillel say to me before I fainted? Lavinia. I couldn't live with the thought of Lavinia doing this to me. It was almost as bad as if my brother had done it. She who nurtured me as best she could in the first few days after the curse descended upon me. Dependable, loving Lavinia, always there when I needed her as a child. Lavinia, who never talked down to me, and who told me about the bandrui.

I made myself ask, "Is Lavinia responsible for my curse then? Did I hear that right? Is that possible?"

"Indirectly, I suppose," said Hillel.

"What does that mean?" I asked.

"You should ask her yourself. It's her story to tell. But I can assure you, she didn't do it on purpose. She does blame herself though."

She didn't do it on purpose. I hung on to that.

"Would you arrange a meeting with Lavinia for me? In the hunter's cabin? At her convenience. Do you think she'll come?"

I wanted to be in my own territory to meet with her. The beast in me felt safer.

"Of course, My Lady," said Hillel.

"One more question. Where is my brother?"

"Lord Gromer Somer and his wife are abroad. They are visiting with Lord Segon Fawr in Caernarfon."

It came as a relief to hear that Somer was away. A wave of sorrow followed, that I should feel this way about my own brother.

"Was this the topic of your second missive? The one addressed to Myrddin Emrys?"

"It was," he said.

I could always count on Hillel for the truth. But it had all been too much for me. The hunter's cabin didn't sound so bad anymore. I needed to retreat, be on my own again, as I had been. I knew two things for certain: My father was *not* involved in the curse upon me, which was a great relief to me. And my father had been murdered on Lady Amunet's order. I would find a way to tell my brother, and he would be horrified, and she would be banished. I would banish her myself. That is what I wished. And if my new magic could help, I would make it so. And then there was Lavinia. But I didn't want to think about that. I was too tired. Bone tired.

"I'm glad about one thing," I said. "It's not my father. He didn't curse me."

"No, My Lady," replied Hillel. "Lord Vortigern loved you. He thought that you should have been his son and that it was a perverse twist of fate that you were born as you were."

"You mean a girl?"

Hillel hesitated, looking down briefly, "Yes."

We were never enough for my father, I thought. Neither I, nor my brother.

"I'm so tired," I said. "May I sleep here by the fire tonight?"

"Of course, My Lady."

"Thank you, Hillel."

"I'll use the cot in the next room. Nos Da, My Lady."

"Nos Da, Hillel."

Hillel retreated to the little closet he called a room, with the cot he slept on when it was too late for him to trudge all the way home. I laid down by the fire, waiting for it to soothe my torn spirit. I searched for the little wren in my pocket and held on to it until I fell asleep.

When I woke up, Hillel was already gone, attending to his duties. The kettle was singing and there was a plate of pice ar y mien, my favorite cakes, on his desk. I ate the cakes with relish, licking my fingers every step of the way, drinking the cider that was left, burping to my heart's content. There was also a pack of food for me and another one for Espoir sitting by the door, waiting for me.

I hurried to the stables to check on Espoir. I hoped he had fared well overnight. I needn't have worried. Espoir nickered when he saw me. He looked all shiny like burnished gold, cleaner than he'd been in weeks, months if I'm honest. And his feet looked neat and trimmed and shiny too. He was munching on some oats. Someone, I assumed Caden, had taken very good care of my horse down to his feet. I looked for my saddle and saw it sitting on the saddle rack, glistening with neatsfoot oil. It had been restored to its original glory. It looked brand new. I must find a way to thank them, Caden, Hillel.

It was astonishing to me how some people went out of their way to be kind and others didn't. Others could be murderous. Human nature was as great a mystery to me as it had ever been. Hillel summed it up quite nicely, *unpredictable.* Like my own divided nature which still baffled me but didn't frighten me as much.

I threw myself into cleaning when I got back to the hunter's cabin. It had never occurred to me to sweep the place or use a rag to clean in the three years I'd lived there. But I felt compelled to do so now. I was covered in cobwebs and dust by the end of my cleaning spree. It didn't sparkle; I was never that great of a housekeeper, having only done it once or twice at Lavinia's insistence that I should know how to clean. But it did look better, like a human being could live here. It was late afternoon by the time I stepped outside, too late to find the little stream I bathed in most of the time. I looked at the knee-deep snow in the woods around me and plunged into it. I gave myself a snow bath. I rolled in it and took great bites of it and chewed on it. I needed pristine snow after my conversation with Hillel.

When I returned to the cabin I was shivering, dripping wet. Night had fallen and it was bitterly cold inside as well as outside. There was a good stack of wood by the front door. I took some and threw it in the fireplace. I stared at it for a while and figured I would try to light it with my new magic. I looked down at the runes on my wrist.

"Come on ladies, time to prove your worth. I don't want to freeze to death in here."

I figured I would ask Ehwaz to find her way to the spirit of fire, bring it back to me and then Ansuz to get fire a message to ignite the wood. It was complicated but I thought it might work. After all, I had Goddess fire and Dragon fire running through my blood now. That was kinship enough to the spirit of fire.

I focused on Ehwaz and tried and tried but it wouldn't work. I would get a meager blue flame that petered out, completely disinterested in the wood in the fireplace. Hearth fire was nothing like Dragon fire. And Ansuz refused to cooperate with Ehwaz. My plan was *not* working.

Necessity fueled by growing frustration and shuddering, I called upon the fire of the Goddess through Ansuz, directing my hands toward the hearth with as much determination in my prayers as I could muster, "Great Goddess clad in gold, I implore you. Rhiannon, giver of boons, rider of the white spirit horse, if I am truly your messenger, *and you don't want me to freeze to death*, then help me now and may the fire ignite into full bloom in this here fireplace where I live—in the hunter's cabin—of the Gwynedd Woods—near Dinas Emrys." I thought I better be as specific as possible. Then I waited.

For a moment, I felt the air suspended around me. My breath was sucked out of me as I became the fire of the Goddess. *Ansuz* leapt like a wild horse onto the wood and flames roared to life in the fireplace. I did a happy soggy little banshee dance, in front of the hearth, singing my thanks to the Goddess Rhiannon: *Thank you, thank you, thank you.*

My singing had more to do with screaming than keeping a tune, but it was heartfelt and made up in sonority what it lacked in melody. I danced and sang until I collapsed in front of the fire.

Chapter Twenty-One

My brother's wife was a murderer. Lady Amunet, whom I had so admired and wanted to emulate, had poisoned my father to death. Not a happy thought to wake up to but it seized my mind and wouldn't let go. Since the night of the curse, Lavinia had become the lady's dresser and dressmaker and never left her side. And she, *my* Lavinia, had sewn the gown that cursed me.

I could not reconcile these thoughts with the feelings I held in my heart. It was enough to drive the beast I was crazy. I paced back and forth in my little cabin for days with no news from Hillel. I knew it might take some time but part of me hoped my confrontation with Lavinia would happen right away. I wanted to get it over with. I couldn't concentrate on formulating a plan to deal with Lady Amunet until then.

I tried to live as I did before, walking the forest floor, foraging for mushrooms or berries, but there was hardly anything to be had in the middle of winter and I found I was not so interested. Perhaps I was too preoccupied or lazy, benefitting as I did from the quantities of food Hillel had deposited in the storeroom which divided the cabin proper from the stable. I let small prey I captured go. I didn't have the same desire to hunt or kill anything. I went on short rides with Espoir. I avoided Dinas Emrys. Mostly I waited for Hillel until I couldn't take it any longer.

I went to find Espoir and told him I needed a long ride. He was happy to meander on the snow-covered paths. The landscape shimmered like a white starry sky. The clouds kept the freezing cold at bay. Compared to these last few weeks, the temperature was mild.

Images of Lavinia taunted me: her washing my wounds on the church floor, wrapping me in her healing salves, holding my repugnant self in her arms. Was it all out of guilt?

Espoir sensed my distress and the wildness that accompanied it and sped through the snowy trails. He had grown so strong from our travels, he could keep going for hours if I let him. We ended up much further south than I anticipated, into a part of the Gwynedd Forest I hardly ever visited, simply because it was so far from home. I dismounted to give Espoir a rest. There was a nice fallen log near a stream. I broke through the ice with my fist so Espoir could take a drink, took some food from my pack and sat down to eat.

I was salivating and about to take a bite into my bread and cheese when I heard a commotion. People, *men*, screaming, chasing something, *there, over there! I see it. No, this way.* Branches cracking. Horses neighing. The *whoosh* of arrows flying close by. Too close. I retreated quickly behind a large rock when a frantic mass of red fur jumped right into my lap. I wasn't sure whether it was on purpose. But there we were, face to face. I saw the scar on the fox's leg. He was one of my rescues. I held on to the quivering furry mass and shoved it inside one my cloak's big pockets along with a piece of cheese. Not that he would eat in his present state, but just in case, better the cheese than my flesh. I commanded everybody - my horse and the fox - to be quiet. They obeyed, to my surprise.

From my vantage point, I could see them going around in circles, disappointed at having lost their quarry. It was a party of hunters. Well-appointed horses caparisoned in gold and silver, hand tooled saddles and cloaks trimmed in fur. Not an ordinary party.

I recognized him first. He was grown into a man. There was no boy left. But the dark curls falling gracefully on the forehead were unmistakable. As was the arresting smile, the sky-blue eyes. It was my Gawain with a retinue of young knights, all handsome, basking in the light of King Arthur's nephew. They were chiding one another for losing their quarry. I squeezed the little wren in my pocket, as I did so often.

"Our lack of hunting skills will give my uncle pause when he visits us," said Gawain.

"Pause?" asked the knight who stayed closest to Gawain.

He cut an impressive figure, all in white and silver on his horse.

"As to whether we deserve to sit at his table," said Gawain.

"*You* needn't worry about that," said the knight. "Unlike the rest of us, your place is assured."

"Not so, Lancelot. I have to prove myself worthy all the time *because* I am his nephew," replied Gawain.

"You are the best of us. The king knows it, brother," said one of the other knights.

"That is kind of you, Agravain. But you've beaten me more than once in tournaments. And what about Lancelot? No one stands a chance against his skill."

Lancelot's modest smile didn't fool me. He knew he was the best.

"Don't worry yourself so much, brother," said a third knight, slapping Gawain on the shoulder like a brother would.

"I'm the eldest. I have to set an example, Gaheris," said Gawain.

"He's right, you know. Your worrying puts a furrow on your brow that would displease many a demoiselle at court," said the youngest looking knight.

I couldn't help but groan inwardly at that remark. It was decidedly offensive. "*Many a demoiselle at court.*" I mimicked the simpering turn of phrase. *They are probably all swooning over his furrowed brow and dark curls.*

"Mind your manners, Gaheriet, or I'll send you to our mother."

And good riddance. Stupid boy.

There was a guffaw from the men. Gawain put up his hand almost as if to guard against their jokiness, "And whose brilliant idea was it to hunt *without* the hounds today?"

"Yours, My Lord," said the one called Agravain.

"It was, wasn't it?" said Gawain, his mouth taking a downturn.

They all erupted in laughter then, including Gawain. The hilarity was genuine. And so was the camaraderie. They were carefree young men, secure in their privilege and in their lives. Gawain had asked about the hounds on purpose, I was sure of it, so his friend and his brothers could make fun of him, and he joined in. It betrayed a confidence in himself I could only dream of. It was lucky for me they hunted without the hounds. They would have detected my scent in no time at all. I retreated deeper into the bushes, the fox squirming under my cloak.

"Hold on. One more minute," I whispered.

The knights dismounted, took their packs off of the back of their saddles and began to share a meal. It was clear they had given up on their hunt, so I released the little fox toward the deep forest, away from the hunting party. He stood still for a brief moment, his stare holding mine, then bounded into the woods. My eyes tracked him until they couldn't.

I was not the only observer of the party. When I turned around, out of the corner of my eye, I noticed a shadow moving between the trees on the far side of the hunting party. His face caught the light between two hawthorn trees for an instant and I was shocked to recognize my brother. He still looked like a lonely ghost, pale and dressed in black, but now his cloak was adorned with a wide silver necklace resting across his chest and a large medallion at the center. It was fit for a king.

Like me, he was observing, intent on not being seen. I didn't attempt to approach him. I wasn't ready. I needed more clarity about Lavinia's role, for one thing, before I could tell him that his own wife had poisoned our father. I wondered what his excuse was for being here until I remembered my brother's reaction upon hearing that our father had gifted Gawain with extensive lands in the southern part of Gwynedd province. Somer had been enraged by it.

The knights departed shortly thereafter and so did my brother. I wondered what Somer meant to do and if I should keep an eye on things, on Gawain.

It was dusk when I returned to the hunter's cabin. I wanted nothing more than to fall asleep by the fire after eating a large amount of bread and cheese and several apples from Bardsey island. But I saw smoke coming from the chimney. Someone was waiting for me inside. It couldn't be Lavinia. Hillel would have informed me first. I left Espoir outside, hitched to the porch rail in case I needed to make a quick retreat, and walked in with some trepidation.

"The place looks nice." Myrddin was sitting by the fireplace, keeping an eye on a stew cooking in the cauldron hanging from the hook above the fire. My mouth watered instantly.

I licked my lips. "I cleaned."

"Did you have a nice ride?" he asked.

"I did. I didn't expect to see you for a while. Weren't you heading to court?"

"I was. But I had to discuss some things with Hillel," he explained.

"You know about Lady Amunet then," I said. "And Lavinia?"

"I do," he said, his black eyes burrowing into my soul.

"Is that for me?" I asked, gesturing toward the cauldron of sweet-smelling stew.

"It's for both of us, if you don't mind sharing with an old friend," said Myrddin.

"I don't mind," I replied. "As long as I get the lion's share, or the *beast*'s share."

Myrddin chuckled. "That goes without saying, Dryw donn."

My heart skipped when he called me that. It had been a while.

"I thought you might be her," I said. "Lavinia."

"When he knew I was coming here, Hillel gave me a message for you," said Myrddin.

"What is it?" I started to scratch this phantom itch at the back of my neck. It was a nervous tic.

"Lavinia will visit with you tomorrow," said Myrddin.

"That's good." My neck scratching increased. It made me mad at myself. I took a breath and stopped even though I really wanted to keep doing it.

"And your brother has returned from his travels," said Myrddin.

"I know," I replied. "I saw him today in the southern forest."

"Good," said Myrddin.

"How is that good?" I asked. "How can I tell him that his wife is a murderer?"

"Don't you think he'd know that?" said Myrddin.

"No, I don't. He wouldn't." My answer came too quick. It hadn't occurred to me that he could know, and I felt defensive, for myself as well as my brother. "No, I don't believe it. I don't think he would have any idea about it, otherwise he would have stopped it from happening."

My mind was reeling with contradictory feelings. I couldn't bear to imagine Somer conspiring with Lady Amunet, their heads together over some potion. Myrddin was wrong.

The druid didn't insist. He was never one to do so. He dropped the subject and instead asked, "What was your brother doing down south?"

"He was spying on Lord Gawain and his knights," I answered.

"Will you be returning there?" asked Myrddin.

I certainly wasn't going to tell him that I thought about it all the way home. Or how it squeezed my heart to see Gawain after all this time or how distressing it was to see my brother again and how I wanted to hide from him.

"I don't know. I just got back. I still need to put Espoir away in his stall."

"Did you happen to hear something about King Arthur visiting his nephew?" he asked.

"Maybe," I said.

"Well, he is. In about a month. I would like you to be there. Would you do that for me?"

"I don't mind," I said, as if I didn't care one way or another. "But how will I know what day or time to return?"

"I will send Eira," said the druid.

How convenient, I thought. *I wish I could get my own avian messenger.*

"Is that my work now? Spying on behalf of the great Myrddin Emrys?" I didn't say that it coincided nicely with my own plans.

"This is as important for you as it is the future of the kingdom, Dryw donn."

There he goes again, speaking of future plans and kingdoms.

"Who am I spying on exactly? The king? My brother? Lord Gawain?" I asked.

"Mostly your brother." He paused. "But feel free to keep an eye on Gawain as well."

Heat creeped up my face. I was blushing, like a real girl.

"Fine," I said. "I need to put Espoir in the stable. I hope that stew of yours is ready by the time I get back. I'm famished. You can have the room if you're staying the night. I'm sleeping by the fire as usual."

"Thank you, Dryw donn. I appreciate that. I'll be leaving early."

"Back to court?" I asked.

"Back to court and its shenanigans," he acquiesced.

I snorted, then it occurred to me. "Did you ride here?"

"I did."

"So is Rhian in the stable right now?"

"She is," he said.

"Espoir is going to be so happy. I'll be right back." I ran out to get Espoir and brought him to the stable around the back. The minute he saw the grey mare, he started nickering excitedly and so did Rhian. I could barely get his saddle and bridle off. I was in their way. Noses touching, like lovers. They couldn't stop smelling each other and touching each other's bodies with their noses as if to say, *it's you, it's really you.* It melted my heart. When I left them, they were grooming each other. I tiptoed out of the stable.

Merlin was dishing out a plate of stew when I returned.

"Rhian and Espoir love each other," I said, eyes filling up.

Myrddin nodded, handing me a bowl of the stew.

I stuck my nose in it and breathed in the flavors. "What's this? Never mind, I know." I closed my eyes and took in the aromas. "Lamb, potatoes, carrots, onion, cabbage, leek." My eyes opened wide. "You made *lobscows*. That stew is supposed to simmer for hours. Were you here all day then? Waiting for me?" I asked.

Myrddin smiled, "I was. It gave me time to cook at leisure."

"It smells good." I began to eat voraciously.

Myrddin dished himself a bowl and said, "You are right. They do love each other."

I stopped eating and tears began to fall into my lobscows.

Chapter Twenty-Two

I sensed Myrddin's absence before I opened my eyes in the morning. There was a deeper silence in the cabin and the emptiness echoed inside my chest. The druid had the uncanny ability to move more silently than a fox hunting in the snow.

Lavinia was coming. I needed to prepare myself for the day. First, I went to the stable. Espoir seemed down, ears listless, head low. I gave him a good brushing and a couple of his favorite apples to perk him up. It helped. He pressed his nose against my chest.

"I know what you mean," I said. "You're saying, *I'm sad Rhian is gone but I'm glad you are here. Taking care of me.*"

Espoir snuffled against my chest in agreement. I scratched his forelock softly with the back of my hand, keeping my claws curled inward and out of the way.

"Don't worry. I'll take care of you. I'm here."

I walked back inside and looked around the cabin. It did look better since I cleaned. I thought about cooking something but gave up before I started. I was no cook. I took out some bread and cheese and apples. That was good enough for me. I sniffed the cauldron still hanging in the hearth just in case and found there was some lobscows left over. Only a little bit but enough for a bowl if I scraped the edges.

The embers were still warm in the fireplace. I called on Ansuz and my status as messenger of the Goddess to ignite the fire again. It worked. I felt a little guilty about using that connection for such insignificant purpose. But I figured if Rhiannon didn't want me to light the fire, she wouldn't help me. The flames worked their magic. I paced back and forth in front of the fireplace, too impatient to wait for the food to truly heat up. I took the cauldron off its hook after less than five minutes and ate straight out of it. It tasted even better than last night.

I was still smacking my lips, trying to finish up every last lick of the stew when I heard a knock on the door. I almost choked. Lavinia had arrived. I dropped the cauldron back on its hook over the fireplace, quickly secured my cloak, drawing the hood close over my face, and waited for her to walk in. I was wondering why she didn't come in when there was a second knock on the door. This time I remembered to open it.

Neither one of us dared look at the other. We stood there until I pulled one of the benches close to the table and invited her to sit, which she did. I sneaked a peek and saw her unchanged. She wore her silver hair in the same plain bun low on her neck. She still favored brown in her clothing. The simplicity of her dress belied the passionate nature I knew she possessed, the one that ran out in the night, hair wild, and danced like a young girl with the bandrui on the solstice.

She broke our silence and began the conversation with more courage than I possessed. "Master Hillel told me of some of your travels with Myrddin Emrys."

"He has?" I asked.

It wasn't surprising as these two were close. Just as I knew Hillel and Myrddin talked regularly. But it bothered me. I didn't want her to know anything of my adventures.

"Yes," she said. "I hope you don't mind. Only in how it related to your search for the weaver."

"Yes. It turns out the weaver had nothing to do with the curse. *Because they didn't sew the gown*," I replied.

That was a deliberate taunt on my part. Lavinia's hands curled into fists. She was angry with me. How dare she? I was the one who had a right to be angry.

"Can you believe it," I said. "I thought my father was responsible. My father, who was dying, poisoned by Lady Amunet."

My last words came out filled with fury. Nostrils flaring, breath short, I could feel my rage fueling the power of the runes. I forced myself to calm down for both our sakes.

"You have every right to be upset, My Lady," said Lavinia. "It was all my fault. I should have known better."

Lavinia was shaking. I was mistaken. What I thought was anger was her trying to control the trembling in her body. My own anger evaporated like ice melting in sunlight.

"Tell me what happened," I said, trying to summon some of Myrddin's serene countenance.

Lavinia clasped her hands together on her lap and began, "When the linen arrived, Hillel was there and so was I. He wanted me to keep it in my room for now. He knew that Lord Vortigern had bought it for you and wanted a gown made from it for your birthing day celebration. But Lady Amunet arrived as I was leaving and asked what I was carrying. I had to tell her. I explained that Hillel had asked me to keep the linen until further notice."

"Until my father got better," I interjected.

"Yes. At the time, none of us believed your father would remain ill for long."

I swallowed hard, unable to speak.

"Lady Amunet insisted that the linen should be kept in her quarters, and I had no objection and no recourse but to hand the package over to her."

I waited for her to continue.

"Your father got sicker and died. Then, a month later, there was the reading of the will."

Lavinia's voice was dull, a monotone. It was hard to listen to it.

"Was that when Lady Amunet asked you to sew the gown? After the reading of the will?"

"Yes it was. She said we'd be fulfilling Lord Vortigern's last wish, to give you the linen gown as a present. For your birthing day. At the time, I thought it was very caring of her." Lavinia scoffed. It was a bitter sound. "I told her I would be glad to sew it."

My patience was running thin. I was no Myrddin Emrys.

"Lady Amunet gave me the linen several days later. I did notice something strange. When the package first arrived and Hillel handed it to me, it weighed nothing at all."

"That's because Fairy Folk clean it," I said.

"But when Lady Amunet handed it to me to sew, its weight had changed. It was heavy, like wool instead of linen. A part of me knew something was amiss then. But I didn't trust it. Instead, I dismissed my doubts as mere fantasy."

"You think the curse weighed down the linen?" I asked.

"I know it did," said Lavinia. "And the lady insisted that I wear special gloves she provided. I made myself believe it was because she didn't want me to stain the linen. Keep it pristine."

"And you got it ready in time for my celebration," I said.

"I did," said Lavinia. "I thought it would be wonderful for you to receive a present from your late father on your birthing day. I was shocked when your brother chose to present it to you as if it was his own gift. But I know there was no love lost between the two of them."

I closed my eyes. It wasn't Lavinia's fault. She had done only what was asked of her with the best intentions. And though she knew something was amiss, she could never have imagined what was about to befall me.

"When I saw you the next morning in your chamber, what you had become, I knew." Lavinia was choking on the words. "I knew then it was all my fault. I hated myself for it. I felt so ashamed and so bad for you, knowing I could have prevented it. Knowing I could have done something. And what they did to you afterwards. What you suffered. I can never forgive myself." Lavinia started to cry. "I'm so sorry. I'm so very sorry, My Lady."

I heard myself say, "It's not your fault, Lavinia. Even if you had told my brother, he would never have believed you. It was your word against his wife's. It was fated."

I did something I had not done in years. I moved over to sit beside Lavinia on the bench and held her in my bestial arms. Me, the monster, held Lavinia in my arms as she cried and sobbed, and I cried with her.

When we both stopped crying, I felt hollowed out but in a good way. I went and got snow in a bucket so we could both wash our faces. I offered her some lunch of bread, butter, cheese and apples. She accepted.

After we settled for our simple lunch she looked at me and said, "Let me take a proper look at you."

I tried to hide from her, but she wouldn't let me.

"You seem well, My Lady," she said.

"That's what Hillel thinks too," I answered.

"Stronger," said Lavinia. "Like you've been touched by the gods."

"I am. I have been." I hid my smile behind a bite of apple.

"And perhaps more purpose in your life?" she asked.

"I don't know about that," I said. "I'm not sure I have found my purpose yet, but I've gathered a few jobs along the way." I started enumerating on my fingers, "Myrddin Emrys' spy, the Goddess Rhiannon's messenger, even though I have no idea what I'm supposed to do about that. And the white dragon shared their essence with me, although that's not a job, so far as I can tell. And, I have received two runes which help me with performing magic, and I have a *lot* to learn in that regard still. But, in spite of it all, I am still a beast."

Lavinia clapped. "How extraordinary. I'm sure some of this will become clear in time."

"I hope so," I said, noncommittal. "And what about you?"

"I have also become a spy," she said, smoothing a wrinkle out of her skirt.

Had I made a mistake in trusting Lavinia so easily again? "For whom?" I asked.

She smiled. "Same as you. Myrddin Emrys and Hillel."

I looked at Lavinia with new eyes. We were on the same team after all.

"Who are you spying on?" I asked.

"Lady Amunet and Lord Gromer Somer," she replied.

Lady Amunet, I understood. Lavinia worked for her. She was in the perfect place for that kind of activity. My brother, I didn't quite understand. And she had not said *your brother* or *Somer*. She had called him by his full name *Sir Gromer Somer* like Hillel had. As if to put a distance between herself and him.

"What have you found?" I asked.

"You should talk to Hillel about it. It's not my place," she replied.

"Not your place? Of course it's your place," I said. "I'm trying to formulate a plan to stop Lady Amunet. I need to know all you know, have all the information I can get in order to convince my brother that his wife is a murderer. And, she cursed me. Maybe she meant to murder me as well."

Lavinia followed me with sad eyes as I paced back and forth, and then, quietly, she called out, "Nella."

Ragnella, Nella, Nella, she'd chanted in a singsong, like a lullaby, until I sniffled and hiccupped and finally stopped crying. I was climbing after Somer, I wanted to be with him in his treehouse, even though he didn't want me there. I slipped; my legs were too short, my hands and feet too small to get a good purchase on the branches which were too far apart. The world slowed as I fell fast and hit the ground with a thud that took my breath away. I heard a crack. My arm was at a strange angle. I couldn't pick it up. And then it started to hurt, and it kept on hurting and I screamed. It was such a vivid memory, it stopped me in my tracks, and I looked up at Lavinia.

I smelled the stillness in the air. I felt heavy, held in the sudden silence. Then I heard Lavinia say, with all the tenderness in the world, while in my mind, I kept hearing *Ragnella, Nella, Nella.*

"He knows. He knows everything," she said.

I had disregarded Myrddin's hints as well as Hillel's, but her statement was so damning, so irrefutable, I could not reject it, as much as I wished to. It was like an arrow that pierced through all my defenses, straight into my heart. It occurred to me in some awakening part of my mind that I was the only one who'd refused to see the truth until now, that they'd all understood a long time ago. But I was still very young, and my brother had been my best friend, my ally and my defender, the beautiful poet of my soul all of my childhood. He was the only family I knew. The only one left. And I would not let go until I absolutely could not do otherwise.

I stood there, rigid with terror and desolation and heard a sound, coming from somewhere else, far away, in the distance. It was the kind of sound a fatally wounded animal makes. A mixture of cry and howl. A wail. It was I. I was wailing from some alien place inside of me. It was not a sound I had made before.

Lavinia was with me in an instant and held me in her arms as I collapsed on the floor. I had held her in my arms and now it was her turn. I wish I could say that I was more mature, better able to handle this revelation than I would have been before. But that was not the case. I shook and trembled and wailed and hid in her arms and banged the floor with my fists and scraped it with my claws. It is a testament to the hunter's skills in building the cabin that the floor remained more or less intact except for the scratches.

When I finally calmed a little, I asked, "Why did Somer do this? Why did he do it?"

Lavinia answered, "Your brother didn't *do* anything."

I dismissed the distinction Lavinia was trying to make as an attempt to soothe my sorrow.

"You said it yourself. He knew. He allowed it to happen. It's the same thing. Isn't it?"

I was determined to face the reality of my brother's deception, even though I had a hard time reconciling the Somer I held in my heart with the one capable of such abhorrent actions.

"Not exactly," said Lavinia. "He was persuaded."

"By Lady Amunet, you mean. Even so. With full knowledge of the consequences for my father, for me!"

"I'm not sure your brother understood how far things would go," said Lavinia. "Where the curse is concerned, certainly, it's hard to control the exact effects on a particular person."

I must be ruthless with myself, I thought, tear down all the illusions I'd held on to for dear life, but Lavinia wasn't helping. She was being too kind.

"And you know a lot about curses, do you?" I groaned.

"A lot more than I used to," she said.

That piqued my curiosity.

"Hillel and I did a lot of research after you curse took effect."

"Did you?" It hadn't occurred to me that they would try to help me beyond what they had done in those first few days and weeks after the curse began.

"Hillel was corresponding with Myrddin about it and also with friends in Rome," said Lavinia. "When Lady Amunet demanded that I be her lady's maid, I knew I had a chance to find out more information. I think she wanted to keep an eye on me."

"I'm sure she did," I scoffed.

"It worked in my favor," she said. "I found her book of spells and curses. It was of Egyptian origin, so I needed Hillel's help with it."

"How did you find her book?" I asked.

"It was not as hard as you think," said Lavinia. "Not everyone is like you, Nella. Most highborn lords and ladies will forget servants are around, after a while. They consider us simple minded, barely above pigs. We become invisible to them. Part of the furniture. Lady Amunet stopped thinking of me as a threat and then stopped thinking of me at all. And one day, I was putting some of her gowns away and saw her unlock a cabinet with a little key she kept in her desk. She wrapped the key in a linen handkerchief I had sewn for you when you were ten. It galled me to see her using it in this way."

"I remember that handkerchief," I said. "I played with it until Somer took it away from me. I pretended I was that great Lady in the tapestry hanging in my father's study."

"Lady Amunet took out the book to read something," said Lavinia. "Perhaps it was your curse, because there was a feather to hold the page when I looked at it."

"Did you find…?" I couldn't bring myself to finish asking.

"I'm sorry to say we didn't find anything to undo the curse," she answered. "We only found how it was done."

"I already know that," I said. "The milk and the linen."

"Well, there is more to it," she said. "And it wasn't meant to work as it did. Your reaction was… excessive."

"Excessive? Maybe that's why Myrddin made me retell so much of that night when I first met with him," I said. "He was trying to understand the effects of the curse on me."

Lavinia nodded. "The curse was only meant to bind you, not transform you. It went far beyond its original purpose according to the book and what Myrddin Emrys explained to us."

"What was it meant to do?" I asked.

"Bind you to stay loyal until your death," she answered.

"But I *was* loyal. Always," I protested.

"Without your own mind. Without any desire for property or marriage or a family of your own. Devoted and dependent on your brother, a virgin until your death," she explained.

We sat in silence for a while after that.

"He wanted all of it," I murmured. "The title, all the lands. He couldn't bear for me to have anything at all. I suppose, coming from a mere girl of fifteen, my offer of half of everything must have sounded arrogant, like a pittance or an insult."

"I believe he was persuaded in that way," said Lavinia.

"You keep using that word, *persuaded.* Lady Amunet played a big part to be sure. She was the instrument." I remembered how she reacted to my proposal that my brother and I share equally. "But she did all this because it's what *he* wanted. Didn't she?"

"I don't know that, My Lady," replied Lavinia.

"Are you saying he is under her spell?" I asked. "Or does he feel so indebted to her? I know she saved his life."

"He takes her counsel in everything and cannot refuse her," replied Lavinia.

"She must be happy then," I said.

"That woman could *never* be happy." The disgust in Lavinia's voice was unmistakable.

"Didn't she murder my father, and curse me, so my brother could be Lord of Dinas Emrys and she, Lady?" I asked.

"No doubt," she replied. "But like I said, that woman will never be satisfied. It is not in her nature. You never met her family. I did. Power hungry, the lot of them. Hillel had to manage them. It's a good thing he is so clever. And your brother refused to sack him. Thanks be the Goddess! That is the only time I ever saw him stand up to his wife. She didn't take it well, let me tell you. It was a good thing too, otherwise most of Gwynedd folk would be starving by now."

"I didn't realize things were so difficult in my absence." *No wonder Hillel looks older.* There was so much weight on his shoulders.

All the tenants and farmers who depended on him to protect them, ensure their survival.

"Do my brother and Lady Amunet know I'm home?" I asked.

"As far as they are concerned you traveled to the Isle of Skye and haven't been heard from since," she answered. "Abducted by Fairy Folk is the story."

"Good," I said, repressing a guffaw. "Let's keep it that way for now. Something must be done. I don't know what or how. But I'll think on it."

"Yes, My Lady," said Lavinia.

"Thank you for having the courage to come," I said. "It can't have been easy for you."

"You've had a much harder time of it, My Lady."

"Some good too." I was surprised to hear myself say so. But it was true. My time with Myrddin had been full of new experiences, challenging, some of them, but in a good way.

We embraced again to say goodbye. It was filled with affection. I didn't want to let go.

"We must visit again soon," I said. I hoped she would be able to, without risking her place at the castle.

"Yes," she answered. "I'm good at coming up with excuses to leave the castle."

"What sort of excuses?" I inquired. I hoped they were smart ones.

"Real excuses. Midwifery," she replied. "I've been helping women with their birthing. The midwife is getting too old to work on her own. I offered my services, and she accepted. It helps to get me out of the castle and find out information."

"About what?" I asked.

"Everything," she answered with a grin. Lavinia always had a special talent for uncovering the best gossip.

After Lavinia left, I was so full of excitement, and fury, and sadness, I couldn't manage so many feelings. I paced around the cabin for a while then had to go see Espoir. We went for a ride, careful to stay away from the main trails my brother might use. I knew the woods well by now, like a beast, by smell and sight and by all my senses. My eyes saw far into the darkness. My limbs could take me to the top of Yr Wyddfa in one day and reach for the highest branch of a pine tree. My claws could tear through flesh and bark with equal ease. These woods were my woods, my home. On the other side of all these feelings was relief, unexpected, glorious, relief. I was glad to finally know all the cruel, sad story. I was no longer so desperate to hang on to my brother's love at all costs. I would be true to myself, beast and all, no matter what.

Chapter Twenty-Three

As winter gave way to spring, a new idea of family coalesced in my heart. Not the one I was born into, but the one made up of people I loved and who loved me and had been on my side all along. Hillel and Lavinia were part of this new idea, but so was Myrddin Emrys and even Morag Ferguson. Espoir was my most faithful friend. That he happened to be a horse made no difference to me. The Laird of Dunvegan Castle was also on my list. In his case, more so because I wanted it to be true than from any certainty that it was. Who wouldn't want to count a giant, kind Norseman with a sense of humor amongst their family? And I liked how he called me Changeling. There was no judgement in it.

Dragon and Rhiannon were in a special category of their own. I didn't quite know how they fit into the scope of my life, but I was in awe of their power and the magic they chose to bestow upon me. Somehow, they found the foul beast girl I was worthy of such gifts. It still astounded me and also worried me, as any gift from the gods would for a creature like me.

After witnessing Myrddin's work with the runes, I felt a great deal of responsibility for what I was given, though not sure how and when I would be called to use it. I did practice as I could, lighting fires mostly. And I was beginning to understand Ehwaz, my spirit horse, the finder of hidden things. Perhaps because I felt connected to Dragon in a different way from Rhiannon, whose uncanny eyes and ability to crack open the underworld unnerved me.

To claim friendship with Dragon seemed almost disrespectful of such an ethereal divinity. But we shared something even deeper than magic; I didn't know what to call it; a mystery to fall in love with, the very essence of aliveness. We had walked together in an infinite field of being and I was left with a piece of quicksilver lightning in my heart, not just on my wrist, that could behold the soul of the world and let me know that I too, belonged to it.

To make a way where there was none before was the magic of the runes. And I was beginning to believe in it. It gave me faith that I would not be confined to the hunter's cabin in the Gwynedd woods forever and might return to Dinas Emrys someday. In the meantime, I waited for news from Myrddin. And I was not so alone as I dreaded I would be, nor so desperate for human company, because I didn't fear being seen as much. As a result, Hillel and Lavinia felt more comfortable when they visited me and would often stay longer than they should have. I was the one who pushed them out the door, reminding them of their duties at the castle and how they better leave before their lateness arose suspicion.

They were right, I wore the curse more lightly and I was more at ease with my monstrous side. Not that I didn't wish for my human form back. But I wasn't plagued by despair and fury the way I had been before my travels with Myrddin. It was another one of his many gifts to me.

During one of our regular visits, I told Hillel, "I miss our druid. I miss Myrddin," as I put away more foodstuff Hillel kept bringing every time he visited. This was for me and for Espoir. Hillel's thoughtful and generous nature still amazed me. I wondered if he was trying to make up for my sorrow over my brother's perfidious involvement.

"I'm sure he misses you too and wished he was away from Arthur's court and its shenanigans," said Hillel.

"That's the word Myrddin uses as well. *Shenanigans*," I said.

"Yes, well. When men and women vie for honors and favors, there are bound to be some troubles," replied Hillel.

"Have you heard anything?" I was curious and waiting was never my strong suit.

"King Arthur has been working hard to bring all the best knights together. It's taxing sometimes. He's looking to get away. He needs a rest from court before engaging in diplomacy with the Saxon leaders."

The king will be heading to southern Gwynedd soon, I thought. *I may see Gawain again.*

I dragged my mind back to the conversation. It was an important topic, worthy of my attention. "Does the king want to end the war?" I asked. This was thrilling news to contemplate.

"He does," said Hillel. "But his young knights are restless, tired of tournaments, more bent on proving themselves on a battlefield than on making friends with the enemy."

Sounds about right," I sneered. "How will he manage them?"

"Separately, I think," said Hillel. "When they are together, they are more prone to act like an ungovernable throng of young men than trustworthy knights."

I snorted. "Like a wild herd!"

"You are being too kind. I'd say, more like a pack of wolves."

Hillel's remark struck me as being closer to the truth. The beast in me shivered or perhaps it was the girl.

Hillel left soon after and I was about to go to the stable and get Espoir ready for our daily ride when I heard a small knocking sound on the shutter. At first I wondered why someone would knock on the shutter instead of the door. It was a steady rhythmic sound. Eira was sitting on the windowsill, her head cocked to the side, as if to say, *It's time. I'm here. Let's go.*

King Arthur was on his way to see his nephew. Or had already reached his destination. Despite my intention to spy on my brother, I had avoided him both around Dinas Emrys and in the southern province. I felt it was an advantage for me to remain out of sight for now. Let them believe I was lost to the Fairy Folk. It was one thing to let all my illusions about our relationship fall away but it was quite another to confront my brother in the flesh.

I came out and told Eira to wait while I got Espoir ready. She followed me to the stable as if to check on my progress and ensure that I was not avoiding her or my errand on Myrddin's behalf. I watched her observing me as I tacked up Espoir. *Eira is the most duty-bound creature I have ever met.* It seemed as if nothing could detract her singular mind from her mission. *No. Not duty,* I corrected myself. *It is out of love. And friendship, and mutual respect.*

The moment I got on Espoir, Eira took flight. This time I knew where we were headed. I didn't worry when I lost sight of her now and then. As a matter of fact, I thought she might head back to Myrddin right away, but no. I suppose she was on her own spying mission as well and would report her own findings to Myrddin so that between the two of us, he would get a complete report. She would give him the "overview," and I would get the "details."

We arrived at the southern end of Gwynedd province late in the afternoon. Eira reappeared and circled several times around me as if to say *stop here*. We were on a hilly part of the forest looking down onto a clearing. I wondered what she knew that I didn't. I dismounted and loosened Espoir's girth.

When I looked around, the forest seemed empty and still. I knew it was an illusion and could feel the aliveness around me but toned down, faint, hiding in the burrows. Eira was perched on a tall oak. Her spring plumage had come in, and I noticed some brown feathers here and there. She was not all white anymore and blended fairly well in the tree. No birds were singing. It was too quiet. Something was disturbing the life of the forest, and it wasn't the sound of a hunt that reached my ear, muffled by distance.

I looked down into the clearing. The king was there, alone. I only had a vague memory of his appearance at my father's funeral rites. What convinced me it was the king, aside from his handsome clothing, purple coat and gold belt with matching brown leggings and leather boots, was his stride, looking around as if he was lost but not worried. And his looks, like an older version of his nephew, same sky-blue eyes and dark curls but streaked with grey. He was hand-walking his destrier. Not wearing armor at all, only a short blade on his side. He was vulnerable.

I picked up a raw scent on the wind. It was that of a predator. My blood quickened, my body tensed to flee or to fight. A knight in full armor on his destrier walked into view from among thousand-year-old yew trees. The black cloak and silver chain with the large medallion gave him away. My brother was waiting for King Arthur. Why on earth wear a full suit of armor? Did he intend to challenge the king in combat?

King Arthur took a step back the moment he sighted my brother riding straight at him.

Somer raised the visor on his helmet. "You are trespassing on my lands, and it is my right to dispatch you where you stand."

It was so shocking to hear my brother speak thus to the king, my mouth hung agape.

To his credit, the king remained composed though he must remember Somer had refused to swear fealty to him. "Sir Gromer Somer, I would not presume to trespass on anyone's lands without their permission. But I'm told these woods belong to Sir Gawain, my nephew, who'll be joining me shortly."

I hope that's true. I hope Gawain is coming with his brothers.

"You are wrong," said Somer. "These woods were stolen from me and given to your nephew without my consent."

This was the old grievance against our father. And also, an excuse to challenge the king.

"As Lord of Dinas Emrys, I am within my rights to slay you here and now," said Somer.

"Are you? Wasn't your sister declared the chosen heir to all of Gwynedd by Lord Vortigern?"

For now, this was only a battle of wits. But the king's last words must be yet another provocation for my brother. His destrier pranced under him, the creature sensing Somer's growing annoyance.

"My sister was cursed three years ago. She no longer holds title over the lands."

"That is not what I've heard," said the king.

That gave my brother pause. But he didn't take the bait. "I am not here to discuss my sister. She's irrelevant."

I repressed a growl. *Irrelevant? Damn you, brother.*

"I will dispatch you forthwith for trespassing," said my brother.

"Sir. Are you not a knight?" asked the king.

That's clever. Appeal to my brother's sense of chivalry.

"I am." Somer stood more erect as he answered.

"Would you not concede that I am at a disadvantage here? Would a knight such as yourself, in full armor, attack a defenseless man in hunting attire?" asked the king.

The king was stalling for time, waiting to be found by Gawain and the others.

"And isn't it true that among the core values of chivalry are honor and the protection of those less fortunate, as well as the prevention of wrongdoing and needless acts of violence, to keep order and succor all who find themselves in distress?" asked the king.

My brother retorted, "Yes, and love of battle, fearlessness, and fortitude. I do know."

"Then you must appreciate that if you slay me here, it will bring no honor to you and yours, only shame, and no knight will embrace you. You will be refused everywhere."

I saw my brother hesitate then. He stood there, his destrier trembling. The king pressed on, taking advantage of Somer's silence.

"I'm glad to find a true knight in you then, and therefore a friend and not a foe."

The king was claiming my brother as a friend and winning the argument. My brother's love for discussion and dialectic had gotten the better of the warrior, or perhaps I should say of the murderer.

His wife would never give the king the opportunity to speak on his own behalf, I thought. *She would have the steady hand and dispatch the king without qualm or prior conversation.*

Somer had not attacked right away and now found himself at a loss. It could not be that easy to strike down your king, even if you'd convinced yourself of the righteousness of the act. Murder or malfeasance was not something Somer did himself. My brother abhorred violence, even as a soldier. And where our family was concerned, someone else had acted for him. He only had to acquiesce. His destrier was making circles around the king, walking my brother's frustration for him. Somer was trying to conjure a new solution. I held my breath as did the king.

"So be it," said my brother. "I will let you live today but only if you swear upon your honor to return to this very place in one year from now with the answer to a riddle. If the correct answer eludes you, I *will* have your head and your kingdom."

A riddle. That was my brother alright. How could the king agree to such a challenge without even knowing the nature of the riddle? But what else could he say? He was in a bind. As a knight himself who had just extoled some of the knightly virtues, he couldn't very well ignore them when they didn't suit him.

"I swear I will return one year from now with the answer to your riddle or I forfeit my life to you," said the king.

A one-sided smile appeared on my brother's face. He saw himself the victor in the exchange after all.

"What is this riddle you would have me solve, Sir Knight?" asked the king.

I was curious and wondered myself what it would be. Some Greek verse only Somer knew the meaning of. A favored quote from Ovid or Plato. Knights were not renowned for the depth and breadth of their education. And Arthur was first and foremost a knight. He had Myrddin Emrys to do his thinking for him. Somer's answer took me by surprise.

"You, Sir King, must answer this," said Somer, "What do women want above all else?" He spun his horse around, shouting, "Remember your oath," and galloped away.

Of all things, I had not expected this. What an odd riddle for my brother to choose. Somer had never concerned himself with women, not until Lady Amunet.

The king was reeling from the encounter, leaning against his mount for strength, as if he had just run through the forest on foot. I could smell the fear now. He was also frowning, a puzzled expression on his face. Who could blame him? He probably expected, as I did, some great riddle from history, like Oedipus, solving the riddle of the sphinx and entering the city of Thebes in triumph. Or like Alexander answering the prophecy of the Gordian knot from the Oracle of Delphi, with a slash from his sword. But no. The riddle was about women. What would a great king care about what women wanted? As a knight it was his duty to protect them, like a farmer protects his flock, his property. And therein lay the problem. Men were not interested in women's affairs. They didn't have to be. It was a dangerous problem for the king. For the riddle must be about more than the obvious: women wanted a family, babies, a good husband.

My brother was always the clever one. But I knew him better than most. I would figure out the riddle. I would help the king. The power of the runes was about magic, and I doubted they could help me in this matter. I would need my wits. The king had a year.

I watched him straighten up as Gawain rode into the clearing.

"Uncle, we lost you. Are you well?" he asked, jumping off.

"I lost myself and I'm not well, nephew," replied the king.

"What is it? How can I help?" asked Gawain.

"I'm afraid you cannot," answered the king. "It is my task alone to face."

"Tell me anyway. I serve you in all things. You know you can trust me."

Gawain could be persuasive. King Arthur relented. "I was accosted by Sir Gromer Somer. You know the one."

"Yes, I know him."

The one who stole my inheritance and my life from me. I growled louder than I intended to. Both looked up.

"We are not alone, I think," said the king.

He stared straight at me through the trees. I stood as still as a dead branch. He looked away and I slowly exhaled. It wouldn't serve to be seen at this moment, but I needed to hear.

"The man threatens my life and my throne if I do not answer his riddle. I am to meet him a year from now in this place with the answer or I lose my head," said the king.

"The insolence of the man. That is no knight! There is no reason to keep faith with such a faithless man." Gawain was outraged as any true knight would be in such a situation. The king put up his hand to silence his nephew. The gesture was familiar. Gawain had done the same.

"I gave my word," said the king.

Gawain nodded. The word of a knight was his bond.

"Alright. What is the riddle?" asked Gawain.

"Find out what women want above all else," answered the king.

Gawain was taken aback as had been his uncle. And I was startled when Gawain began to chuckle. "I'm sorry Sire. I don't mean to laugh but what a strange question to have your life depend on. Don't they all want the same thing? Don't they all want to be wed?"

I shook my head in disbelief. I wanted to strangle Gawain. I knew he was better than that, but I worried court life had changed him.

"It is a riddle. It must be about something else besides marriage," said the king.

At least the king had some sense. I could see Gawain thinking, as he caressed his chin.

"We'll travel together throughout the kingdom and ask all women what it is that they want most of all. We'll gather our answers in a book and return three days before the appointed time to discuss our discoveries and decide upon the best option."

"That's an excellent idea, nephew," said the king, putting his arm around Gawain. "But perhaps we must divide our efforts, and each go in separate directions," said the king.

"You are right, uncle. We'll collect more information that way."

The rest of the party arrived, happy to be reunited with their king. Arthur put his arm around Gawain's shoulder, and they began to plot the itinerary of their respective travels.

I looked up at Eira. "They have no idea. They are doomed. No woman will give a true answer under the circumstances, not to a king or a great knight. She would be too afraid, afraid to displease, afraid for her life."

Eira looked at me, cawed once, and flew off. I had done my duty as a spy, but I was of no help so far. I would have to come up with the real answer myself and find a way to tell the king, to ensure he kept his head and his crown.

On the ride home, I contemplated yet another truth about my brother. Dinas Emrys was not enough. Gwynedd province was not enough. My brother wanted King Arthur's crown. And his lady wanted to be queen. It was treason, pure and simple. And it was greed. And it was ugly. My father and I had been merely pawns in their game. That was the word Lady Amunet had used to describe her arrival in Thessaloniki with her family: a game, a great game to raise her father's fortune to its pinnacle, that of private physician to the emperor. I shook off the malice of it all, worse than any bestial skin. Hillel would have some ideas. His counsel was always sound.

Witnessing my brother's nefarious intentions toward the king and the kingdom drained any reservations I still held that he might be in Lady Amunet's thrall. He had stood in full armor against the king and threatened his life. But why should it surprise me? He had agreed to his father's murder and to making a beast out of his own sister. In the process he had destroyed all of my most beloved childhood memories, the ones I treasured and held onto for dear life during the last three years of my ordeal. These memories kept playing all night long in my dreams, including all of our games, the ones where we guessed quotes in Latin and Greek. And Eira kept flying in and out of my dream as well. It was not a restful sleep.

The morning sun flooded through the window, caressing the floorboards of my cabin. I needed to get rid of the cobwebs that hung on from the dreamtime. I walked and ran through the woods. And walked and ran, drank from a stream. My limbs softened into themselves, my mind quieted and I took in the generous flowering of the season. I slowed down and breathed more deeply. I picked flowers, snowdrops and daffodils, primrose and sweet violet growing along the hedgerows. I hadn't done so in years. A beast didn't pick flowers. But the girl in me wanted to. The one who still yearned for Gawain. Not that I wished to resemble any of those genteel demoiselles of King Arthur's court.

I knocked on Hillel's door and opened it without waiting for an answer. I should have waited but Hillel was always ready for my visits. I walked in with my news and my flowers and froze. Hillel and Lavinia were holding on to each other in an unmistakable embrace and separated as soon as they saw me. I apologized and turned around to make a quick exit.

Hillel called out, "Wait, My Lady. Don't go."

I stopped, sheepish, embarrassed. I handed him the bouquet of wildflowers. "Here you go. I picked them on my way over here."

"Thank you. They are lovely," he said, handing the bouquet over to Lavinia.

She got busy putting the flowers in a small pot and adding some water from the pitcher on the table. She was trying, and failing, to conceal the beatific smile on her face.

"We've been meaning to tell you," said Hillel.

I rushed to interrupt. "You don't need to tell me anything. This is your private life."

"My Lady, Lavinia and I got close over the last three years. We find. Ourselves. Aligned. In many respects." Hillel was struggling to find his words for the first time ever.

Lavinia intervened, "You're like a daughter to us. We searched everywhere for answers to the curse. Our love for you was our guide toward each other. We didn't expect it at our age."

"I'm happy for you," I said, stumbling over my own words. *How did I not see it? I was so blinded by my own predicament. Their relationship completely escaped me.* "You are the perfect match," I said with utter conviction.

Hillel offered his hand to Lavinia, and she took it. They smiled at each other with such fondness, when they finally turned their gaze onto me, I burst into tears. They encircled me.

"No. No. I'm fine," I said, defending myself. "I'm very happy for you. Truly I am. I'm glad you found each other. It seems obvious now that I see the two of you together."

"We have kept it a secret," said Hillel, still holding on to Lavinia's hand.

"We need to be careful," said Lavinia, looking at Hillel with her serious eyes.

"I understand," I sniffled, wiping my nose with the back of my hand. "And I agree. My brother and his wife cannot know. It could be dangerous for both of you."

"Please sit," offered Hillel. "You have news."

Like Myrddin, he had the knack of turning questions into statements. I sat down.

"I saw my brother confront the king in full armor. He meant to slay him right there, *for trespassing on his property* he said. What rubbish! The king was clever enough to turn things around. Instead, Somer gave King Arthur a riddle. He must return a year from now with the answer or forfeit his life."

"Do you know what the riddle is?" asked Lavinia. "Is it difficult?"

"I do. It is. For men, certainly," I said.

"Why so?" asked Hillel.

"Because it's about women. What they want above all else."

"And why would that be so difficult for the king?" he asked.

I glanced over at Lavinia. She rolled her eyes then turned to Hillel, "Because he is a man and a king. And no woman will speak her truth to a king."

I jumped in. "Exactly. She would be too afraid to lose her life. She will tell him what she thinks he wants to hear, and he will lose *his* life instead." It was all horribly plausible.

"We'll not let that happen," said Hillel. "You are at least as clever as your brother."

"Maybe so. But I don't have the answer," I replied.

"Not yet," said Hillel. "But you will. Find out why Sir Gromer Somer asked this particular riddle, and I wager the answer will come to you."

I let the tension in my shoulders slip a little. Hillel was right. If I knew why my brother asked the riddle in the first place, I would be able to figure out the answer.

"Well, I have almost a year to find out." I sighed.

"That is a good amount of time, My Lady," he said.

"Do you have cider left?" I asked. "I would celebrate your relationship."

"I do." Hillel served us and himself.

I raised my cup to them. "*Byddwch yn falch.*"

"Byddwch yn falch," they answered in unison.

We all drank heartily. I was thrilled for them and felt sorry for myself. Seeing them tugged at my heart. I wanted this, the secret handholding, devoted looks and conspiratorial happiness. It hit me with the full force of a summer storm in the mountains: I wanted something I could never have.

I ran all the way back to the hunter's cabin, chasing the darkness, giving my bestial strength free rein, not caring when branches scratched my face or thorn bushes scraped my calves, my eyes glowing in the dark, the runes dancing around me in the double spiral of their fire. I was a mad demon. I ravaged the contents of my storeroom that night.

Hillel came to check on me the following week. I was a surly beast, ready to retaliate at the slightest provocation. He was kind and said nothing about the decimation of the supplies he had recently brought me. Two days later, the storeroom was full again, not just full, filled to the ceiling with oats, a mountain of apples, wheels of cheese and loaves of bread for twenty people, instead of one unhinged creature.

Hillel and Lavinia still came to see me separately as if nothing had changed. But I knew better. They were together as much as they dared, in Hillel's office mostly. The scent of their love, like a bouquet of forget-me-nots, was inescapable. It wrapped itself around me and wouldn't leave. I didn't run from the shards of loneliness stuck in my throat. I felt them all.

Chapter Twenty-Four

Thanks to Eira, news of the kingdom and of the king's travels arrived regularly at Hillel's doorstep. Gawain and the king had each gone on their singular journeys. No one at court knew why and speculations ran high: They went hunting for the grail and got lost in the wilderness. King Arthur had abandoned his kingdom, converted to Christianity and entered a monastery. Or he was studying with a bandrui on Bardsey island. Only Gawain knew and he was gone too.

I would have laughed at such wild tales except the knights were restless and wanted to have a tournament to determine succession for the kingdom. The Saxons leaders wondered, like many at court, if the king would ever return. They all ranted at Myrddin Emrys while he tried to put out fires among the knights fighting about who would make the best king.

My brother may not have killed the king, but he'd created a lot of instability in the realm with his challenge. Fall and winter dampened the spirits somewhat. There is nothing like a downpour of heavy rain or a blinding snowstorm to keep people close to their hearth and stop them from attempting to steal the crown.

I was glad I was not Myrddin, trying to keep all the pieces together in the king's absence, like a juggler at the fair. What upset me was my own lack of answers. I asked Lavinia what she thought. She was in love, so her answer was *What I want most is to make a life with Hillel.*

I kept dreaming about my childhood with Somer, how he challenged me to think better, how Somer always found me when we played hide and seek. *If you don't want me to find you so easily, little sister, you must stop your silly giggling.* But I wanted to be found.

I figured there must be a clue hidden in those dreams for them to be recurring in this way. I was missing something, something that was probably obvious once I figured it out. My brother was tricky and smart, but when I thought about why he had chosen this particular riddle, I felt certain it must be about him. I just didn't know how.

The winter celebrations came with the year's end. Myrddin made a special trip to preside over Hillel and Lavinia's secret wedding ceremony at Myrddin's stone circle. That's how I thought of the place. His own magic had the same green scent. I was the only witness. Myrddin did the handfasting and we lit candles to remember all our loved ones. They wore simple wreaths of winter leaves on their heads. And Lavinia had a bouquet with myrtle leaves for luck and fidelity. Not that she needed them, the way Hillel looked at her. He would have faced the lord of death himself to defend her. It ended with Lavinia and Hillel jumping over the broom together. We, druid and beast, congratulated the happy couple on this auspicious day, their wedding day.

"*Llongyfarchiadau ar eich priodas*," said Myrddin to Hillel.

"Llongyfarchiadau ar eich priodas," I repeated, embracing Lavinia.

"Thank you for doing this," said Hillel.

"It was my pleasure," he answered.

I noticed the strain around Myrddin's eyes. Managing all the knights who aspired to become king was taking a toll on him. Not to mention avoiding another conflict with the Saxons.

The ceremony took place during the *Mari Lwyd*, the Grey Mare feast. We drove back to the old midwife's cabin together in a carriage Hillel decorated for the occasion and Lavinia had supervised. I hid between them under my cloak with assistance from Myrddin's spell. We fit right in with our little bells jingling and colored ribbons floating in the breeze. Folks, mostly children with a hoster to guide them, danced around us. They held up the skull of a horse adorned with ribbons and baubles from house to house, singing and causing mischief until they were allowed in to bless the household for the new year. Cakes and ale were exchanged. Lavinia and Hillel couldn't stop smiling. The priest from

Beddgelert followed the children, full of himself, giving his benediction over and over. I dug my nails into the palms of my hands.

The Grey Mare referred to the Goddess Rhiannon and her white horse, but the priests had imposed their new Christian traditions on top of the old rituals. It was the same with Wassail, my favorite feast as a child. We'd pour spiced ale or cider around the roots of the trees to wake them from winter slumber, with much clattering of pots and pans by the children to ward off evil. That was my favorite part which I joined in until I was twelve when the priest took over Wassail with his solemn mutterings and holy water. I never liked it after that.

Myrddin and I spoke after the ceremony. I was having a plate of my favorite pice ar y maen the old midwife had baked for the occasion.

"Hillel told me there is a church being built in Camelot. Is that true?" I asked.

"Yes it is. It's been happening for some time now," he said.

I'll have to apologize to Hillel. I had not believed it at the time. I told Hillel he must have misheard the conversation between Somer and his guest, a baron who'd been present at my birthing day feast and did my brother's bidding for a tidy sum. Hillel paid him out of the estate accounts, however much it galled him. The baron had been to Arthur's court to spy on my brother's behalf on the pretext of swearing allegiance to the king.

That church was an affront to Myrddin, the greatest druid of our time and King Arthur's most valued councilor.

"How do you tolerate it?" I asked.

"We must try to embrace what is happening, in order to keep abreast of it," he answered. "It is a growing movement. And it seems even more unstoppable than the Saxons."

I shook my head in disgust. The priest in Beddgelert had tortured me and I could never forgive or forget. I thought as my father did, their god was a pale copy of our gods. It was a conundrum that these people who had suffered under Roman rule, some dying as martyrs for their beliefs before the emperor converted to Christianity, were turning into tyrants themselves.

Myrddin's equanimity was beyond me. He was witnessing the destruction of his way of life. The new religion would render him obsolete. Yet here he was, being so calm. He interrupted the tirade in my head.

"Have you discovered the meaning of your brother's riddle yet?" he asked.

"I haven't," I replied. "But it must concern my brother personally. He wouldn't pick a random riddle."

"That sounds about right, Dryw donn. You'll get there," he said.

"What if I can't? What then? Can you figure it out?" I asked.

"It's your task. Dragon made it clear," he said.

"Not that clear," I grumbled.

"You have everything you need to solve the riddle. Do not underestimate yourself."

I had heard this before. He was also trying to bring me back to what was in front of me, instead of attempting to solve the unsolvable riddle of Christianity ravaging our way of life, household by household. Of course he was right, but I was still mad about it. I felt powerless to change it and I hated that feeling. It was the same feeling I had when the curse was first upon me. The helplessness was terrifying. Complete powerlessness over my own life. I never wanted to feel like that ever again. I would rather die. And I would have if I hadn't found my way to the druid.

We toasted to the newlyweds' health a few more times before they left. They were staying in the village tonight at Lavinia's friend. The old midwife was off to visit her little sister, herself pregnant with her tenth child, after two still births. I couldn't imagine what it must be like to go through ten pregnancies with no assurance that the child would live beyond infancy. It was one of those things that made me glad to be a repulsive beast instead of a woman.

"Myrddin, will you stay the night?" I asked. "The bedroom is yours. I never use it. And you know Espoir will be thrilled to share the stable with Rhian." I could hear myself begging, my voice unsteady with the sudden onslaught of loneliness.

"I was counting on it. Thank you," he replied.

I was so relieved that he wanted to stay, I squealed and did a little happy dance. He laughed out loud. It pleased me to see the twinkle in his eye for the first time since he arrived.

I laid down in front of the fire, closed my eyes, and slept more soundly than I had in months. I always felt safe when the druid was around. He was gone early in the morning as was his custom. I didn't envy him returning to court.

The frost moon came and went and my nineteenth birthday with it. Hillel and Lavinia celebrated with me. Lavinia brought a magnificent pale-yellow gown with pearls and jewels sewn into it. It was ludicrous for me to wear it in my present condition. But Lavinia insisted that the gown would have its time and place.

"You must wear it when you meet the king," said Lavinia.

"I agree, My Lady," said Hillel. "You are more than a cursed beast. You are the Lady of Dinas Emrys."

I snorted. *Of course, Hillel agrees with Lavinia. She's his wife.* "Not really. Not anymore," I said before I accepted the gift. I refused to put it on. I was more comfortable in my tartan and cloak.

"For when I meet the king," I said. "To witness his demise if I don't solve the riddle."

"You will. It's only a matter of time," said Hillel.

"Yes. It is. And I'm afraid I'm running out of it," I replied.

"You must succeed," he said. "There is much at stake here."

"Don't remind me!" I exclaimed.

A part of me loathed that it had become my job to save the king. What did I care about the affairs of men? They cared nothing for me. If my brother would be king then let him. He would make a mess of things and would be murdered in his turn. I told myself I wanted nothing to do with any of it. But it was a lie. I cared about Myrddin Emrys, and he cared about Briton, and was devoted to King Arthur. And Arthur was Gawain's uncle and if something happened to Arthur, what would become of Gawain and the rest of his family? I didn't need to be a seer to know they could all disappear. The Saxons would move in, only too happy for the chaos. And the priests, glad to get rid of this half Christian half pagan king, would surely choose one of their own. I didn't want to fail Myrddin.

I had been going over my childhood memories. I kept navigating back to my games with Somer. Anything that resembled a puzzle or a riddle. But it was as if I was blind. The same way I had been blind to my brother's role in my father's murder and the curse placed upon me.

I watched the daffodils pierce through the snow as spring came around again. Out of desperation I got on Espoir and told him to take me where I should go. He was an inspired finder of paths since I had received Ehwaz from Dragon. It was a damp foggy day which made it hard to see. But Espoir was surefooted. He knew where he was going, and I trusted him with my life. I didn't apprehend where we were until the stones rose out of the mist. I laughed and dismounted, patting Espoir on the neck, "You are a clever boy, aren't you?"

We were back at the stone circle where I first met Myrddin. The mossy stones were standing as if they had been waiting for me all this time. I crouched down near the altar. My hands caressed the earth, muddy, half covered with melted snow. My instinct told me to draw my two runes on the ground, the way the druid had done it on our first meeting. But instead of a stick, I used the sharp nail on my pointing finger. And I waited.

The stones began to hum, and I attuned myself to their song until it became the song of my body, and I heard it resounding throughout the forest all around me. The stones were multiplying the power of the runes, and I surrendered, inviting all of their magic to unfold like a flower, letting it take over my body. I fell to my knees and raised my arms in invocation. I prayed before language was taken from me:

"I call upon Myrddin's eyes, help me see more than I have ever seen. I call upon Rhiannon's gift, the great sufferer who walks through all the worlds, make the message clear to me. I call upon Dragon's wisdom, more ancient than time, share your understanding of the past with me. Please, if I am truly your messenger and your servant, help me save the king." I closed my eyes and whispered the last words I would utter that day, "Show me what I need to see in order to understand the riddle."

Ehwaz and Ansuz began their spiral dance of blue silver and red fire. Dragon and Rhiannon were two wild horses, galloping around the stone circle. I was swallowed into the rapture of their dance before I had the chance to change my mind or decline their invitation. I was thrown into the darkness of all that had been.

I relived three moments of my life. In the first I was with Somer during one of our games. A game we only played once and memorable for that reason. My brother played Socrates and I, Crito. I remembered every word, every feeling. *I yield to the sovereign laws, even unto death. For that is better than a bare life. I will drink the poison.* Somer's performance was so convincing, I was terrified. The second moment, I was on the floor of the church being whipped by the priest, the lowest, most wretched point of my life. It was such agony, such helplessness, the only thing that kept me alive was the beast, her instinct for survival and her rage. And the last one, I was with Myrddin and Eira at Dunvegan Castle. Eira was the messenger and the message.

When the visitation of the past ended, and I was thrown back into the present, I knew. The message was clear. I had been misled by my brother's cleverness. I believed that it was about women only. But it wasn't. My brother saw himself as the injured party which infuriated me. Because he had done to me, in the worst possible way, what he believed was done to him.

I knew I had the answer and would be able to help the king who must be on his way back to the southern province. He'd want to meet with Gawain and compare their findings, as the time of reckoning was fast approaching.

Before I left the circle, though I was past coherent thought, I managed to mumble my thanks. "Thank you, Myrddin. for being my mentor, my friend, and the best seer this kingdom has ever known. Thank you, Rhiannon, Goddess of horses, who understands suffering and being ostracized out of family, out of home, and out of love. Thank you Dragon for your endless wisdom and generous nature. I am grateful. Thank you stones for singing the song of the runes so I could hear it. And thank you Eira for being yourself." I did smile a little at that last one. Eira was a shining example for all who cared to see who she really was and for me in particular.

I had opened myself to more magic than I ever had before and felt as if my bones had been sucked out of me. This must be what Myrddin had endured after the battle on our way home. Espoir took us right to the stable. I untacked him, ensured he had some food and water, dragged myself to the cabin, stumbled to my knees in front of the hearth, barely managing to start a tiny excuse for a fire, and fell into a dreamless sleep.

When I woke up, I felt refreshed and worried. I had no idea what time or day it was. I also wondered if I wasn't being arrogant in assuming that neither the king nor Gawain would be able to garner the correct answer. I was ravenous and ate a bushel of apples with sheep cheese.

I was readying slowly to seek out Hillel for news when I heard a knock. Before I could answer it, Hillel and Lavinia walked in. Something I would have done in the past.

"We received a message from Myrddin Emrys. You must leave at once," said Hillel.

"Did you solve the riddle finally?" asked Lavinia. "You'll need help with the gown. I came along to dress you."

I was still dazed from my deep sleep. "Alright. Fine. No need to rush me."

"There *is* need." Hillel, not anxious by nature, sounded anxious.

I looked at both of them and became suspicious, "How long since our last visit?"

"Five days, My Lady," answered Hillel.

"Five days?" I repeated in disbelief. I thought maybe three days at the most. My eyes opened wide as dinner plates. "That means I slept for two days straight." *Magic does have its price.* "The world could have ended, and I wouldn't know it," I said.

"I came looking for you before, and knocked on the door but couldn't wake you," said Hillel. "I saw through the window that you were fast asleep by the fireplace. I thought it might be due to the effects of magic. I would let you rest but Lavinia convinced me to come back and attempt to wake you."

Hillel knows about the effects of magic. Friendship with a druid will do that I suppose.

"What's happened?" I asked.

"King Arthur is back in the southern province with his nephew. He returned early."

"And?"

"Myrddin Emrys doesn't believe they have the correct answer," said Hillel.

I nodded. *I was right. I knew they wouldn't have it.*

"Do you have it?" Lavinia was looking at me, kneading the front of her dress with her hands and I realized I hadn't told them yet.

"I have it," I said.

"Are you quite sure?" she asked.

"Sure as I can be," I replied. *Is certainty ever possible?*

They looked visibly relieved and smiled at me for the first time since they came in.

"Let's get you ready," said Lavinia.

"Are you set on this?" I wasn't thrilled about putting on this gown over my beast body. Lavinia was convinced this was the best way to make a strong impression on the king and get him to listen to me. I thought my monstrous self was quite enough but there was no talking my ancilla out of an idea when she made up her mind and Hillel simply shrugged his shoulders; they behaved like an old couple already, which, I suppose, they were.

We went into the bedroom I never used, and Lavinia dressed me. I came out and saw it all on Hillel's face. It was revolting.

All he could manage was, "This is quite a study in contrast."

"You mean, it's obscene," I groaned.

He corrected me. "It commands attention. No doubt about it."

"And that's what we want?" I asked.

"That is exactly what we want," said Lavinia.

"I think I'm going to throw up," I said.

"Not on my gown, you don't!" Lavinia could be very bossy when she wanted to.

"What do they say about me?" I asked, once I recovered.

"What do you mean?" Hillel was pretending not to understand.

"You know what I mean," I growled. "What manner of monster am I in people's minds?"

Hillel would not speak. It must be worse than I thought.

"Come now, no one else but you two and Myrddin see me as Lady Ragnell, Lord Vortigern's heir to Dinas Emrys. That person vanished the night of the curse. What do they whisper about the monster I have become?" I asked.

"Well," he said, clearing his throat, "They call you the Cursed Lady of the Gwynedd Woods. You know."

"Yes. But there must be more," I said. "I need to know what kind of reaction to expect from the king. Even Lord Segon Fawr was frightened of me. There was no Lord Vortigern's heir for him. All he saw was the Cursed Lady, the monster hiding under the cloak. He didn't want me at his table. He just couldn't say no to King Arthur's Magician."

Hillel looked like he was standing on hot coals. His voice barely audible. "They say you have tusks for teeth, and snot that comes out of a huge nose."

He cleared his throat, "And warts." He fell silent again.

"And?" I prodded.

"And you are wide as a barrel with breasts than hang down to your knees."

"And?"

"Hair in a clump of twigs. And a hump on your back."

"The hair bit is true enough," I acquiesced, touching the brittle mass of hair on my head.

"And claws for hands."

"I do have sharp nails." I showed off my nails for emphasis. A part of me was relishing this. "What else do they call me?"

"Do I have to say?" Hillel looked pitiful but I was unrelenting.

"Yes. I wish to know. All of it."

"Foul, evil, wretched, hideous."

Lavinia offered her own contribution, "I've also heard demon spawn. And a witch."

"Everything I've thought about myself at one time or another," I said. "Is there more?"

"No, My Lady. Not that I can think of."

Hillel didn't look quite certain. I pressed on, "I said I wished to know all of it."

He let out a big sigh. "They also say that a mere glance from your eyes, a touch from your hand or a word from your mouth can curse a man where he stands and turn him to stone."

"Is that so? Wish I was as powerful as the Medusa!"

I eventually gained control over my laughter. "It does make approaching anyone, let alone the king, a challenge. He will be frightened out of his wits when he sees me. Believe I've come to turn him to stone. I shall have to speak very quickly in order to make my case. I'm not sure if the gown will hurt or help me but I will wear it. It *is* fit for a queen."

"As it should be. It is your due. And the queen has nothing that comes close." Lavinia was proud of her work. If I had to guess, she wanted to make up for the calamitous linen gown.

"I must be going then. I wish Eira was with me," I said.

"Myrddin's crow is already on her way," said Hillel. "She will find you."

It was reassuring to know Eira was keeping track of everything, like having a bit of Myrddin around.

I went to the stable to get Espoir, and found him ready to go, resplendent in his hand tooled Iberian saddle, brushed to a golden shine.

"I took Espoir to our stables three days ago when I couldn't wake you and asked Caden to take care of him," said Hillel. "We brought him back this morning."

"Thank you for looking after Espoir, Hillel. Please, thank Caden for me, *again*." That anyone of our house had kept faith with me despite the curse amazed me.

I mounted Espoir astride despite the gown and found Lavinia had made extra wide invisible pleats so I could do so. It was ingenious and practical. The pleats only came to view if riding astride and revealed more of the exquisite beading all along its sides.

"I knew you'd be riding like this, so I made provision for it," said Lavinia with a smug little smile.

"That is quite something. You outdid yourself." It was wasted on me, but I didn't say so. It would be harder to hide from my brother in this gown. It would be harder to do anything in Lavinia's golden dress. My leathery, furry skin rubbed against the fabric, and it made me itch and sweat. I should never have accepted to wear it. It also constricted my movements, despite the extra pleats for my legs. It was miserable.

Chapter Twenty-Five

Riding to the southern province, all I thought about were the varied and numerous ways things could go wrong. The king could be so frightened by my appearance, he'd refuse to talk to me. Somer could be filled with rage and strike the king even if he gave the correct answer. Would I be there soon enough to meet alone with the king before the appointed time? Would I be able to stay within reach of the king, in case he needed my help, without my brother seeing me? How could I be sure I had the correct answer to the riddle in the first place? And on and on.

Espoir kept snorting at me. For his sake, I tried to set my mind on more uplifting subjects and found it wandering back to the Isle of Skye. My mind returned to the place, like it was inescapable. Like that waulking song about the famous wedding of black-haired Morag.

'Si Morag, 'Si Morag
A rinn a' bhanais ainmeil

Once the song came into my head, it wouldn't leave; as if I was on my way to a bhanais, a great wedding, instead of danger and possibly death, mine or the king's or both. It did work to distract me from my more pessimistic views of the situation I was about to face.

'Si Morag, 'Si Morag
A rinn a' bhanais ainmeil

I urged Espoir on and we made good time. According to Hillel, King Arthur had returned early to look for more answers to the riddle. He wasn't satisfied with the results he had already gathered. That told me he was clever enough to know he didn't have the answer and that would help my case. *He may listen to me.*

Eira made her appearance once I arrived in the southern woods. She was my north star to the king's whereabouts. I hoped he was out there still searching for something he couldn't find on his own. The woods were vast, and I kept looking up to track Eira's flight between the trees. She led me back to the clearing where King Arthur had first encountered my brother.

The king had returned to the scene of the crime, so to speak, where it might all end. He was sitting on a log, looking down. His destrier was nosing some grass nearby. I loathed to interrupt but it was now or never. I ushered Espoir into the clearing. It was a bold move. King Arthur looked up and stumbled backwards over the log he had been sitting on. He regained his balance quickly with a light step. There was strength in him despite the greying hair. No sight of the pregnant belly older men often wear after a life of indulgence. He was still first and foremost a knight and a leader of men, with a vision for Briton. He stood bravely, facing something he had never encountered before. The shock and revulsion were plain on the king's face. But also, a kind of wide-eyed curiosity and a studied calm only a protégé of Myrddin Emrys would possess under such circumstances. He had no magic of his own that I could detect, but I could smell blessings and protections galore surrounding him. My brother would not have an easy time killing him if it came to that.

"King Arthur, I have come to save your life." I thought I better get straight to the point. "I advise that you speak with me before you meet with Sir Gromer Somer."

He recovered his wits enough to speak, "Why should I believe such a one as you?"

He meant such a beast but wouldn't utter the words.

"I see that you value your prejudices more than your life then. Our mentor, Myrddin Emrys, will be disappointed in you. Goodbye and good luck to you, Sir King."

I had summoned Myrddin's name because, in that moment, it felt like my strongest tie to the king. I turned Espoir around and made to leave. It was a gamble. I didn't like the way he spoke to me. I had come to save his life after all.

"Wait! You know the druid?" he asked.

"I do," I replied. "You are not his only protégé."

I could see he was puzzled by my answer, curiosity and revulsion battling it out on his face. There was no doubt that the glamour of my gown and splendor of my horse confounded him further. His eyes kept darting from one to the other and back to my face and away again.

He was trying to figure me out. The dress was itching worse than ever. I was sweating but trying my best to sit straight. And Espoir was annoyed with me, prancing about. I claimed to be Myrddin's protégé, but who could believe it? I wouldn't.

"King Arthur, we both know you do not have the answer to Sir Gromer Somer's riddle, and he will have your head in three days' time."

"Who told you that?" he asked.

"A little bird told me." I almost smiled, thinking of Eira.

"I believe I'm close to it," said the king, straightening himself to his full height.

"*Close to it* will not save your life," I replied.

He enumerated on his fingers, "Women want to be surrounded by beautiful things to reflect their own beauty. They want to be admired. They want love in their life."

I interrupted, "Very nice. But you will still lose your head. Unless I tell you the true answer to the riddle."

"No doubt you'll want something in exchange," said the king.

He is used to people seeking favors from him. I doubt it's ever been in exchange for his life. As I contemplated the king's words, Myrddin explaining what the curse had done and what it would take to get it undone came into my mind: *a man would have to marry me of their own free will as I was.* I heard the Goddess Rhiannon whisper the wedding song in my ear and urge me to take charge of my own life. *Go on little beast. Now is the time to turn the tides of fate in your favor. Trust your heart's desire. Ask.* Today was not a day for timidity. Timidity did not change curses or fate. I would not only save the king's life but my own. I spoke boldly then. "For saving your life? Yes, I will give you the answer if you agree to make a covenant with me."

"I don't like your words. Nor your way of speaking. But tell me and I'll decide."

The king was no doubt unused to people speaking to him without flattery or reverence. Although, I could not imagine Myrddin being obsequious with him, like a courtier.

"Here is the covenant I would make with you," I said. "If the answer I give you saves your life, grant me marriage to your nephew, Sir Gawain. Consider carefully, Sir King, but decide quickly. Unless you agree, I can assure you, you will die."

King Arthur shook his head. "Even if what you say is true, I cannot make such a promise on my nephew's behalf. He alone can decide to marry you. There may be prior arrangements."

I growled. I couldn't help myself. *Prior arrangements. He's lying, to protect Gawain.*

"Be assured, I will appeal to Gawain," he said. "But the decision remains entirely his."

Good. He remembers his life depends on it. "Well then, you best go home and speak fair words to him," I said.

"I know my nephew, he will be loath to refuse my request, but I would regret causing him any pain."

"Will you regret it more than losing your head to my bro…?" I almost said *brother*. It was quite involuntary. I simply was not used to calling Somer by his full title. I corrected myself immediately, "To Sir Gromer Somer."

"What did you say?" the king asked, frowning.

"You heard me," I said. Did the king hear the mistake? I prayed he didn't.

"I will speak with my nephew and meet you in three days' time before I am to meet with Sir Gromer Somer."

"Let's meet early in the morning. You're meeting Som…" *I did it again!* "Sir Gromer Somer in the afternoon. But he might be eager and arrive early. I prefer my help to remain hidden from him."

King Arthur nodded, and we parted ways. Him, to his nephew's house, and I, to mine.

Hillel and Lavinia were waiting for me upon my return, with warmth in the hearth and a stew on the table. I was too tired to speak, and I wanted to get out of that gown. Lavinia helped me out of it, and I put my tartan back on. We sat and ate in silence. Or rather I ate, and they watched and waited.

"He's coming back in three days, early in the morning, and I will tell him the answer then," I said between mouthfuls.

"You didn't tell him?" They both asked at the same time.

I could hear the worry in their voices.

"We made a covenant," I said.

"You bargained with the king?" Hillel asked, eyebrows raised.

I couldn't tell for sure if he was shocked, or proud of me.

"I said I would give him the answer to the riddle if Gawain agreed to marry me."

Hillel and Lavinia looked at each other.

"It's something Myrddin said about the curse," I explained. "The only way to lift some of it is to undo what it has made me."

"Unfit to be married," they both said at once.

Speaking with one voice, like an old married couple.

"Yes," I said. "A man would have to marry me as I am, as a beast, of their own free will. Myrddin said there was more to it, but he couldn't ascertain what it was."

They seemed dumbstruck so I continued, "It was an opportunity I never saw coming, but the Goddess whispered it in my ear, and I seized upon it."

"The king agreed to ask his nephew to marry you?" asked Hillel.

"He said he would ask but would not force him," I replied.

"To save the king's life, he will," said Lavinia.

"That's what the king believes as well. There is something else."

"Something else? This whole meeting sounds like it was *something else*," said Lavinia.

"He may or may not know who I am. I forgot to refer to Somer as *Sir Gromer Somer* and almost said *brother* instead."

Hillel turned to Lavinia. "What do you think, Love?"

He calls her Love. How lucky they are. I'll never be so lucky, I thought.

"Not necessarily a bad thing. But the king must not tell your brother about you," said Lavinia. "And wear the gown again next time you meet."

"Fine." I knew better than to argue with Lavinia.

They left me to finish the food, which I did. All these adventures made me anxious and left me famished. It was hard not to speculate. If things worked out and my answer saved the king's life, I would marry Gawain, and if that happened, it might lift some of the curse. And what would that look like?

I was taken with a frenzy of cleaning over the next couple of days. And when I wasn't cleaning, I was devouring the foodstuff in my storeroom. I kept scratching my neck and stopping myself the moment I noticed I was doing it again. It was an endless circle of crazy. I was a thoroughly mad creature, and I knew it. I was terrified that it would work, and that it wouldn't work, that I had the answer to the riddle, and that I didn't, that Gawain would marry me and that he would not, that the curse would be lifted, even if only partly as Myrddin had suggested, and that it wouldn't be. I felt caught like a fish on a hook and I hated it. The feeling of helplessness was deeply abhorrent to me. I could feel my hackles rise and rise and they stayed that way for the whole time.

The dice was cast. There was nothing I could do now but be back in that clearing in the southern woods at the appointed time and meet with King Arthur again; find out whether Gawain had agreed, and if he had, which he must, give the king his answer. And then I would watch the meeting with my brother unfold.

I told Hillel and Lavinia that I would meet the king early in the morning on the third day, which meant I had to leave in the middle of the night. I trusted my eyes and Espoir's as we could both see well enough in the dark. I never expected it, but they arrived a little after supper. Hillel brough two packs of food, one for me and one for Espoir. Lavinia helped with the gown.

"You may come back a married woman," she quipped, fastening the gown on my body.

It was a confusing thought which I had not entertained in four years, not since my birthing day celebration. I liked that she thought of me as a woman not a beast.

"Or a dead one," I muttered. "If Somer finds out I helped the king."

"We'll make sure he doesn't leave until later in the day," said Hillel.

"How are you going to do that?" I asked.

"I'll keep him busy with some business that requires his immediate attention," said Hillel.

"Be careful, just the same," I warned. "Both of you," I said, looking at Lavinia.

We embraced and said our goodbyes.

"*Pob lwc*," said Hillel.

"Thank you, Hillel," I replied. "I'll take all the luck I can get."

I got one final hug from Lavinia, and they were gone.

I shoved my tartan in my pack and gave a squeeze to my little wren before securing it in the hidden pocket of my cloak. It felt momentous, like the eve of some great change that would come to pass for good or ill. I prayed to Rhiannon and to Dragon that it was for good.

The quiet of the woods calmed my restless spirit. The air was cool and soft against my skin. There was a good sliver of moon, enough to help light our path, not enough to betray our presence. The creatures of the night were quiet as we passed through their territory. The owl stopped hooting, the wolf stopped howling. The nightingale stopped her summer trills.

We were a strange sight. The beast in the golden gown on a destrier adorned like a king's mount, stepping silently through the darkened woods. Like a waking dream. And I was dreaming in it. Images of the past crowded my mind. Somer and I discussing philosophy like equals. Father and I riding wildly through the woods. Myrddin telling me about being betrothed to Gawain before the curse and the certainty that my life was over, that I'd missed my chance at happiness. Lady Morgause. How she could level a man with her eyes. The Fairy Queen who chose to leave husband and child and return to her own life. Eira, the white crow, who chose to serve Myrddin but only because she wanted to, out of love. What would the world look like when I truly awoke, afterwards, I wondered. And would I fit in it?

The king was already at our meeting place when I arrived with the dawn. Barely above the horizon, the sun filtered through the trees, surrounding the clearing with a golden light. It made it hard to see anything, but we knew each other. The birds were singing their morning greetings. It was a wonder despite the gravity of the moment or perhaps because of it. The king did not look a mere huntsman anymore. He had come to his death, or to his rebirth, a king, from the Hermine on the hem of his cloak, to the red dragon emblazoned on his surcoat and the circlet of hammered gold on his head.

"Good morrow," said the king.

"Well met, Sir King," I answered.

"I have accomplished my side of our covenant," said the king. "Sir Gawain has agreed to marry you despite my objections. As long as you have the answer that would save my life."

I knew Gawain would agree but still, I could barely contain my smile, or snarl.

"Did you tell him who I was?" I asked.

"I told him what you looked like, but he said that you could be the spawn of Satan, he would marry you. He would do that for me."

I snorted. "He's very loyal, isn't he? Reminds me of someone."

"Someone I know?" asked the king.

I was thinking of my father but didn't answer. Instead, I said, "Never mind. It is important that you not tell Sir Gromer Somer who helped you."

"I won't," said King Arthur.

"Be sure you don't. He'll have me killed," I said before I could stop myself. The idea that my own brother would hunt me down was both absurd and tragically believable.

"I understand," said the king.

Did he understand? Did he know who I really was? He had a confident serenity outlined on his face, just like Myrddin. It was annoying.

"Let us digress no longer, Sir King. You gathered many answers in your year of travels, that women desire to be beautiful, to be seen as young and fresh, not old, that women can be won through flattery, and pretty things. That they desire to be wed and have a loving family."

I paused and looked at his face which he kept carefully blank. The king had nothing better to offer.

"And these are all true as far as they go. But that's not what women want above all else."

"What is it then?" he asked.

I could tell he was reaching the end of his patience with me.

"I could name a hundred more, but the truth is there is only one that counts for you today, Sir King."

"Yes. Which is?"

"What women want above all else is *sovereignty*, Sir King. Sovereignty over their own lives," I said.

He looked at me blankly, then frowned and said, "It is the same for men."

I could hear the confusion in his voice. Annoyance even.

"No, Sire. You are mistaken," I said.

The king raised an eyebrow and shook his head. "Truly, you must be a protégé of the druid. Daring to say anything."

I snorted, surprised. But he was right. Only one of Myrddin's students would find such strength in themselves, such belief, that they would challenge a king and speak their truth. Myrddin was a man of faith and once he put his trust in you, nothing could alter that. His faith in you could make you believe in yourself when no one else did, when you didn't, even if you were a monstrous beast and wanted to die.

"Proceed," he said. "Explain yourself."

He couldn't help himself and still had to order me about, but now that he confirmed for himself I truly was Myrddin's pupil, he was more attentive, and I continued.

"Men are raised in a society that grants them sovereignty by virtue of their sex, simply because they are born male," I explained. "What most of them seek, therefore, is sovereignty over *other* people's lives." I truly felt like the messenger of the Goddess Rhiannon for the first time. I was lit from within, holding her knowledge of death and rebirth, as I named the unspoken truth. "Women are born into the same society but without sovereignty over their own lives. Which is why they yearn for it above all else. Anything else they might gain with their wiles, be it power or position, through inheritance or marriage, is but a poor bargain, a pale substitute for what they truly yearn for, the freedom to choose their own life, be who they truly are. They will live with what they can get, even convince themselves that they love it, but it is only pretense, rooted in fear, not love."

I could see the puzzlement on his face. He had no idea. He was a man and a king. How could he know what it was like to not be in possession of your life? I had more to say on the subject, but I knew it wasn't to the king I wished to speak it, it was to my brother. I wondered if I would ever get the chance.

"Trust me," I said. "It is the truth. Remember your promise." I held my breath.

"I will trust you," he answered after a while. "I will remember."

I nodded and left him to ponder my explanation. I retreated far enough away that my presence would go unnoticed but close enough to overhear. Once I took my place behind a thicket, Espoir and I waited. It was a very long day.

The sun hung low in the western sky when my brother finally appeared. Hillel must have kept him back as promised. Somer too had chosen magnificent apparel for the occasion. No longer armor, but richly adorned, like a king himself, though he still favored gloomier hues, a dark wine cloak with black embroidery, a grey surcoat with an embossed eagle, a design reminiscent of the Roman legion.

The silver medallion laid on his chest like a piece of armor, and it shined with a light of its own. It held power I had not detected before. I sniffed shadowy magic emanating from it, sour and sweet enough to make me gag. My tongue recognized the taste and was revolted by it. Goosebumps coursed over my skin. The strange song of the medallion invaded my ear, a hiss, full of dissonance. My body was remembering something I didn't know I had heard and smelled before, for I had been in the grip of a deathlike sleep. This would cause trouble, I knew, but not what kind or what to do about it.

The two men approached slowly from opposite directions, until the flanks of their mounts almost touched each other. The king immediately took out two books from the satchel hanging off the horn of his saddle. He handed them to my brother who wasn't expecting them and found himself unprepared. One hand was on the pommel of his sword, the other held the reins of his horse. He put down the reins and tried to pick up the books but realized he needed both hands. Somer seemed almost clumsy. He looked displeased. This wasn't going the way he planned.

"Sir Knight, I have brought the compilation of all the answers I received over this last year. Pray, do me the honor of looking through them. See if your answer might be in there," said King Arthur.

"You expect me to look through all these answers?" Somer sounded genuinely surprised.

"I thought you might," said the king, with the same serenity I had observed before.

My brother started to leaf through the books then abruptly handed them back to the king. "Do you take me for a fool? I only need one answer. At any rate, I do not see it in your books."

The king took his time to place the books properly back in his satchel. Again, I admired his calm. A lesson from the druid I never mastered myself.

"Let me give you another answer, one that is not written in the books, hoping it might please you enough to spare my life," said the king.

"Get on with it. Let us hear it now," growled my brother.

Watch it brother, you are beginning to sound like me on a bad day. Though I would never use the royal "we" to refer to myself.

"If I had to summarize it in one word," said the king, "That word would be *sovereignty*."

He said the word slowly and with a great deal of emphasis. It was a word well suited for a king. Sovereignty was the essence of who he was.

Somer froze. He opened his mouth, and nothing came out at first. "Impossible," he said. "You cannot know this."

"I take it I have the correct answer?" asked the king.

"You had help," said my brother. "Was it that loathsome druid? May he burn in the fires of hell."

My brother the Christian. He thinks it was Myrddin. He can't imagine it could be a woman, let alone a beast.

"Loathsome?" asked the king. "I would never call him that."

That's what you called me.

"I did receive help. You never said I couldn't." The king was defiant in his words and stance, even in this moment.

Careful, Arthur Pendragon. Even if your father claims kinship with dragons, it doesn't make you one. Remember your promise.

Somer backed up his horse roughly to get away from the king. He was seething and the medallion's hum turned into a roar. It was urging my brother to act. He unsheathed his sword. Before I had time to think, I unleashed Ansuz and Ehwaz. They rushed out like two serpents and began to weave their own song around the medallion. I hoped they might mitigate whatever nefarious influence it was having on my brother.

The king stayed imperturbable. He didn't move a muscle, and neither did his horse. It was quite a sight. My brother, on the other hand, didn't stop moving, and his horse prancing about. His sword, no doubt guided by the medallion, was fighting the unseen fires of the runes. Somer looked like a puppet with the sword in charge of him. The king didn't know what to make of it, though he knew something was afoot. Somer was now fighting with his own sword as the sword was fighting with the power of the runes. He was still brandishing his sword at the king, his arm rigid with the strain of fighting the runes' magic, when he spoke at last. His voice was hoarse with fury, and it hurt me to hear him.

"God help me!" he cried out, "You are free to go for now. But be sure, next time we meet, death will fall upon you."

"Be sure that next time we meet, Sir Knight, you will not find me at such a disadvantage," replied the king. "Thank you for honoring my answer to your riddle. *That* was worthy of a true knight."

Not without the magic of the runes, he wouldn't have. The runes had done exactly what I hoped they would to contain the medallion as well as my brother's reactions. I was so pleased I'd trusted my instincts, I wanted to do a jig and shout. I didn't. I promised my creature self I would do one later.

"Keep your thanks. I refuse them," said Somer.

My brother wacked his destrier and the poor creature lunged into a gallop. They headed north at full speed, down a trail, through the trees, and soon were swallowed in the wooded landscape. The king slid off his horse, put his arms around the animal's neck and buried his forehead into its mane. I gave him a moment then walked over to the clearing with Espoir in tow.

The king raised his head the instant he heard us approach. "Oh, it's you," he sighed.

He hoped I'd disappeared and spared his beloved nephew marriage to a bestial bride.

"Congratulations. You live," I said. "Now, take me back to court to marry Sir Gawain."

"Will you give me a minute?" he protested.

"I did." I was brazen, shameless. I could see it in his eyes; how he shook his head, hair falling over his face so I wouldn't see his pursed lips. But I didn't care. Not anymore. I knew who I was, and embraced all of it, the curse, the loathsome lady of nightmares, messenger of a Goddess, loved by a dragon, protégé of Myrddin Emrys, full of unhinged appetites and vengeance, dressed like a queen on my caparisoned palfrey.

"Lead the way Sir King. I will follow," said I.

"I can arrange for the two of you to meet and have a secret ceremony," he offered.

"No, thank you," I said. "Didn't Gawain agree to marry me of his own free will?"

"He did," the king nodded.

"Then I will not hide," I said. "I want to marry on the solstice at High Mass. A banquet to follow with the court in attendance. It has to be official with no denial possible."

"You are a careful beast," he said, climbing back onto his destrier.

"I've had to be," I replied, mounting my palfrey.

The king shook his head, more or less resigned. "I must thank you for my life, though I am sorry for the cost to my nephew."

Though it hurt to hear him say so, I understood his feelings too well. “You’re welcome.”

King Arthur led the way down the trail toward Camelot. I could hardly believe it.

Chapter Twenty-Six

Gawain was the only sweet memory I kept of the night of the curse, and I had held on to that little carved wren ever since. It had been my companion, my talisman when there was nothing else. It was a terrible thing I was about to do to him, but I had no other choice to find out whether my curse could be broken. And Gawain would forfeit his life for his king, his family, marry a wretched worthless hag if need be.

I was also curious of King Arthur's famed castle which was located at the border between North Wales and Hen Ogledd. The Romans had called the fort Camulodunum, and when Arthur had built his castle there, he re-named the place Camelot. So many wild stories I'd heard, I wanted to see it for myself. Myrddin never mentioned anything about it, only talked of courtly shenanigans which seemed to be numerous and kept him busy. I hoped he'd be in attendance to help me get through the ordeal of facing the king's court.

The air was mild, but the night was late, and we were still too far from any village to find refuge in an inn or even a peasant's hut. I could see the king was getting worried about finding somewhere to bed down for the night.

"Shall we find a place to sleep?" I asked.

"How? Where?" King Arthur looked around. We were still in the midst of a forest, thick with oaks and hawthorns.

I closed my eyes, extended my arm out and called upon Ehwaz to find a safe abode for the night. My silver horse reared into the summer dark and sped through the trees.

"This way," I said.

The king spotted the runes on my wrist when I moved my arm. "You are full of surprises," he said. He didn't expect a beast to possess such magic.

As we followed the silver trail marked by the rune, we soon came upon a cave as I expected. It was one of the old druidic hidden places. They would be used again to hide from the Christians who would hunt down the bandrui to sell them back to their priests.

The king marveled at it. "Amazing. We could not see it until we were right upon it."

"Yes. That *is* the point, Sire."

The king started a fire the old-fashioned way. I let him. He went about gathering kindle wood. He had flint he carried in his pouch and struck a flame with it. He shared his food with me which was not enough. So, I went hunting. He asked me if I wanted to borrow a knife.

"Don't need it," I said, showing off my nails.

I did ask him to help me get the gown off of me first, which was even more embarrassing for him than for me. I took my tartan out of my pack and put it on quickly, while he pretended not to watch. I sauntered into the night. It was quiet, warm, with a cool breeze. Perfect for hunting. I smelled the hare on the wind, placed myself in its path and slit its throat with one nail before it had time to scream, while holding it down with my other hand. It was a fat one. Arthur didn't mind eating it after it was cooked but he kept an eye on me and my claws.

"You seem proficient in the art of putting on a tartan," he said.

It was not what I expected him to talk about.

"Yes. Someone taught me how to wrap it," I replied.

"Someone from the Highlands?" he asked.

"Yes," I answered.

"Interesting. For a beast who has survived in the Gwynedd woods, you do get around."

"I suppose I do. It does happen when one is…"

He finished my sentence. "When one is a protégé of Myrddin Emrys?"

"Yes."

"You are not very talkative," said the king.

"Not unless I have something to say," I replied.

"Right. And then no one can stop you," he said, ruefully.

"That's true enough these days." I could tell the king had something on his mind, but I wasn't clear whether it had to do with me or not. "Is there something I can help you with?"

"I'm trying to make out your character, and I find it rather baffling," said the king.

"I wouldn't worry about it, Sire. Most of the time I don't understand myself. It's hard when one has two such opposing natures within one body. Nos Da, Sire," I said, as I laid down.

"Nos Da, My Lady."

It was the first time the king called me *My Lady* without it sounding like a question.

"I know you are set on a public wedding," he said to me from his sleeping corner. "But the court will be a hard place for you."

I detected a note of genuine concern in his voice. I knew it would be a trial to get through, but I had navigated and survived more than one difficult situation by now.

In the morning, the king was cheerful, no doubt because he was going home to Camelot. I requested his assistance again to get back into the gown. His disgust didn't get as much in the way of his help. I could tell he had some practice with such matters.

The closer we got to his castle, the faster his pace. I, on the other hand, was in no such hurry. My own reluctance lodged in my throat. Even good change brought its own set of fears along with it. We emerged out of the forest and were surrounded by meadows. King Arthur pointed out the dwellings and farms sprawled around the castle. Camelot rested on top of a hill, alongside a river.

He pointed. "We set the castle on top of the hill for protection."

Like my father did for Dinas Emrys, I thought.

The castle was surrounded by ramparts and palisades. It was built to endure any siege. The whole hill was terraced, and each terrace had wooden walls and earthen ditches. I had imagined Camelot in my mind my entire life. It was supposed to be a fairy castle, but it was just another hillfort like Dinas Emrys, mostly built out of wood and reinforced with stone.

What took my breath away, though I would scarcely admit it to myself, was the cathedral which appeared in the glowing rays of sunset as a soaring stone monument to the glory of the Christian God.

"Saint Stephen cathedral is our newest building. It took us years to complete it. And the interior is still not entirely finished."

There was pride in his voice as he commented on the building. "It is unique in the kingdom." He pointed out how white the stone was, how it gleamed in the sunlight.

"Do you not find a conflict in this?" I asked, as I tried to contain the seething within me.

"A conflict?" he asked.

"Yes. Being a pupil of Myrddin Emrys, following the old ways, and this?" I asked, pointing to the cathedral as we were riding by.

The king reflected on my question for a while before he answered, "I admit it is difficult to straddle two worlds as I do. But it can't be helped. It is the times we live in. And if I want to continue to rule and strengthen this country, I must include all Britons."

Spoken like a politician. I understood being of two worlds, but my two worlds were internal, not like his, opposing forces of the society he lived in. I was glad not to be a king.

I wore my cloak like an armor as we rode into the outer courtyard of the castle. I dismounted as a couple of grooms came to take our horses. I asked if Rhian, Myrddin's grey mare was here. A trembling young attendant stammered a "yes."

"I would like Espoir to be stabled with Rhian or next to her, please. They know each other and I want him to have someone familiar near him in this new place."

The boy looked to the king who gave a nod of approval, and it was done.

News of his return spread throughout the castle. The king dismounted and handed his destrier to the other groom. I stayed a careful distance back from the king, my cloak wrapped close around my body, the hood hiding most of my face, as knights ran toward us. Gawain was first at his uncle's side, concern and relief both clear on his brow. Gawain's brothers and Lancelot I recognized but not the others.

I looked up to catch my breath and noticed the flags floating in the wind, not only on the towers but also in the courtyard. They all bore the mark of the red dragon. I wondered if my dragon of the Fairy Pools was still alive. I thought yes, and that I would know it if they weren't.

A small crowd of the king's closest friends, knights mostly, had gathered around him, hailing him a hero, and I was reminded of the traveling performers I had seen as a child in Beddgelert. The acrobats were doing somersaults to amaze the crowd, and make the children scream with delight. But here, all of it was done to impress one person only, King Arthur.

A herald posted himself at the gate and announced, "Make way for Queen Guinevere!"

The knights parted. She paused at the top of the stairs. Her veils floated in the evening breeze. She looked an apparition. The softest smile drifted on her plump pink lips. And all the men stared at her in admiration. She seemed the personification of grace. Several demoiselles surrounded the queen. Her attending ladies looked so dainty, dressed in their fineries.

A blur of white and silver passed me by as Sir Lancelot rushed to the top of the stairs and gave the queen his hand so she could safely walk down to meet her king. There was such a look between them as their hands touched, it would take a blind man not to notice the devotion there. I looked over at the king, and his eyes were riveted on his queen. The love on his face was plain. Her beauty measured fairly against the Goddess Rhiannon, beyond that of a mere mortal. It's not good to make the gods jealous. They don't take it well. Unlikely for it to ever be my problem.

The king embraced his queen and turned to address the crowd. "It has been a long year, and it ended with an ordeal. I am most happy to be home amongst my dearest friends, fellow knights and lovely ladies." He kissed his lady wife's hand then.

Everyone cheered and applauded.

"I have brought back with me the one who saved my life. Though she may be cursed, she is wise. Please treat her as an honored guest and my friend, the Lady of the Gwynedd Woods."

In one sentence, the king had extended his friendship and protection to me before a small circle of favored courtiers and knights. I thought well of him then, despite his divided loyalties.

I could no longer remain anonymous in this crowd. All eyes were on me. I was still hiding inside my cloak though some of the gown showed and of course, I had caught the covetous glances at Espoir's perfect confirmation and effortless stride when we first arrived. I pushed the hood off my face for a moment and saw the growing horror around me. Faces bright with curiosity and fear. I heard cruel whispers as refined as the tempered blades the knights carried on their side. I told myself I didn't care, that I would not disown the beast I was, not anymore. And how many among them could say they'd saved the king's life?

Several of the courtiers stepped back and a few of the demoiselles fainted prettily into the arms of willing knights. I noticed the Queen managed to not stagger but she was next to the king on one side and leaning against Sir Lancelot on the other. Gawain's face remained carefully blank, but I had seen the flash of horror cloud his eyes. He was stoic but for the slight tremor in his mouth, the tension in his jaw, and the overall dread that darkened his countenance.

It was only my first test and with a small gathering at that, but it was getting to be too much for me. I pulled my hood forward and was looking for an escape, a way to run into the nearest clump of trees, when I saw the druid advance toward me. I sighed with relief at the sight of him. Myrddin Emrys walked up to the king and told him he would take care of me until the wedding. The king had failed to mention Gawain's oath. Perhaps he hoped there would be no wedding. I had my own doubts.

Myrddin turned to me, "Welcome to Camelot, Dryw donn."

"I'm so glad you are here," I whispered. "I just about had enough of this…"

"Pomp and pageantry?" he offered.

"I was going to say traveling fair, but yes," I replied.

Myrddin took me to his apartments. I checked the hood of my cloak was secure over my face to walk through the castle. I wasn't about to subject myself to any more scrutiny. I knew more would come with the wedding and the banquet. It was easier to observe that way, instead of being observed. There was a wealth of tapestries covering the walls of the castle. Other than that, I could detect no great difference between what I saw here and what I'd seen at other castles.

What made it unforgettable was the experience of the place, the chatter and the music. As we walked through the halls, I heard groups of people arguing and laughing, others playing music and singing. Some were discussing the stars. Others recited poetry, while practicing their sword fighting! As we passed by an interior courtyard I saw women having a wager about who could hit the bullseye with their bow and arrow while others played cards in a corner. It was an intoxicating mixture of wonder and mayhem, full of cheerful noise. Something I had never heard before, except at a feast, maybe. Though there were a few curious glances in our direction, Myrddin's presence, and his magic, quickly turned their eyes aside. I thought they were much too interested in their own lives to pay attention to me. That would come later, at the wedding.

"There is a tournament tomorrow morning," said Myrddin.

"I've never seen one," I replied.

"More mayhem," he said. "But it's a good place to observe the currents of power. Unfortunately, the knights are always intent on proving themselves and I have to prevent the worst and patch them up."

"Sounds like a lot of work," I said.

"You wouldn't believe it," he replied.

I did believe it.

"Perhaps you can assist me," he offered.

"Why not," I said. "I need to talk to you first."

"That's why I'm bringing you to my chambers."

"Like old times," I said.

It was nothing like *old times,* but the druid smiled at me in response. "It's very nice to see you, Dryw donn."

I could smell the green sap of Myrddin's magic before we arrived at his apartments, which were in proportion to his status at court. But I didn't detect anything of Myrddin's in it. He answered my question before I could pose it.

"You won't find anything of mine in this place. Better that way."

"You are a cautious man, Myrddin Emrys."

"At court, always. But I have something for you." He opened a closet and took out a stick. He handed it to me. "This is yours."

It was the branch from the two-hundred-year-old rowan tree he had cut for me so long ago during our travels and carved with my runes. I took it from him. It was polished to a shine. I noticed only the two I already had, Ansuz and Ehwaz. "Thank you. Isn't there a third one?"

"Room to grow, Dryw donn. Room to grow. It will come to you when you are ready."

I laughed at my own impatience. "It's beautiful. I thank you."

"Do not let anyone take it from you," he cautioned. "The staff is an extension of your power."

"I won't," I said.

"Most people do not enter my apartments without my permission. You can leave it here during your stay at court."

"I could smell your protections on the door from down the hall," I said.

He chuckled. "A few simple precautions."

The mossy greenness of Myrddin's *simple precautions* reminded me of the Gwynedd woods. I navigated toward a table where water, cider and various foods were set. I took an apple.

"Tell me Dryw donn, what's on your mind?" he asked.

"You mean, aside from saving the king's life, my wedding to Gawain and the possibility of my curse being lifted?"

He chuckled again. "Yes."

"Somer was wearing a medallion. I saw it once before, but this time its magic made me nauseous. I sent my runes against it to mitigate its power. I can't be certain, but I think it saved the king from my brother's wrath. Somer didn't appreciate being bested at his own game."

"I'd have to see the object to know exactly. But I can believe it."

"Do you think this medallion could be a spell on my brother?"

"Possibly," said Myrddin. "But not one done without his consent, I wager, even if the entirety of its meaning was concealed from him. Curses and blessings are the two sides of the same coin. Sometimes it's hard to distinguish one from the other."

"That brings me to my second question regarding my curse."

I took a few bites of the apple and swallowed before I continued.

"Lavinia told me the curse was not meant to transform, only bind me and control me."

"Yes, that's true," he replied. "When we examined the writing about the curse there was no mention of any transformation."

"So why did it happen?" I asked.

"As I explained to you at the time, you were particularly vulnerable to the curse because of your circumstances," said Myrddin.

"Being motherless," I said.

"Yes," he replied. "But that's not all of it. In fact, I now believe that the transformation occurred to protect you."

"To protect me?"

The thing I abhorred most about myself for years now, the thing I had resigned myself to accept, grudgingly, because I could not do otherwise, could have been a protection. It was hard to believe.

"Your creature self, your wildness, rose up in your defense against being bound, and took over, to protect the freedom of your mind and the integrity of your soul," he explained.

I closed my eyes to take in Myrddin's words more fully. They rang true to the core of my being. My skin was covered in goosebumps. The beast had risen up to protect my spirit, my freedom, and prevent my mind from being stolen from me. I began to feel a level of gratitude for this monstrous part of me I had not experienced in four years. Dragon's words, the ones I had dismissed as just another riddle, came to the forefront of my mind.

"It's true," I murmured.

"What is?" asked Myrddin.

"What Dragon told me."

Myrddin waited for me to find my words. They cut through the silence like quicksilver lightening, like dragon fire. "The curse is the cure. They told me that."

I started to sniffle and wiped the snot with the back of my hand.

"The curse is the cure," I repeated. "The beast was protecting me from the curse taking hold of my mind. Nobody expected me to keep my wits, did they?"

I started to cry, and cough and sniffle and laugh. "The curse is the cure," I repeated.

Myrddin laughed out loud, "Indeed it is, Dryw donn. So, you see, it doesn't matter what happens on the night of your wedding. You are already free. You always were."

I did a mad jig then. The jig I had promised myself I would do after the runes worked to contain the magic of Somer's medallion. When I regained my breath sufficiently, Myrddin helped me out of the gown.

"It's perfect for a royal wedding," quipped Myrddin. "Lavinia outdid herself."

"Yes. But not today. Not until the solstice," I said.

If the curse could be lifted at all, the solstice, because of its inherent magic, was the best time to try, and I wanted all of the help I could get.

"You do like wearing that tartan, don't you?" he said as he watched me wrap myself in it.

"I do. It's comfortable," I said. "It fits my body no matter what it looks like."

"You'll be safe from prying eyes until the wedding here," he said.

"Thank you. I don't like crowds. They make me itch." My hand went to scratch my neck without thinking. I stopped myself.

"Then perhaps you better avoid the tournament," said Myrddin. "It is a very popular pastime among the nobility."

"Perhaps you are right," I said. "I think I'll keep to your chambers until the wedding."

"Wise decision. You'll have enough to contend with on the day."

I snorted like Espoir. "Would you do me a favor and organize a meeting with Gawain for me? I think that the look of me shook him up. It got the better of his natural forbearance."

Myrddin smiled. "He's all right, but yes, I will do that for you."

Beyond wondering whether our covenant still held after witnessing Gawain's reaction at the gate, I was beginning to have doubts about the wedding myself. Was it fair to hold Gawain to his word under the circumstances? Or marry him, or any man, who was so filled with revulsion at the sight of the beast I was? A beast, I now realized, who had rescued and protected me from the worst effects of the curse. Maybe fear was running away with me on the eve of great change.

"I'm glad you are here," I said to the druid. "I don't think I could go through with this if you weren't. Could we send word to Hillel and Lavinia about the wedding?"

"I will send Eira," said Myrddin. "They'll receive the news even if they cannot be here."

"Thank you," I said.

"I must attend to the king, inform him of all that happened while he was away," said Myrddin. "We can have supper together tonight."

"I will see you then," I said.

"The window has a good view of the field where the tournament takes place tomorrow," he said, pointing to it. "You'll be able to see quite a bit of the mêlée from your vantage point."

"What's a mêlée?" I asked.

Being a soldier as much as anything, my father had despised tournaments, thinking them a frivolous pastime, not real practice for war, and so I never saw one growing up.

"Groups of opposing knights fighting, stealing each other's destriers, or capturing another knight for ransom," he explained.

"That sounds very unfair and dangerous," I said.

"It's quite violent. But the jousting is worse. You'll see it tomorrow," he said. "Get some rest, Dryw donn. You've had quite a journey to get here."

We smiled at each other, or rather I snarled, and he smiled; then Myrddin let himself out. The door swung shut behind him with a definite thud. I felt quite safe but more lonely than I had been in a long time. I did need rest. I was tired. The events and revelations of the last few weeks, not weeks, months, were catching up to me. I laid down in front of the fireplace as was my habit. The hearth was filled with brand new logs that remained unlit. It was too warm for a fire. The summer heat had arrived in time for the solstice.

I wasn't certain I'd be able to fall asleep in a strange place, but I could smell the cool, mossy fragrance of Myrddin's magic all around me. It was like being submerged in a bath of green trees or cradled within the stone circle of the Gwynedd Forest. Sleep gathered me into its arms, and I yielded to it. My brother walked into my dream. He was wandering in the woods, lost. I called out to him, but he couldn't hear me or see me. There was a thin red scarf tied around his throat. I woke up with a gasp, upset with myself that I still cared so much about Somer, he could invade my dreamtime in such a way, after everything.

Chapter Twenty-Seven

The air was cooling, the sunrays lengthening on the horizon. It was late in the day. I walked over to the window, pushed open the shutters still fastened against the heat and took in the view of the meadows, a field shorn in preparation for the tournament, the red dragon looking down from the banners on each side of the stands erected for the occasion.

I heard a light rap on the door and wrapped myself in my cloak, pulling the hood forward to hide my face. I was glad I did because Myrddin walked in with Gawain.

Gawain planted himself by the door and stood still as a statue. He kept looking at the ground as if fascinated by it. I wanted to touch him but how could I with my beastly hand?

How do we get through this? How can I help him? I better speak plainly, I thought.

"Sir Gawain. Well met," I said, more boldly than I felt.

His head jerked up. It was the same surprise I saw on my brother's face. I sounded almost normal, more human being than beast.

His looks still mesmerized me, the sky-blue eyes, the dark curls. I got hold of myself and focused on what I meant to say. I'd loved Gawain since I was fifteen years old. I had done all I could to make him my husband so I could change my fate, but I was coming to the realization that in doing so, I was making him a prisoner.

"I've asked Myrddin Emrys to bring you here to speak of our wedding. You have agreed to wed out of duty to your king which is commendable but now that you have seen the face of your bride, you must have second thoughts. I would understand if you felt it was beyond what you can endure. I would release you from our betrothal. I wish for you to be happy, Gawain."

To speak truly, there was no absolute guarantee the curse would be lifted by our wedding. Then what would I be doing to both of us? The man I loved would be repulsed by the beast I could no longer hate. And I would grow to resent him or even despise him. I couldn't bear the thought of learning to hate the man I'd loved for so long. I'd rather stay a beast until my death.

I saw Gawain stare at me, as comprehension slowly grew. I saw the struggle inside him. He looked around the room as if asking for help from invisible allies. Myrddin said nothing but I noticed the uncertainty clouding his brow. Gawain closed his eyes and let out a big sigh.

"My Lady," he said. "You are gracious to offer me a way out of my oath, but it is done. I would never renege on a pledge taken on my king's behalf. That would be an offence I couldn't live with, as a knight or as his nephew."

I nodded. "We are all bound by something, aren't we?"

Gawain didn't expect my answer and looked up from behind his dark curls, blue eyes widened by surprise.

The wedding is still happening then. It was a shock, for both of us perhaps. I thought Gawain would take me up on my offer to release him from his oath. My heart was beating fast.

Gawain bowed and hastened toward the door.

"I would show you something before you take your leave," I said.

Gawain slowed his gait and turned toward me. Resignation draped his body. I took my little wren, my constant companion out of its hidden pocket and showed it to him.

"This has been with me since the night I was cursed. Do you recognize it?" I held it flat in the palm of my hand so he could see it.

Gawain observed my offering, then took it from me gingerly, only hesitating a moment as he appraised the length of my nails and the furry aspect of my skin.

I saw the recognition on his face. The astonishment. What it meant. Who I really was. And then sadness and pity followed, like shadows on his brow. I hated seeing his pity but marshalled my feelings.

"It has been my most precious possession until now," I said. "A reminder of what I was. And what I wished for."

Gawain regarded me with new understanding in his eyes.

"It traveled with me from Dinas Emrys to the Isle of Skye. It's meant everything to me."

My last words hang in the air between us. I saw Gawain receive the truth behind them. *It's meant everything to me.* His sky-blue eyes filled. I could hear his heart beating like a drum against his chest. I held my breath with the unexpected tenderness of the moment.

"I remember," he whispered, handing it back to me. I stopped him.

"Keep it."

Gawain beheld the wren again with a kind of reverence for how his little wooden sculpture had helped me through my darkest times.

"You can return it to me on our wedding night," I said.

He stopped mid-step. I instantly berated myself. *Why did I have to mention the wedding night? Why couldn't I keep my mouth shut? Stupid, stupid, beast.*

He pocketed the wren then surprised me by taking my foul hand and kissing it, "Lady Ragnell," he said. "I shall see you on the solstice at High Mass."

Hearing my name on his lips left me shaken. I nodded, "On the solstice, Sir Knight."

Gawain bent his head in a short bow and walked away. I collapsed on the floor as soon as he was gone, all strength gone from my legs.

"You took quite a risk, Dryw donn," said Myrddin. "You had me worried there for a moment."

"I had to be sure," I said.

Myrddin nodded, "Of him?"

"Of myself," I replied.

"You'll probably get more visitors over the next day or so," he said.

"To let Gawain out of his oath?" I asked.

"At the very least to convince you to have a small wedding and no banquet," he said.

"If I'm going to go through with this wedding, it needs to be as official as possible. "So there's no doubt as to its legitimacy."

"That's wise," he acquiesced. "So be it."

"I do worry that my brother will find out. Hillel mentioned a spy at court."

"The baron received a note from Hillel three days ago telling him to return to Dinas Emrys on urgent business for your brother."

"That's a relief. Thank you Myrddin. I'm not ready to face Somer. Not yet."

"You will have to if you are ever to reclaim your title and your land," he said.

"Can I do that?" I asked.

"Yes, you can. And you should. They are yours by right. It was your father's wish. And you'll have the support of the Pendragons. You won't be alone."

I observed Myrddin as he poured himself a glass of cider and remembered that the person he loved most was King Arthur and by extension, his family. That he thought it was a good thing for Gawain to marry the beast I was, I took as a sign of his regard for me as well. But there was something else, something a part of me knew all along but that became clear in that moment.

"If I claim my rights over Dinas Emrys back from my brother, the instant I become Gawain's wife, all of Gwynedd becomes his property by law. Isn't that so, Myrddin Emrys?"

Myrddin looked back at me with his fathomless black eyes, "Would that be such a terrible thing, Dryw donn?"

I didn't answer his question right away. "I think that is what my father wanted all along. It's so ironic that he was ever called a traitor. For there was never a more loyal man. Not to his family or his children it turns out. But to his king. He disinherited his own son for the crown. He knew the moment he arranged for my betrothal, it would all go to Gawain and therefore to the crown. My father had it all planned out before my fifteenth birthday. He just didn't plan for his own murder or the curse that befell me. And to answer your question, no, it's not the most awful thing that could happen. But I wish someone had told me. Anything else I ought to know?"

He hesitated only for the briefest instant. "There is one thing. I would like you to be present at our negotiations with the Saxons."

I knew why. My mother. "You would use me, my birth, to make your peace with them?"

"I would, if you'll allow it," he replied.

"You ask a lot of me," I said. "I'll think about it. When is this meeting to take place?"

"The day after the wedding," he answered.

I snorted. "You don't waste any time, do you."

"You are here," said Myrddin. "And we need peace. At least for a little while. The Saxons question whether we still have a king at this point. But they are also tired of war."

"So, we must make peace with them before they want to return to war."

"Yes," he said. "That's about the scope of it."

"I have one request," I said. "Would you organize a bath for me? I would like to be clean at least on my wedding way."

"There are no Roman baths here, I'm afraid. But I will arrange for you to have one."

"Thank you," I said. "And will you walk me down the aisle on the solstice?"

"It will be my honor, Dryw donn. The bishop might not approve."

"Well, I doubt I will have his approval either."

"Yes. A singular bride, a unique wedding, to be sure."

"To be sure," I agreed.

The Saxon delegation arrived early the next morning and Myrddin went to meet them with the king. I decided to watch the tournament from my window. Hundreds of people were in attendance, but the tournament was delayed until the king and queen finally appeared with their entourage. I had a constant reminder of Dragon with the red dragon banners floating everywhere.

It all looked absolutely inane to me. Exactly what privileged young men with too much time on their hands would do, to be seen and admired by the ladies. Although there was a lot of screaming and cheering during the mêlée, the crowd grew quiet when came time for the joust. It was a more serious affair with real danger for both knights involved despite the bluntness of the lances and the heavy armor. I recognized Sir Lancelot right away in all his white and silver. He rode forward and approached the stands, stopping in front of the box where the king and queen were seated. He extended his lance toward the queen who stood up and approached the balustrade to favor him with a flimsy piece of red scarf which matched her gown. He took it from his lance and kissed it. He was her champion and sworn protector, but I thought it excessive. The king didn't seem to have any objections and applauded vigorously.

The other knight was Gawain. He was dressed more simply. The red dragon on his white cape gave him away as the king's man. He was bowing to his sovereign when a lady near the queen rushed up to the balustrade and bent over to give him her handkerchief which she attached to the end of his lance. It occurred to me then that Gawain might have other arrangements after all, a love that preceded his oath to the king. The girl was very young, as I had been that fated night. She was pretty, a freshly blooming flower with a smile sweet as cream. My clawing hands flexed of their own volition. I wanted to rip the skin off of her lovely face.

The two knights faced each other on opposite sides of the tilt barrier, readied their lances, and charged each other at full gallop. I couldn't take my eyes from them, even though part of me didn't want to watch. I thought I might lose my husband before I had a chance to marry him. His lance broke against Lancelot's shield. Gawain's squire, who was standing at the ready at the lists, in front of the stands, immediately handed him a new lance. The knights went at each other again. Lancelot's lance broke, and he was thrown from his horse because of it. Gawain dismounted and the fight continued on foot with swords that looked too sharp for a game. Watching them was exhausting. I started panting.

These two were close friends. I had observed their banter with my own eyes. But they were going at each other like sworn enemies. They were evenly matched in skill. But Lancelot had the advantage in height and weight. I couldn't bear to watch any longer. They were slowing down, getting clumsy with their strokes. I saw Lancelot's sword cut into Gawain's armor at the joint between arm and shoulder. The impact stunned Gawain and his sword fell from his hand with a clatter like thunder against the greave, the piece of armor that protected his shin. I stifled a scream. I was not the only one.

The king stood up and cried out, "Enough Sir Lancelot. You have proven yet again you are the best of us. Do spare my nephew on the eve of his wedding day."

He smiled, pleased with himself, but the crowd was not amused. They heard about the monstrous bride-to-be and felt sorry for Gawain.

"Yes, thank you, Sire," said Gawain, holding his wounded arm with his other hand. Then he turned to Lancelot, "Or do you wish to replace me as groom tomorrow?"

A wave of shocked remarks and hushed recriminations flooded the crowd. The queen almost stood up.

"You are the better man, my friend," said Lancelot, bowing out with a flourish and a sarcastic smile on his face.

The young girl who had given her handkerchief to Gawain fainted and was promptly rescued by the other ladies. Gawain's squire helped him make his way toward the lists. I saw Myrddin walk down to meet them. Gawain made it to the lists and slid down the wall to the ground next to his squire. The man was struggling to get Gawain's armor off. I hoped he was not seriously wounded so he could stand next to me at the altar.

A knock at the door took my mind off my worries. I quickly put my cloak back on and pulled the hood close over my face.

"Who is it?" I asked.

"Your bath, My Lady."

"Come in."

With Myrddin's protections in place, no one set on causing mischief could come in, but I ran into the bedroom anyway as they walked in. I didn't want to frighten them or interfere with whatever they had to do. I opened the bedroom door a crack and saw an army of servants walk in. The first four of those held the actual bathing barrel. It was made of wood and lined with a sheet, to protect from splinters. Then came the rest who proceeded to fill up the container with hot water. Finally came another servant, a housemaid, with salts for the bath. She left another piece of cloth over the side of the bath. It was such a to-do I felt somewhat guilty, but not guilty enough to stop them.

Last to leave, the housemaid shouted in my direction, "Your bath is ready, My Lady."

"Thank you," I answered.

I waited a moment to make sure everyone was gone then came out. I tested the water with my fingers, and it was quite hot, so I waited a while. The barrel had been converted from its previous use for cider. I found the drawing of an apple on its side. It didn't smell bad, but the scent lingered despite the salts. I stepped into it and found a little stool at the bottom for me to sit on. It was quite comfortable, and I was able to submerge myself in it.

I must have dozed off because next thing I knew Myrddin walked in. I swallowed some water which made me choke and cough. Not a satisfying end to my restful bath. I never let anyone take me by surprise like that and it unnerved me.

"Sorry to have disturbed your bath, Dryw donn."

"I fell asleep."

"I have to attend the dinner, but I asked to have food brought up here for you. You best get out of the bath before it arrives."

"Yes. I will. How is Gawain? Is he alright? He seemed quite hurt."

"More his pride than his body. The wound was superficial. The armor deflected the blow. All I did was make sure it was clean and wouldn't get infected."

"They were like two brutes fighting," I said.

"Yes. They have to prove who is the best. But their friendship is sturdy, so goodwill generally prevails."

I kept quiet but thought it was something more serious than fighting skills. Myrddin left and I jumped out of the bath, dried off with the cloth and wrapped myself in my tartan. The food arrived soon after. I repeated my escape into the bedroom while servants laid out the meal on the table and left. I was about to come out of the bedroom when there was another knock. More servants returned to take the bath barrel away.

It all looked really good, a meat pie in a crumbly pastry, juicy partridge in mushroom sauce. Mashed turnips. Fried almond cakes and spiced fruit. But I wasn't hungry. Very odd for me. What I needed was to get out of here, see Espoir, head for the woods and ride. I couldn't bear to be confined inside for any length of time. I was used to roaming the woods. I started pacing. I approached the door more than once but in such a foreign setting, I didn't dare venture out. Eventually Myrddin returned from the king's feast.

He rested a critical eye on me. "Are you alright, Dryw donn?"

"No, I'm not. I need to get out of here. I don't like this place at all. And I need to go ride Espoir. Will you help me?" I pleaded.

"I can arrange it in the morning."

"I need to get out now," I said, panic rising in my voice.

"That is not feasible. Tell me what ails you, Dryw donn," asked the druid.

All my resolve to collect myself, my feelings, crumbled. I was a sniffling muddle.

"I don't belong here. I'm a beast. I belong in my cabin in the Gwynedd woods. That's where I feel safe. That's home."

And it was true. That hunter's cabin had become my home. I had Hillel and Lavinia who visited on a regular basis. Espoir was my best friend. It was enough.

"You are frightened. That's understandable," said Myrddin with that serene tone that could so irritate me.

"I'm not sure I want my life to change anymore," I said.

"It already has. And you know it, Dryw donn. Do not let your fear keep you from your destiny now. There are many who would prefer you not marry Gawain at all."

I recalled the lack of enthusiasm at the king's sense of humor, starting with that swooning gangly girl. So like me at that age. I'm sure I was just as taken with Gawain back then as she was. But I didn't embarrass myself quite in the same outrageous way. I thought about Lady Morgause and how she surely had other ideas for her son than to marry an ugly beast. And my brother of course would be furious to know I was still alive and marrying the very man my father had planned for me. The

Fates had an ironic sense of humor. I wondered how many other people at Arthur's court didn't want this wedding to happen.

There was another knock at the door. We looked at each other and Myrddin shrugged. "I'm not expecting anyone."

"Do we have to let them in?" I asked.

"We must."

"Do you know who it is?"

"I have a strong suspicion," said the druid.

Two guards opened the doors, followed by the queen herself and Sir Lancelot a few paces behind, at a respectful distance. My throat dried up. I could barely swallow.

"Your Royal Highness, what a pleasure to see you again so soon," said Myrddin.

"Spare me your nonsense, Magician. I would speak with your beast." The queen didn't like him. I'd say the feeling was mutual.

"She is not *my beast*, Your Majesty. She was my pupil. May I present Lady Ragnell."

"Be that as it may, she looks like a beast. If this unnatural wedding is to take place, it must be done simply. No High Mass. No banquet. It would be impossible to eat in her presence."

Queen Guinevere may be a famed beauty, but her character was disappointing. She looked at me directly, disgust plain on her face.

"I've been informed that you understand language. Would you spare us from such a public spectacle? There will be such shame in it for poor Gawain. If you have any love for him or for your king, whose life, I'm told, you successfully bargained for, you will not do this."

"You mean whose life I saved, Your Majesty," I said, daring to correct her.

"If that is the truth of it, you cannot wish to save a life in order to ruin it," she retorted.

I felt my hackles rise and the runes burn. Any doubt I had about the wedding evaporated.

"I couldn't ruin the king's life," I said. "I'm not intimate enough with him to do that."

The queen's cheeks lost their glow for a moment. Sir Lancelot kept his face carefully blank but gripped the hilt of his sword.

"I wish to have a wedding befitting my station, that's all," I said, trying to master Myrddin's trick of sounding serene no matter what.

Once she recovered, the queen scoffed at my answer. Sir Lancelot eased his hand away from the hilt of his sword.

"You wish to proceed with this abomination then?" she asked.

"I don't see my wedding that way, Your Majesty," I answered.

The queen turned to Myrddin. "Your pupil is a most disagreeable beast. Unsurprisingly."

She walked out, her scarf floating behind her. Sir Lancelot led the way. The guards closed ranks behind their queen. I blew out a breath, relieved they were gone.

"I don't think that's the end of it," I said.

"You may be right, Dryw donn. But I'm glad she came."

"Why?" I looked at the druid. I saw a knowing little smile etched on his face.

"She convinced you to go ahead with the wedding better than I could ever have."

I snorted and he laughed. He was right of course.

Chapter Twenty-Eight

Myrddin woke me at the crack of dawn. "If you want to go for a ride it's now or never."

"Why so early?" I grumbled, half-asleep. Threads of a blissful dream about Gawain and me in my human form still occupied my mind.

"Because you'll have to get ready for your wedding after that."

I panicked. "It's tomorrow already?"

"Tomorrow has come," he acquiesced. "The solstice is tonight."

"It's too soon. I'm not ready," I whimpered.

Myrddin looked at me with such commiseration, I wanted to kill him. "Don't look at me like that," I growled. "You better take me to the stables now. I must see Espoir before I can face this day."

I wrapped myself in my tartan and adjusted the cloak over it. I followed Myrddin out the door and around the corridors like a shadow. There were only guards and servants about, and they knew better than to ask Myrddin Emrys where he was going or with whom, with the sun scarcely out of its slumber. They averted their gaze at the stranger in the cloak. Was it Myrddin's magic? Or did they always look the other way when someone from court walked by? Perhaps ignorance was safer.

When we got to the stables I was pleased to see Espoir and Rhian together as I'd asked. They seemed to be well taken care of. One squire, with an unruly mop of red hair and freckles all over his face, was in the process of feeding the horses their morning oats.

"Would you mind getting our horses ready?" asked Myrddin. His eyes became fixed on the boy, as if he was seeing through him. It was a long exchange which made me look twice.

The youth was not bothered by it. He stared back at the druid like a dare. I could detect no shyness in him. He must have been twelve or less but knew his business with horses. He started brushing Rhian. I asked for a body brush, and he handed me one. I saw his shock when I put out my hand to take it from him, but he also remained silent. He darted a look at me, and I saw eyes of midnight. They reminded me of Myrddin's eyes. But where the druid's eyes were an unknowable mystery, the boy's eyes were guarded, obscured by mischief. I thanked him and proceeded to brush Espoir.

"I get the feeling I'm not the first strange thing these people have seen," I said to Myrddin as we got started on our morning ride, heading toward a thick green wall of forest.

"You are a most strange thing, Dryw donn, but they are used to keeping quiet about courtly shenanigans," he answered.

"Like the queen and Sir Lancelot." I didn't mean to say it. It just came out. But Myrddin pulled Rhian to a standstill and yanked Espoir's reins out of my hands. He looked more upset than I had ever seen him.

"Do not speak, or even think, such a thing, ever. It is treason."

I was completely taken aback by the intensity of his reaction and immediately apologized. "I'm sorry Myrddin. I won't say another word about it. I promise."

The rest of our ride was quiet. Myrddin was lost in his own thoughts, and I dared not intrude. The woods were thick with trees and songbirds, but it wasn't Gwynedd Forest. Here, the woods seemed almost tame by comparison. Large, manicured trails populated the forest which was full of hunting game. Partridges, pheasants, deer. I felt sorry for them. I urged Espoir into a gallop and began to breathe easier. Myrddin gave Rhian her head so she could keep pace with us.

By the time we returned, I felt better. Espoir was the best medicine I knew. We left our horses in the care of the red-haired squire and walked back to the castle, still waking up, and still peopled mostly with servants and guards. The nobility stayed in their rooms until there was some fun to be had. Today it would be the wedding at High Mass. Myrddin sneaked me in through a side door and we rushed through the corridors and back to his apartments.

I hesitated when he offered to help me get back into Lavinia's yellow work of art. I thought about staying in my tartan. What did I care about the court and what they thought of me? But in the end I decided to wear it one more time, to be the beast in the golden gown, a study in contrast. The druid was my dresser again, a far cry from his usual duties. I wrapped my cloak over it. I looked for my Auseklis in my hidden pocket. It wasn't there.

Myrddin put his hand on my shoulder, "You gave the little wren to Gawain, remember?"

"That's right. I did." I was relieved it wasn't lost but I wished I could hold it right now.

We waited. The breakfast was unappetizing, some gruel and stewed spiced fruit. I missed my Welsh cakes. Myrddin looked uneasy, pacing back and forth across the room.

"I'm counting on you. Churches are not my favorite place."

"Nor mine, Dryw donn," he answered.

"Tell me," I said. "If I hadn't solved the riddle, you'd have helped me. Wouldn't you?"

"Dryw donn, it was your task. Not mine," he replied. "No one but you could have come up with the answer to the riddle. You know your brother best."

It wasn't what I wanted to hear. I was still contemplating Myrddin's answer when we heard a knock at the door. It made me jump but it wasn't the guards come to fetch us yet. It was a manservant with two missives for Myrddin. He opened them right away and read through them quickly. He handed me the first one.

"Congratulations from Hillel and Lavinia."

Their note put a smile on my face. "At least they know," I said.

"Yes," he acquiesced.

"What's the other letter about?" I asked.

"A confirmation of the meeting with the Saxon leaders for tomorrow. It's what I was waiting for."

"Do they know about me?" I asked.

"They don't," he replied. "I wouldn't say anything until you agreed to meet them."

I was grateful he hadn't. Myrddin was a man of his word.

"I will come to your meeting," I said to him. I wasn't really going to refuse Myrddin. I just wanted to feel like I could.

He seemed relieved to hear me say so and gave me a smile that reached his black eyes. I didn't want anything unfriendly between us on this day of all days. And his anger this morning had shaken me.

The guards came to fetch us eventually. As we approached the cathedral, I felt dwarfed by it. It was built to impress, taller than the castle, with its white stone gleaming in the summer sun, almost blinding. The flag with the red dragon floating from the tallest spire seemed out of place. My step became hesitant. The old urge to run and hide came up strongly in me. Myrddin squeezed my elbow to comfort me.

We walked into the shadows of the central nave. The coolness of the place was a relief. A choir was singing. The music was a somber hymn. The bishop was holding up the cup of the Goddess to his dying God. And hundreds of pairs of eyes were upon us, upon me. The eagerness and the revulsion with which the people of Arthur's court stared was only surpassed by a certain disappointment. My looks didn't match the stuff of nightmare they expected and somehow they felt cheated which increased the viciousness of the commentary. As I walked past the pews toward the altar where my betrothed was waiting, they whispered loudly: *That dress looks grotesque on her. Is it even a "her"? What is it? Some bear must have coupled with a sow. Look at those teeth. Those nails. That fur. It's not human. It can't be. Poor Gawain. He must have been bewitched. Poor dear Gawain. She is a monstrous witch. Burn the thing. That will free poor Gawain. How did it not burn the moment it entered sacred ground? Look who is standing with her. The devil and the demon. A perfect match.*

I heard all of it, the sickening sneers and repressed guffaws, but I was walking toward my destiny, and I would have the last laugh. I hoped. My transformation awaited me at the end of our handfasting if I could get through the ceremony. The bishop's reaction, as he took one look at me, made it clear he too was revolted by the idea of our wedding.

"This is an abomination. I cannot bless such a union in front of God." He timed it perfectly, as I joined Gawain at the altar. Myrddin had stepped away to stand by the king. The humiliation reached into my bones and out onto my skin. I began to itch all over my body. The entire proceeding came to a standstill. The music and singing faded to nothing. All the murmuring and snickering ceased, replaced by a silence full of eagerness and malice. The bishop had no idea. I was no longer the helpless beast on the floor of the church in Beddgelert. I was standing free. And I could rip his tongue out with one nail. I clenched my jaw to stop the rage from engulfing me. I thought my teeth would crack. I looked at Myrddin. I was trying to catch his eye, but he was glaring at the queen. A small smile floated on her sweet plump lips. A faint flush caressed her cheeks. She looked innocent and mischievous at the same time. I wanted to turn her face into pudding. King Arthur tried to stand up out of his pew, but the queen put her arm out to stop him.

I was so relieved when Gawain began to speak, I didn't care what came out of his mouth.

"Priest, there is no abomination here," he said. "Do not insult my betrothed, *Lady Ragnell of Dinas Emrys*. She may be cursed but her generous heart is beyond what most are capable of. We shall be married this day. It is ordained."

His words provoked a collective gasp. I wanted to kiss Gawain for whatever chivalry prompted him to utter such words. He had given me my name back in front of the whole court.

"Sir Gawain, would you not prefer to be spared the indignity of such a union?"

"There is no indignity here. My uncle, *the king*, approves."

Our marriage had all the sanctity required. The king approved.

The bishop was relentless, "Is anyone forcing you? What about the use of spells?"

"No spells. No force. The lady is known to me four years since. She is kind, intelligent, forthright. And she has a rare appreciation for fine woodworking," he said in a loud voice.

Gawain glanced at me. I knew that last remark was for my benefit.

"Please, proceed," he said to the bishop.

I could not have asked for more. Gawain's gallantry embodied the spirit of chivalry. I could practically hear all the demoiselles in the church swooning with envy.

"Very well. If there are no objections, from anyone, I shall proceed." The bishop looked out at the assembly, hoping for help from someone, then his gaze fell directly upon the queen who made to rise from her pew, and it was the king's turn to put out his arm across her chest and stop her. She was hissing mad but kept her peace.

I don't remember any of what was said after that, except for the handfasting, which I'd asked Myrddin to participate in and made the bishop so uncomfortable, he stumbled over his homily, fear and forbearance alternating on his face. I was hoping that Myrddin could add his power to the handfasting ritual. I kept staring at my bestial hand wrapped in a white handkerchief with Gawain's flawless hand. I waited for it to turn back into a woman's hand. But nothing happened. I was unchanged at the end of the ceremony. There was no beginning of transformation, not even a hint that the curse was lifting.

Disappointment does not express what I felt. I was so mad, my whole body was shaking. I wanted to rave and scream at the heavens and all the Gods. I was especially mad at Myrddin, for he, above all, had given me hope that this wedding was the unmaking of my curse. Nothing. I was as much a beast as ever. I had fussed and fretted about the gown after my transformation. If it would become too big for my human body and fall down. What a waste of worry. Maybe the Fates meant for me to be a beast forever. I couldn't wait to get out of the bloody golden thing and wear my tartan again.

The full force of the gossiping demoiselles hit me again on the way to the banquet hall. They dabbed their eyes with dainty handkerchiefs like preening hens, making a show of their grief. *Surely, the bishop is right. There's a spell on poor Gawain. How else could he marry such a monster. The queen tried her best. There is only so much she can do. A sad day for Camelot.*

We reached the hall when Gawain stopped in front of his parents, King Lot of Orkney and his wife, Lady Morgause. I hesitated. Lady Morgause had made an impression on me at a young age and that impression was unchanged. She was a bandrui, a druid in her own right. What would she think of a monster as wife for her son?

Her hair flowed down her back in waves. Her golden bracelets, inscribed with runes, jingled on her wrists. Lady Morgause looked into my eyes without a word, then seized my wrist to examine it. The half-smile on her face reminded me of the Goddess Rhiannon. She simply nodded as if she expected to see what she saw and then said, "Congratulations."

That was all. I was speechless. She was only interested in looking at the runes on my wrist, as if seeking confirmation for something she already knew. No recrimination. No remarks about my appearance. The husband took his cue from his Lady wife and said nothing as well, but he was clearly agitated. And as soon as they were out of ear shot, he was gesticulating and shouting grievances at his wife while she remained calm as a lake at dusk on a summer night. I noticed a boy nearby. It was the young squire with the red hair and dark eyes I had seen earlier.

"Who is that?" I asked Gawain.

"My youngest sibling, Mordred." Gawain's tone was strained as he spoke. "A difficult boy." There was more to that story, but he didn't wish to speak of it. I didn't insist. The boy looked like no one but himself. I could smell the magic around him, like burnt resin, but I wasn't sure if it was his or protections around him. Both perhaps.

We sat at the head table with the king and queen as well as Gawain's parents. Thanks be the Goddess, Myrddin was seated on the other side of me.

I whispered to him, "Nothing has changed."

He answered, "Be still, Dryw donn. The solstice night is not over."

"That's easy for you to say. The reversal of the curse was supposed to happen during our handfasting. It's the most sacred time."

"You don't know that," he said.

But I did know, and I had no hope that it would happen later. It was a cruel fate, and I felt most sorry for Gawain to be trapped in this way. Perhaps it was the rage I felt, combined with the rabid gossip and cruel comments in the church, but my wanton appetite was unleashed with a vengeance at the banquet. The demoiselles could feel superior with their dainty fingers and minuscule nibbles, I didn't care. I slashed my way through mutton and pheasants with my nails, cramming down mouthfuls between my teeth and grabbing handfuls of bread sopped in sauces that I drowned with cups of ale.

A few dared to stare with a kind of disgusted fascination that they might lose control and do the same. I was curiously aware of what I was doing and had no desire to stop it. The queen was suffering as though through a great ordeal and didn't touch a morsel. But she did accept a dance with Sir Lancelot when the music started, after the feast was over. The king asked for a dance with Lady Morgause who accepted graciously. My hackles were raised at the whole spectacle that everyone seemed to find acceptable. I couldn't wait to extract myself from such sticky company. I followed Myrddin when he stood up to leave. Gawain followed me.

"My Lady, where are you going?" he asked.

"Back to my apartments, with Myrddin," I answered, as if it was obvious and Gawain a fool for asking.

"It is customary for newlyweds to spend their first night together," he said.

"Oh. I wasn't… I didn't… You must think me very rude."

Very rude. Very drunk. Very ugly. You name it. I am a beast, after all, I thought.

"I don't," Gawain replied.

I wanted to disappear, vanish from the world. I suppose part of me didn't believe I was really married because it hadn't worked. I was still cursed, and still a beast. I had put myself through this charade for nothing. I could have gone on drinking for the rest of the night, if truth be told. I would have preferred to do it with the Laird of Dunvegan Castle and Myrddin Emrys, with my friends.

"Shall we go to your chambers then?" I asked my new husband.

"If it pleases you."

Gawain's unfailing kindness was getting on my nerves. He should be more upset. I was.

"Why not. Lead the way, Sir Gawain." I was a sarcastic drunk, but he said nothing. Gawain's apartments were a long way away, it turns out. Or I was drunk enough to make it hard to walk. I stumbled and he caught me. By the time we arrived, I had sobered up quite a bit. I wanted to crawl in front of the fireplace and fall asleep. A fountain of sorrow rose up inside as I stared at the two chemises displayed on the bed for us.

"Can you help me out of this gown?" I asked. "I don't want to call on servants at this hour. And I don't want to frighten anyone unnecessarily."

"Yes. I can do that," he said. Gawain averted his gaze as I took off the gown and slipped on one of the chemises.

I shivered.

"Are you cold?" he asked.

Gawain was gentle and thoughtful, and I couldn't bear it. Here was a man I had loved since I was a girl. A beautiful kind man. A knight in every sense of the word. And I couldn't be with him as a woman. It was too sad for words.

"No. I haven't worn a sleeping gown since the curse."

"I see. It must be hard," he said.

"It has been," I replied. "I'm going to lay down by the fireplace. That's where I sleep."

"Are you sure?" he asked.

"I'm sure," I answered.

I saw Gawain undress and put on the other chemise. His body was perfect. His skin smooth except for a scar near the right shoulder. There was still bruising around it, where Lancelot had struck him at the tournament, but it was mostly healed thanks to Myrddin's magical ministrations. I yearned to touch him. I curled up on the carpet instead, a sorrowful beast. I stared at the logs burnt almost to ash in the fireplace with a few crackling embers here and there. I heard him lay down on the bed. I was exhausted and soon fell asleep.

I woke up a few hours later at the blackest time of night, between matins and lauds. A time when the faithful pray. Lady Moon painted the wood floor of Gawain's bedchamber with her milky whiteness. Attracted by the shimmering light, I got on all fours, praying to all the Gods I knew and some I didn't. It was a simple prayer: "Please. Goddess of the moon. Goddess of suffering and redemption. Rhiannon. Please, help me. Silver dragon. Please, help me. Lift this curse from me. See the man on our marriage bed. He chose to marry me as I am, a beast."

I laid down on the moonlit floor as I had laid on the church floor. Although this was a surrender, not torture. I let the moon wrap me in her lambent sheen. I wished for the chains of the curse that had held me in its prison for the last four years to be released from my body. I had no ill will toward the beast. I was thankful for her. She had protected me in many different ways. I was simply done. I was done with my penance, whatever it was meant to be. I said so to the moon and to the darkness. *I'm done. Please help me. Thank you for everything. I'm done. I'm done.* I went into a trance between waking and sleeping, steeped in the milk of the moon. I don't know how long it was, but I heard a click. Like a key turning in a lock. I heard a voice like a breath made of fire and silver softly in my ear: *This is the first of three.*

I didn't move for a long while for fear what I sensed would disappear. Slowly, I turned my body etched in silver light onto my back. I was reminded of the Fairy Pools, of Dragon. I brought my hands up to my face. My eyes witnessed the bare flesh of a woman's hands with smooth skin and nails flushed with the pinkish hue of human blood. I touched my face with my hands. It was a woman's face. I touched my lips. I explored the inside of my mouth with my fingers. My canine teeth no longer protruded but were level with the rest. My hair was long and silky. I sat up and began to giggle and then burst into tears, my hands cradling my head.

Gawain shot out of bed and was kneeling next to me in an instant. I opened my hands and, like an offering, raised my head up to him.

"Gawain. Do you see what I see?" I asked. It was a plea more than anything.

"I do. I do." Gawain studied my face, unable to say more. His eyes kept darting back and forth, up and down my body, blinking as if they had trouble taking in what they saw. He swallowed, his breath ragged.

His hands hovered near my face and down my hair, as if touch was too intrusive or too bold. "You are more beautiful than I remember. You are more, more alive, I cannot say. I have never seen such entrancing beauty," he murmured.

A peal of laughter burst out of me, breaking the spell of the silver moon, "No one has ever called me *entrancing*."

"They will now." He sounded sure of himself. He finally dared place his hands on my arms, and I felt the heat of them. "Tell me. How is this possible?" He gazed into my eyes, and I felt his desire burning me like a torch.

"It's too much to explain all of it," I said. "But you agreeing to wed me while still a beast was the main reason."

He was almost as shaken up by the experience as I was, both yearning to embrace my human form and fearful of it. It was the first time I witnessed Gawain tremble. As best as I could judge, it seemed to be hope, fear and desire, all rolled into one. Perhaps I judged poorly because they appeared to be identical to my own feelings.

"Is this real? Is it a permanent change?" he asked, hope straining his voice.

"It is a gift of the solstice night," I answered. "It is not real. Not yet. But it could be, I think. For now, it is a trick of moonlight. It will disappear in the light of day. Or else, it will become a trick of sunlight and disappear with the rising of the night."

My words came from another part of me, as if something or someone in me knew more than I did, the Dragon part of my soul, maybe.

A look of despair shadowed his face, "What are you saying?"

"It is, I believe, a matter of choosing. I can be like this, my human self, in the dark, for you alone. And a beast by daylight at court in front of others."

I stopped myself. This was the Goddess Rhiannon speaking. Or it was me, but as her messenger. I could feel her voice behind my own, her golden glory surrounding me. I was delivering a message on her behalf. I was not quite sure yet what it was or what it meant. I kept going, "Or I can be my human self at court during the day so everyone will see that you did not marry a monster after all, and you can be proud of the wife at your side."

"And they would envy my stupid luck in marrying the most entrancing woman in the realm," he grinned like a young squire.

"And I would be a beast at night when we are alone," I said, my words soft as an echo in the quiet of predawn.

He looked at me crestfallen and shook his head, "That's an impossible choice for me to make."

"You must choose," I said. "Or I'll go back to being a beast forever. I'm certain of it."

"I cannot. You have suffered too much. I heard some of the comments today. My heart was breaking for you." He looked at me with his sky-blue eyes, still mesmerizing to my fifteen-year-old self. "It is your choice alone. Your life," he said. "You must be the one to decide."

The moment he said those words: *Your choice alone. Your life,* I heard the second turn of the key, the click, and the rest of the shackles from the curse were removed from my body. I felt it as strongly as if I had been tied down to the floor with real chains again. The message of the Goddess had been delivered and received, a message of freedom. I felt alive and full of light, and I laughed as I imagined Rhiannon did too. This was the essence of her wisdom, that all creatures, beast, crow, dragon, or woman, deserved the freedom to choose their own life. Though I knew there was one more turn of the key, I couldn't imagine anything else of importance changing and put it out of my mind.

"You have done it, Sir Gawain. The curse is lifted."

"What did I do?" he blinked in confusion.

"You gave me back sovereignty over my own life. Quite ironic really, since this was the answer to the riddle that saved your uncle's life."

"Indeed. Your life is your choice, My Lady."

"Gallantly said, husband. Though the world we live in would disagree with you."

"It will be so where it counts, between us," said Gawain.

"I will hold you to that," I said.

It was only then I let all my longing and desire for him bloom, "Will you take me to our bed that I may enjoy some of those wedded privileges now?"

Gawain lifted me into his arms and carried me to our nuptial bed. We spent the rest of the night and late into the morning, playing those games best known to newlyweds, sometimes tender, sometimes shy and sometimes like a tempest filled with laughter.

I did notice that my senses were as sharp as ever, smelling the passion of love, the sweat of a man's desire, an unerring feel for those places on the body that love to be touched. The more feral aspect of my nature reached out to Gawain during our love making. It surprised him but he found delight in it, after some hesitation. We both ended up with some bite marks, but they were only human teeth and the bites easily hidden beneath clothing. The stronger legs and arms of the beast also remained, though without their furry covering. My hair had almost doubled in length and reached near my knees. My appetite was not entirely tame either. I would never be a lady of minuscule portions or proportions. During a pause in our coupling, I threw myself on the fruit and cheese left for us as a collation for our night of wedded love.

I had a moment of trepidation as the first rays of sun streaked across our marriage bed. But I remained my human self and jumped up and down on the bed, doing a little mad jig of thanks to Rhiannon. Gawain laughed in astonishment, and I fell back into his arms.

The sun was past its midpoint when we contemplated getting out of our nuptial bed, without much enthusiasm. I looked over at the discarded golden dress in dismay. "I cannot leave our chamber in the same gown. It won't fit me now."

"We'll have to remain here then," said my husband, not at all upset at the prospect.

I made a face at him, and he took me in his arms again with a growl worthy of the beast I was so recently.

Once we both calmed down, my new husband, eager to please me, asked, "Should I go find one of the maids for you? Or perhaps a lady of the court could assist you?"

"No. I think not." To have one of those vicious gossips come to help me was unthinkable. There was only one possible choice. "Would you mind fetching Lady Morgause?" I asked.

"My mother? Of course. I will go right now, my dearest solstice silver moon miracle." He kissed me and I giggled. I pressed both hands over my mouth. I hadn't giggled in ages. I wasn't sure I liked it.

Gawain fetched something from his surcoat pocket. "I kept it for you as you asked. I'm returning it now." He handed me my little wren.

I set her down on the bedside table with a kiss. “My treasure.”

“May you receive many more treasures and may I be the one to gift them to you.”

We kissed as he tried to dress, hopping from one foot to the other, pulling his breeches on, then his boots. He was out the door while I still helped tuck his shirt in and tame his curly hair. It was such a thrill, running my human hands through his hair. I could never tire of it.

Chapter Twenty-Nine

I walked over to the window to witness this newly made day, with me, newly remade in it. Eyes closed, I hugged myself, while rays of sunlight washed over my human form and stood there a while, reveling in all of it. I looked over at the unmade bed, smiling to myself and walked to the table holding leftovers from last night. The blackberries gleamed darkly in their bowl. I crammed a handful into my mouth.

I heard a brief knock. My husband walked in with his mother. I stood up too quickly, scrambling for my cloak. The bowl fell from my hands and broke. It was still my instinct to hide myself from people. I was not yet used to my remade self and despite the sleeping gown, felt too naked without my usual covering.

Lady Morgause looked me up and down, "Gawain told me to bring some gowns. He wouldn't say anymore. But he couldn't stop grinning. I can see why now."

"Thank you for coming," I mumbled, shoving the last of the berries into my mouth. "Your Highness," I added. "Mother?" I wasn't sure what to call her.

"Call me Morgause, or Lady Morgause when in company. But not mother. Please."

"Yes, Lady Morgause. I need your help."

"You do," she replied. "It takes more work to be a girl than to be a beast. Especially at Arthur's court." She turned to her son, "Gawain, go to my rooms and keep company with your father while I deal with your wife. And make yourself presentable."

Gawain didn't argue with his mother. "I'll be back soon," he said, blowing me a kiss. He grabbed some clothing from a trunk and withdrew from our chambers.

"Not too soon. Adorning real beauty is slow work," said the lady, mostly to herself. She cupped my chin in her hand and looked into my eyes like a Bandrui would, with her soul, seeking what lived in mine. I could not move until Lady Morgause let go with a satisfied little grunt and I could breathe again.

The lady fetched two housemaids waiting outside the door. They walked in with creams, washcloths, combs, clothes, jewelry boxes and went to work on me. They were efficient and precise, soaking the washcloths in the water basin to clean me, combing my hair, and finally dressing me. Lady Morgause dictated all of it.

"You need a simple dress. Let's not hide your beauty," she said, as she picked a silver gown made of rushed silk. It was tight on me.

"It is meant to fit snugly," she said. "It shows the figure to advantage when you have one. And you do."

It was praise indeed. The lady had an exquisite figure. The dress must fit her perfectly.

"Your hair is better than any jewelry," she said. "No fancy hats or veils required. Let's find something to keep it out of your face."

She took a thin circlet of gold out of a jewelry box and set it on my head. Finally, she brought out a necklace with a single ruby that she clasped around my neck. The stone was warm against the hollow of my throat. It gave off a calming feeling to the touch.

"The ruby is charmed for protection. Even your mentor would approve," said Lady Morgause with a half-smile.

I should have realized she knew about me being Myrddin's pupil. She was a Bandrui.

Lady Morgause gave me a pair of soft leather shoes that matched the dress. They were a bit big on me, so one of the maids added an extra piece of leather that she cut to fit the shape of my foot and placed inside each shoe.

The lady took another look at me, "I think you are ready to deal with any court or even the Saxons."

A wave of dread clenched my throat. "The Saxons! I forgot. Myrddin wanted me to attend a meeting with the Saxons."

"Not to worry," she replied. "The meeting was postponed till this afternoon, which is to say, shortly."

"How do you know?" I asked, still worried. I couldn't bear to disappoint the druid.

"Myrddin Emrys came to see me when neither you nor Gawain were visible this morning or for the noon meal. I suggested to postpone the meeting till later in the day."

I held her hands in mine, relieved. "Thank you. I'm grateful for your help."

She shook her hands away. I might have squeezed too hard.

"No need. I was actually on my way to you when Gawain intercepted me." She took a critical look at me. "You're ready."

Gawain walked in and stopped in his tracks, not saying a word.

"Well?" I asked. "Will I do?"

"You will do very well, my Lady wife." He grinned, again, and offered me his arm. His mother took the other.

I had no idea what kind of comments I would get from the courtly demoiselles and their knights now. I hoped once again Myrddin would be close by. It was between noon and vespers when we walked into the Great Hall. The courtiers were all busy, listening to a bard strumming his lute, playing cards, reciting poetry. Queen Guinevere was officiating, Sir Lancelot ever at her side. I saw no Myrddin and no King Arthur and began to panic.

Gawain squeezed my hand. "Never fear. I will not leave your side unless you wish it."

I took a breath. Everything stopped. And once again all eyes were on me. The wide eyes and opened mouths spoke of shock. There was no warmth in it, but it wasn't like the previous revulsion. There was speculation and envy in the stares. And then we were surrounded, as by a flock of screaming birds.

Many who had scorned me and vilified me came to congratulate me: *It must be the sanctity of the wedding ceremony. God took pity on you and took you back into the fold. You are blessed.* Many of the comments were for Gawain: *We were so worried about you. I hope the transformation happened before marital consummation. It turns out you are still a lucky man after all.* There were a lot of slaps on the back and snickering from his fellow knights. *No wonder you didn't appear for the noon meal.*

We reached the queen who stood up and gave a charming smile for all to see.

"Welcome to Camelot, Lady Ragnell. You belong here after all."

Everyone applauded and the music resumed after a signal from the queen.

I didn't care for her benediction, but I made a perfunctory curtsy. If I belonged anywhere it was in the Gwynedd woods. They accepted me because I looked more like them now.

"Where is the meeting with the Saxons? Do you know?" I whispered to Gawain. I was eager to get out of here and find Myrddin.

"Not to worry," he said, squeezing my hand.

Despite his conspiratorial blink, I worried until the three of us left the banquet hall. Lady Morgause led the way. The inane exaltation of the courtiers cheapened the sacredness of what had happened on the solstice night, and I didn't believe a word of their unctuous praise. I hated having to keep a smile pasted on my face as Lady Morgause had recommended I do: "Think what you want and keep smiling. It's the only way to navigate Queen Guinevere's court."

I didn't want to navigate such shallow waters as slanderous gossip or scheme my way to advantage with the queen. The thought of it made me gag, like having to return to that church for mass on Sundays.

I was still pondering all the things I might have to do that I didn't want to in this newly made life when we arrived at King Arthur's Hall of the Round Table. Sentries opened the double doors for us. I saw more people crowding the room than could fit the twelve chairs meant for the table. Some stood apart in groups. All the knights were easily recognizable as they wore the white cape with the red dragon on it. The only noticeable difference between Arthur and his knights was the crown on his head. And my runes shimmered, attracted by the power of Myrddin's protections, wrapped all around the king. I covered my wrist with my other hand to quiet the rising of my magic. No one noticed. They were too agitated, speaking loudly and interrupting one another until they saw us, and talk fell away.

"My lords," said Lady Morgause with a grace and aplomb I could never hope to match, "I've brought Lady Ragnell and Sir Gawain to sit with you, as was requested."

I made an attempt at saying hello, gesturing with my hand, and stood there. Myrddin bore his unfathomable black eyes on mine and then a smile as big as a rainbow broke out all over his face. He stood up and everyone else followed suit.

Myrddin asked, "Will someone offer their chair to Lady Ragnell?"

They all offered their chair at once. I didn't know what to do.

Gawain whispered, "Entrancing. I told you."

"I think it best for the lady to sit next to me," said Myrddin.

And so, I did, thanking the knight who gave up his seat. I recognized Gawain's brother, Agravain. Lady Morgause retired, after a nod at the company who all bowed to her.

"You must thank your mother for me before she leaves," I said to Gawain.

"You can thank her yourself later," he said. "She won't be going home quite yet."

I was glad to hear him say so. I would need her wisdom in this place. Gawain kissed my hand and left my side to sit by his uncle.

King Arthur spoke, "Lady Ragnell. It is good to see you looking so… Like yourself. Some of us were led to believe you were abducted by Fairy Folk." He gave a pointed look at Myrddin.

"That's one way of putting it," I said. It came out rougher than I intended but everyone laughed and the tension in the room eased.

The king turned his attention back to the assembled knights. "My Lords and Gentle Lady, we are here to discuss the terms of peace."

I wasn't sure there was anything *gentle* about me. If there was, I had forgotten it.

A tall Saxon man with a rough beard stood up. His weathered armor was made from pieces of leather sewn together. He smelled of brine and smoke. He had the look of a warrior, not a politician. "How can you guarantee that you will respect the peace terms? There is nothing to keep you from betraying us the moment we accept. What insurance can you give us?" His guttural accent fit his untamed appearance.

Myrddin answered, "There is something that would keep us from breaking the peace agreement between our tribes."

The Saxon warrior motioned for Myrddin to go on.

"This Lady right here," said Myrddin as he gestured towards me.

The Saxon man scoffed. "None can deny her beauty, but isn't she already married?"

"That she is," answered Myrddin. "To Sir Gawain, the king's own nephew."

"Why should that matter to me?" the Saxon warrior blurted out.

"Because she is your blood," replied Myrddin.

The Saxon glared at both Myrddin and me as if treachery was afoot. No one dared speak.

I swallowed my fear, "Myrddin Emrys is correct. I am granddaughter to Hengist, your great warrior and chieftain."

"No," said the Saxon leader. "There is no granddaughter."

I took another breath. "I am not known to you because my mother left your family before I was born."

Though he veiled it quickly, the shock of recognition broke over the Saxon's face. "Rowena's child," he murmured.

"Indeed, I am Rowena's child." It was the first time I claimed my parentage so publicly and I felt it keenly. I grabbed hold of the table to steady myself.

The Saxon struggled to master his own emotions. The room was filled with silent anticipation until he spoke. "My name is Oeric." He hesitated. "I am your uncle."

It was my turn to be unsettled by the encounter. I did not expect to meet actual family members. A family who had ostracized my mother.

"I never knew what happened to my sister," said Oeric.

Somer's description and my own experience in the bath at Caernarfon were too tender to discuss in such a setting.

Oeric turned to Myrddin who was waiting, with a perfectly bland expression on his face, when I knew he had been scheming for years to bring this peace treaty about.

"My men and I need a moment to confer." The Saxon leader summoned his tribesmen. There was a mere instant of hesitation at the door, the guards waiting until the king gave his permission to let them out. The Saxons withdrew and all of us waited.

The king addressed me, breaking the anxious silence, "Lady Ragnell, it gives me much pleasure and relief that I was finally able to fulfill my oath to your father. His greatest wish was to unite our families."

He remembers. Did he know all along who I really was? I wonder. He can't have. He was appalled at the idea of Gawain having to marry a beast. Still. Arthur was hard to read. I saw, for the first time, the shrewd politician behind the warrior and the knight. He was Myrddin's pupil in more ways than I could ever be, essential to the druid's vision for Briton.

"Tell me, is there anything you would like for a wedding present?" he asked.

King Arthur was eager to make up for his previous lack of enthusiasm and for the lack of generosity and graciousness offered by his wife and the court on my wedding day. Before I could answer, the Saxon delegation returned. They stood as one, while Oeric eyed the whole gathering, until his gaze settled on Arthur. The silence deepened.

"If you think so highly of our blood as to marry this one to your nephew," said Oeric, pointing at me. "Then, we have an agreement."

Myrddin was so pleased, he applauded the Saxon and everyone else followed suit. It was as he hoped. Never mind that I'd saved the king and devised the marriage to save myself. None of the men in this hall could fathom that peace was achieved because of me.

The king lifted his cup, "Let us drink to peace and to the power of blood to unite us."

And just like that, the Saxons became our allies. They recovered the kingdom of Kent in the ensuing treaty that was ratified right then.

As the meeting broke up, King Arthur came over to congratulate us on our marriage. It was a more wholehearted greeting than before. Then Gawain took it upon himself to get further acquainted with my Saxon relative and introduce himself officially as my husband.

The king turned his attention to me. "We were interrupted before. I would bestow a wedding present upon you. What do you wish for?"

"Since you ask, Sire, there is something," I said. "I have seen your banner with its red dragon everywhere. It would please me above all else to meet the real dragon."

Disbelief drew itself on the king's face. He, no doubt, expected something in the order of jewelry or gowns.

"Our dragon has grown ill-tempered. It hides from us, despite our bond. I fear it might attack you."

I forced myself to smile. "I'm not afraid. Dragon nature is known to me."

The king glanced over at Myrddin to confirm such an assertion.

The druid nodded. "Tis true, Sire."

"Very well," said the king. "It is an unusual request but if that is what you really want."

"It is," I affirmed.

"Then you shall have it." He announced it like a decree, the kind only a king would utter. "Will you let me know if you receive any communication from the beast?" he asked.

It irked me to have any dragon referred to as a beast. But then, I had been called that, and worse, but a day ago. I forced a smile again. "I will, Sire."

"I'll order some of my archers to accompany you," said the king.

"No need. Myrddin Emrys knows the way, doesn't he?" I asked.

"He does," replied the king.

I turned to the druid. "Will you come, Myrddin?"

"I will, My Lady," said Myrddin.

It was odd to hear Myrddin call me anything other than Dryw donn. He was being formal in front of King Arthur and his men. The Saxon delegation was invited to the evening meal, but I said I would go now to see the red dragon. I had no desire to sit at another banquet quite so soon.

"I know many who will be disappointed by your absence," said King Arthur.

He meant to flatter me. It didn't. "I'm sure they'll get over it," I said. I saw a frown form on the kingly brow and quickly added, "With so many distinguished guests in attendance and my husband by your side."

King Arthur smiled, shaking his head, as if I was an unruly child he was willing to indulge for now. Gawain returned from speaking with my uncle and stood next to the king.

"I know you will be safe with Myrddin Emrys," said Gawain. It sounded more like a question to my ear. "But it seems a foolish errand."

"Will you take back your word so quickly, husband, and forbid me do as I please?"

Gawain blushed. "I will not. But I would prefer that you not walk into danger needlessly."

"I would not do that. I would not have survived the last four years if I had. Methinks that is the province of fearless young knights." I meant to say foolish, but I didn't want to be unkind.

My Saxon uncle walked over to speak with me. As he got closer, the feral part of me could smell the animal in him. He walked like a wildcat, an easy stride that belied the power of his thick muscular legs.

"I hear you are going to challenge the red dragon. I would watch," he said.

"No, it's a peaceful meeting," I replied. "Like the one we attended."

"It seems you have family and magician to protect you, My Lady wife." Satisfied that I was safe, Gawain kissed my hand and together with the king, rejoined his fellow knights who swarmed around him with a hundred questions.

My Saxon uncle bared his teeth into a smile. "You interest me. I've heard so many tales about you. I don't know what to make of them. You have the look of your mother. Rowena was more a mother to me than my own mother before she was *sullied*."

The runes began to burn on my wrist. I felt rage rise up in me. The insult was pointed. My hand flew to my throat as the ruby sitting there began to cool the intensity of my feelings. Protection, Lady Morgause had said. She meant protection against my own, more volatile, feelings.

"I have offended you. My apologies, Lady Ragnell." There was no contrition in his voice.

"Not at all," I answered, having regained my composure. "My mother found more love and understanding in the last year of her life than she ever did among her own people."

The Saxon surprised me with a grin. "A true daughter of Saxons. I hope you never become so tame as to forget yourself Lady Ragnell."

"I don't intend to, Uncle Oeric." It was the first time I owned our kinship. I felt his equal in that moment. Tension began to leave Myrddin's body. He had kept quiet the whole time. But I could tell he worried I might destroy his entire peace plan in my one interaction with the Saxon.

"If we are done with this conversation, shall we go before it gets dark?" asked Myrddin.

"Lead the way, druid," said Oeric.

"The cave of the red dragon is a distance from the castle. We must get our horses," said Myrddin.

"Oh. I'll never be able to ride in this." I looked down at the silver gown. "Do you have my tartan?"

"I do," he acknowledged. "I had it cleaned. I thought you might want to wear it again." He knew somehow that, although it was hidden now, the beast was still here, part of me.

"Can we go to your apartments first then?" I asked.

"We can," he said.

We made our way to Myrddin's rooms, Oeric in tow. I told my Saxon uncle to stand outside the door when we got there. I was comfortable enough undressing in front of Myrddin but not with the Saxon warrior, uncle or no. Myrddin helped me untie the dress. I went into his bedroom to take it off and put on the tartan. It was such a relief to wrap it around my body. There was more cloth now than before, but it worked fine. I kept the shoes which fit me well. I put the cloak back on, more out of habit than real need. I was ready.

Oeric was waiting for us as we walked back out. He took one look at me and nodded, "This is more who you are. Isn't it?"

His observation startled me, but he was right. The transformation was so new, I still felt unsettled in myself.

"It's more practical," I said.

We reached the stables. Young Mordred was nowhere to be found. Other squires helped us get Rhian and Espoir ready. The Saxon found his mare. I had expected a stallion.

Catching my stare, he said, "My mare is more agile and smarter than any old stallion."

We rode out of the stables, galloped through the meadowland and took a left turn into the woods. This is where I felt most myself, riding Espoir, in the woods. My uncle was correct.

I worried Espoir might need time to adjust to my latest incarnation, but his eyes were soft, his lower lip loose and there was no tail swishing. He knew me regardless of appearances. He knew my touch, my voice. He knew me better than I knew myself. I broke first into a gallop.

"You ride like a Saxon lad," said my uncle, as we slowed to a walk. He sounded pleased.

"Forgive me, but I ride like myself," I replied. "And like I love my horse."

Oeric grinned. "Well said, my niece. It's the only way."

I didn't think I'd like him, but I did. He was a man of strong spirit and stronger opinions.

"You are fiercer than your mother was," said Oeric.

He petted his horse's neck. I held my breath.

"My sister was made of gentler stuff than the rest of our tribe and did not fare well with our father. I loved her and I *am* sorry for the way she was treated. She didn't deserve it."

That was all he said. But it lifted a burden from me I didn't know I still carried.

Chapter Thirty

Myrddin led us through the woods to a cave which didn't look big enough to hold a dragon. We stepped inside and began to walk downhill. My eyes still held enough of the beast to let me see in the dark. I found it reassuring.

The Saxon grumbled behind us, "Will one of you light a torch? I am not blessed with your all-seeing eyes."

Myrddin and I smiled at each other. The druid took a torch from one of the sconces in the rock wall of the corridor. He spoke the words of fire to light it. My runes responded to his call with a frisson up my spine and a tingling on my wrist. The corridor meandered endlessly, and I began to wonder if we were heading for the underworld. The Saxon was a man of sun and sky and struggled with his breath. Eventually we reached the end of it. The cave opened up. It was larger than the one at Dinas Emrys. The lake was smaller, but it shone like obsidian dotted with starlight. I heard the Saxon unsheathe his sword.

I turned on him, anger flaring. "Put that sword back in its scabbard now, Saxon. I am here for a conversation. If you cannot get that through your head, get out."

If my tone surprised him, he didn't let on. He smiled a little. "Forgive me. It's a bad habit of mine when about to face a monster."

To his credit, he did comply. I could feel his nervousness, as he kept huffing behind me.

"Stay back. You too, Myrddin. I wish to go alone."

"Are you certain, Dryw donn?" asked the druid.

"I am, Myrddin."

As I walked away, I overheard the Saxon ask Myrddin, "Is it courage or madness?"

"Neither. It is love," answered Myrddin. He was right as always.

The rumbling reverberated throughout the cave and doubt crept into my mind. What if the red dragon was nothing like my white dragon? What if I was making a huge mistake and would pay for it with my life, after everything? I calmed myself or the ruby did its work. *No. I am what I am. It will be all right. And it's much too late for such considerations.*

The red dragon appeared like a moving mountain out of the darkness. They were lit from within, burnished scales glowing. Eyes like two suns. So different from the white dragon. And yet there was kinship in the towering shifting slowness; another creature of before time, such different divinity from the Gods, bearing no resemblance to humans or human aspirations. Incompatible with this new Christian era infecting us like the plague would in a few short years.

"Who dares intrude upon my rest?" they growled with a voice like rolling thunder.

"No need to speak so loudly. I can hear you perfectly."

My casual tone surprised them. They stopped and stretched their neck toward my face and sniffed, like any creature would, except it was a squall and blew me on my back.

"Who are you? I can smell Dragon in you," they growled.

I was still recovering, righting myself, when they yelled, "Speak!"

I did my best to remain calm and remember all that I was. "I am Ragnell. Dragon is my kin since I was on the Isle of Skye."

That disclosure completely changed their demeanor. There was no diffidence after that. Only eagerness. They laid their head down next to me.

"You know my love on the island. There is a piece of my love in your heart. Isn't there?"

"There is," I said.

"How is my love of the Fairy Pools?" they asked.

"I dare not say." A dragon's reaction could start a fire storm.

"Say it." They were growling and pleading at once.

I couldn't refuse. "They are dying."

The red dragon sighed. It was a storm. "So am I."

"Is there anything I can do for you?" I asked.

They paused then said, "We wish to be set free and be with our love before we die."

"You are bound to King Arthur."

"He can unbind me."

"I will ask."

"Thank you, Dryw donn."

"How do you know this name?"

"You are that druid's kin as well, *Emrys*."

There was such contempt in their voice, I couldn't understand it until they said: "The one who bound us to the king."

I'd forgotten Myrddin's role in the binding. In many ways, it must be similar to the binding intended for me: make a slave of us in mind and body. *No wonder Myrddin knew so much about its effects on me and what it should or shouldn't do,* I thought. "I'm so sorry. I suffered from a similar binding myself, until recently."

"There are remnants of its stink clinging to you still," they said.

"Will it ever go away?" I asked.

"I cannot say," they answered.

Cannot say or won't say? "I'm sorry about Myrddin Emrys doing this to you. He's not a bad man."

"He's a beast. Like us. And he was a fourteen-year-old boy, trying to save himself." The red dragon managed to have contempt and compassion for Myrddin at the same time. "I can smell the runes on you both. And that Saxon whelp. Your kin as well."

"We are all kin, in some way," I said with a half-smile.

The red dragon moaned, "If only human folk knew that."

I could say nothing in response. But my whole body shivered with it. *If only human folk knew that, indeed.* I thanked them. "I will relay your message and attempt to convince the king."

"Is there anything you wish from me?" they asked.

"Nothing. Your presence is gift enough for that part of my soul which is Dragon."

A tear fell from their eye. They turned around and shuffled back into the darkness.

Myrddin and Oeric waited where I left them. I was in no mood to speak. No one said a word until we were back outside. In the distance, a red glow illuminated the castle with the last rays of the setting sun.

Oeric broke our silence. "You're braver than any of my warriors."

"If you think that was bravery, you're a fool, Saxon," I snapped.

He tensed but didn't retaliate. Gave me a wide berth after that.

Myrddin was gentle with me. "You don't need to speak. Not unless you want to."

I turned to face him. "You must help me set them free."

"That would not be wise, Dryw donn," he argued.

"They are *dying*."

"You do not know what you ask," he argued.

I could still see the dragon's tear falling from their eye. I knew the image would haunt me until I accomplished what they asked of me.

"I do know. Their suffering is my suffering. I am determined."

Understanding reached Myrddin's eyes. "Only Arthur can undo it," he said.

"He will listen to you," I said.

"Not anymore. He's a grown man," he replied, a trace of worry circling his words.

Upon our return I took my leave of my Saxon uncle and Myrddin. I headed for Gawain's apartments. My attire surprised him.

"What happened to the silver gown?" he asked.

"I left it in Myrddin's rooms," I replied. "I needed something comfortable to ride."

Gawain shook his head. "You cannot present yourself at court like this. You know that?"

"I understand. But at home or to go riding, this is what I will wear."

He sighed. "As you wish. But perhaps we can work on a more presentable version of this clothing?"

"I'll do my best, husband." Being conciliatory was tiresome but appeared necessary.

"My mother has a great seamstress in her employ. I'm sure she'll work with you on an outfit that fits your needs, whatever you desire."

"I thank you, husband."

Lady Morgause did send over her seamstress, and we came up with a combination that gave me the freedom of a tartan with leggings underneath but could look like a dress from the back with sleeves and a surcoat. It worked so well, I had her make me a few of them. Lavinia would have been intrigued.

When King Arthur requested my presence in the Hall of the Round Table, I put on a proper gown embroidered with flowers and gold thread. The attire was generously provided by Lady Morgause once more.

"Be sweet, be clever, use your wits and your charm. And don't let him bully you, or any of them," she admonished as I took my leave.

"I don't know that I have your gift for courtly manners," I said.

"You'll be fine. Trust your instincts," she said.

"*That* I can do." I curtsied and left.

I looked around the hall at the knights, including my husband, and felt outnumbered. I wondered if they would listen though I knew that chivalry dictated they must. Myrddin was not seated with them but rather stood beside his king. He gave me a nod of encouragement. So did an older knight with graying hair. It took me a moment to recognize Uncle Kay, my father's dearest friend. He was absent at my arrival, and I had not seen him at the church or the banquet. But here he was, though changed. His presence lifted my spirits. I smiled and nodded back. He had the worn-down look of someone beaten by the Fates, with eyes full of sadness.

"Will you tell me of your encounter with the red dragon, Lady Ragnell?" asked the king. "Myrddin wouldn't say a word, that it was your story to tell."

"They request their freedom." I was doing my best to restrain myself and be polite.

"And why should I grant it?" he asked.

"Because they have served you for many years and it's time. Because they are dying."

I saw the surprise on the king's face and around the table.

"The red dragon is the symbol of our country," said the king. "Would you have us be without it?"

"You have it on your flags and banners. Isn't that enough?"

I heard the shocked murmurings. I wasn't being sweet enough in my answers, not like the demoiselles they were used to. But I wasn't like them. I could never be.

When the noise died down, the king said, "These beasts have lived for thousands of years, as long as the earth itself. Even if what you say is true, they might take years to die."

"If you were dying, would you want to spend your last years in fetters, in a cave, alone, or would you prefer to be free?"

The king narrowed his eyes. "You do speak plainly, My Lady. But you cannot compare us to that…"

"To what? That beast? That monster?" I took the words out of his mouth, challenging him, as we both knew such a creature I was called, not two days before. "A creature with more divinity in each of their breath than we can ever hope to attain."

My words shocked the assembly and elicited a communal intake of breath. Had I gone too far, placing dragons on a higher plane than men?

"Enough!" He raised his kingly hand. "I'll consider your request."

"Not my request, Sire. Theirs."

"I stand corrected," said the king. He was trying to be amicable but was losing his patience with me.

"How do you know the beast is dying?"

I turned to face the questioner. Sir Lancelot was standing. He towered over the assembly, his white cape with silver filigree shining. The rest of them looked drab by comparison.

"Because they told me so," I answered with a calm I didn't feel.

"They told you so? You speak with dragons then?"

He was mocking me. There were a few chuckles around the table.

"Yes I do, Sir Lancelot. Some of us are more gifted than others."

He might have been the greatest knight of Camelot, but I did not trust him or his shiny cloak one whit. I must have been glaring at him because he looked away and pretended to laugh.

Lancelot was not one to give up easily. He addressed his fellow knights, "I'm with our king on this. It would be wrong to let the symbol of our country desert us on a whim."

I felt the power of the runes, fueled by the rage of the beast I once was, surge at the word *whim. How dare he?* I thought. Myrddin and Gawain each tried to catch my attention, shaking their heads, to warn me or stop me.

"This is no *whim*, Sir Knight," I said between clenched teeth.

Lancelot turned his gaze upon me. A sneer lingered on his lips.

"Do you not understand the pain of loss, the terror and fear of never seeing your beloved again, being wrenched away from your one true love? When your only wish is to spend your last hours with them. Does that mean nothing to you?"

Lancelot froze and turned pale at my words. He swallowed hard and sat down silently. It was so unexpected, I knew not what to make of it.

King Arthur interrupted as I was about to press on. "Lady Ragnell. There is something else I would speak with you about."

I tried to breathe and calm myself down. I put my hand on the ruby for solace. It helped.

"Now that you are my nephew's wife, you must reclaim your full status," said the king.

Here we go. I must claim my lands back from my brother so Gawain can inherit it all.

"We wouldn't want to deprive your children from their inheritance, would we?"

Claim my future children as well as my inheritance. Why don't you. "How do you propose I do that?" I asked. "My brother won't relinquish what he believes is his due and his right. He went to great lengths to take it from me."

"Yes. I've heard the details of his conspiracy from Myrddin Emrys," the king answered. "Which is why I believe he needs to be made accountable in an official capacity."

He wanted to chastise my brother publicly. "We can find a pretext to invite him to court," suggested the king. "And then we present you, so he realizes that he has failed."

"I'd have to willingly participate in humiliating my brother."

"Don't you want revenge for all you suffered?" The king was surprised by my hesitation.

"I did. But I'm not so certain anymore." I surprised myself. The whole story was so sordid, it made me itch. I wanted no part of it anymore.

"The man wanted my head and my throne. You know that well enough, Lady Ragnell. He must be taken to task. A knight must take responsibility for his misdeeds, one way or another. I'm asking you to claim your lands back. Anyone else would leap at the opportunity."

"You want me to claim my lands back for Gawain's sake, and I don't have any objection to that." I wanted him to be aware that I knew why he wanted me to do this. But it was the natural order of things for the king, and he didn't find anything wrong with it. He had already forgotten the answer to the riddle that saved his life. I decided to play my last card.

"On one condition," I said.

"Woman, you have a bad habit of bargaining with your king," he said, banging his fist on the table. My father had done the same.

"I'm sorry, Sire." I looked down as if contrite. I held my wrist marked with runes to temper their power activated by the intensity of the emotions running through my body.

The king looked at Myrddin, shaking his head, as if to say, *your pupil is more trouble than she is worth*, but I wasn't more trouble, I was a prize, with the entire Gwynedd province at stake. It was the easiest way to grab a huge swath of land and place it into the hands of the crown. He glared back at me and raised his arm in the air in frustration. "Go ahead, ask."

"I will claim my lands from my brother if you free the red dragon," I said.

The king addressed his nephew, exasperation writ large all over his face, "Nephew, have you no control over your wife?"

Gawain bit down on his lip. He would not stand against Arthur, not for anyone, but he didn't speak against me, even though I shamed him in front of his king. Would even one of these knights speak on my behalf?

"Sire, can we not grant Lady Ragnell her wish? There's no urgency for the red dragon's service as we enter this time of peace. Lady Ragnell has suffered much and does not ask anything for herself."

My heart soared with affection for the older man. Though I thought of him as family, Lord Kay was not my kin but Arthur's. He was the king's uncle. "Lady Ragnell," he said with a bow. "I missed all the recent proceedings but heard the news of your wedding and your miraculous recovery. I am glad of it for your sake and your father's."

My eyes filled. I could kiss him. We all waited on the king's answer.

"Your words are hard to ignore, uncle," said the king. He turned to his favored knight, "Lancelot, what say you?"

Lancelot cleared his throat, subdued, unlike himself, and said, "Sire, I believe the lady's character to be worthy of your clemency."

They all gawked at Lancelot, including me. It was clear the king expected a different answer. He scoffed, "Lady Ragnell, you are persuasive. You will have my answer shortly."

I was dismissed and the meeting adjourned. It was all I would get from the king. I saw Lord Kay speak further with him and Myrddin as I left the Hall with my husband.

"Take care, Ragnell. Do not make an enemy of Sir Lancelot or any of the king's knights."

"It's not my intention, husband," I replied.

"You have a privileged position but speak too plainly, and act too forcefully," said Gawain. "As if the rules of courtly manners do not apply to you."

"It's who I am." I said. "You didn't seem to mind between the sheets."

Gawain grinned, then pressed my hand against his lips with a great deal of fervor.

A few ladies of the court strolled by, giggling. I wondered if they had heard us. I realized I didn't care if they did. It was a liberating feeling. I had the urge to kiss my husband.

"I say this for your own sake, because I love you," he said, his sky-blue eyes shining into mine. Eyes to get lost in if one wasn't careful.

It was the first time he told me he loved me, and my heart swelled, for I had loved him from the first. Yet I felt the hackles rise on my back though I didn't have them anymore. The urge to kiss him died. The phrase *for your own sake* bothered me. I thought he said those things more for his sake than mine. I didn't want to start an argument, so I changed the subject.

"Tell me, husband. Why was Lord Kay absent until today?"

"He was burying his son," he answered.

"What happened?" I asked. Lord Kay's grieving eyes made too much sense now.

"His son was fighting the Saxons. The king thought it best if Lord Kay stayed away from the peace talks."

"Understandable," I said.

I held on to the hope that Lord Kay's intercession on my behalf and Lancelot's change of heart would work in my favor, and the king would be persuaded to free the red dragon at last. If King Arthur acquiesced to my demand, my instincts told me it would require some sacrifice on my part. But I was blind to what it would entail in the end.

Chapter Thirty-One

The peace held. I feared the king had forgotten my plea for the red dragon, because months went by without an answer. I became pregnant. It was a new experience that was joyous and yet fraught with uncertainty and fear at the same time. All these questions kept whirling in my mind: *Will the baby be human or catch whatever remains of the curse and the beast? Will I die in the birthing bed as my mother before me?*

Gawain was overjoyed. But I was alone most of the time. My husband was either attending meetings with the king and the other knights, or joining tournaments to win more fortune, or he went on quests of one kind or another. Apparently, he wasn't participating in as many tournaments as he used to before our marriage. And the other knights chided him, saying he spent too much time with me. It was hard to believe but he had no reason to lie about it.

When he was home, we attended banquets with the king and queen. I kept pasting a smile on my face and thinking my own thoughts as Lady Morgause had recommended. She was the only one whose company I sought but she went home with her husband a couple of months after the wedding. She left me the silver gown and the ruby necklace.

"Keep the ruby on you at all times. Your spirit is too unruly for this place. It will help keep your emotions in check."

"The fifteen-year-old girl I was would have loved it here, all the dancing and feasting and tournaments," I said. "Now I cannot bear it."

"You will find your way. I have no doubt," she answered.

Her eyes were so full of fire, I wondered how this life was enough for her. But she also had a secret life, as a bandrui. Her departure left me bereft, without a friend.

I asked Myrddin if Lavinia could attend to me as midwife for my baby. "What if I tell Gawain I want Lavinia to be my midwife? And we say that the king's nephew requested her for his wife, without naming me? What can they say?"

"That's a possibility," said Myrddin. "It could even open a path to invite your brother for the naming ceremony when your child is born."

"No. That's too much," I said. "A banquet would be more suitable."

"I'll speak with the king about it," said Myrddin.

"Will you remind him about the dragon, that I'm still waiting on an answer?" I asked.

"I will try, Dryw donn," replied Myrddin. The druid had wrapped so many protective charms around Arthur, that he could no longer influence his kingly protégé. It was frustrating.

I escaped into the woods as often as possible, riding Espoir. It was my solace, but I felt lonely. Myrddin was gone, traveling on the king's behalf, bringing the news of peace wherever he could. Lord Kay had returned to his home, dragging his grief behind him, like a heavy load of unwashed laundry that could never be cleaned.

Lord Kay was the one who brought me the news before he left. I hadn't noticed the deep grooves on his face before. They were a shock up close. His hair had turned white. His body had shrunk, become old. He explained that the king agreed to free the red dragon after the naming ceremony, and after my brother atoned for his despicable behavior, unworthy of a knight.

"Were these the king's words?" I asked.

"Yes, Lady Ragnell. Those were his words exactly," he answered.

"Am I the one to punish my brother or will it be the king's prerogative to do so?" I asked, fuming.

"He believes you both have cause to want him punished. And that you should confront him first and then he will do his part."

"And what of my brother's wife, Lady Amunet?" I asked. "She played a powerful role."

"The king doesn't believe Lady Amunet had any part in it."

I found *that* hard to believe. "Does he not know the lady provided the poisons and made the curse?" *I know she must have pushed Somer toward his worst tendencies, where he was only leaning. And I could see that priest in Beddgelert pushing him as well, in the name of his God.*

"He has been made aware of the details," said Lord Kay.

Since I'd seen the medallion on my brother's chest, I thought as Lavinia did, that Lady Amunet played a substantial role to control my brother's actions and wield his sword.

"You can tell the king I disagree, and that I'm certain Lady Amunet had a strong influence on my brother."

"The king doesn't believe in a woman's influence on her husband as it is not her place."

"Really? Queen Guinevere has no influence at all on the king?"

She had done her best to put a stop to my wedding. She was in charge of all court proceedings. And the queen begged Arthur to leave Lancelot behind every time he left court. She'd smile sweetly at her husband, say she didn't feel safe without Lancelot by her side and that was it. The king would capitulate. I couldn't stomach it. I'd feel queasy watching them and take my leave, blaming my pregnancy. Being pregnant was very useful to get out of courtly life.

"I cannot speak to this," said Lord Kay. "He loves her. Love can be an influence by virtue of its mere existence."

"Indeed, it can be, and also make us blind," I retorted.

Lord Kay would not argue with me. He was too good a man for that. He bowed and kissed my hand and took his leave and his grief with him.

An official letter with the king's seal was sent, requesting Lavinia's presence at my bedside, stating that her renown as a midwife had reached Arthur's court. I was not named in the letter but only referred to as the wife of the king's nephew. The letter also hinted at some sort of pardon if my brother acceded to the request. I wondered if that was maneuvering on the king's part or if it was a real offer. I didn't know and couldn't ask Myrddin about it as he was absent.

I wondered what Somer would make of the letter, but his wife was my greater concern. She would find a way to turn the king's request to her advantage. I thought Somer would be more inclined to refuse but Lady Amunet would persuade him otherwise. If Lavinia did come, I would have to test the accuracy of my theory on her. Thinking about my dear Lavinia gladdened my heart. I hoped and prayed for her arrival.

Despite pleading from my husband and various doctors sent over by the queen, I would not stop riding and refused to be put into any kind of confinement. I threatened to turn the doctors into toads. It was an empty threat, but I was finally left alone. Once on Espoir, my whole body would soften. He was particularly attentive and careful with me. He'd put his nose against my belly and snuffle on it, as if he knew what was happening. He developed a new gait, all of his own, a slow canter really, a motion between walk and trot that was neither and rocked my back gently. I enjoyed it and I could tell the baby enjoyed it too. He kept giving little happy kicks in rhythm with my horse's gait. But there came a point when I was too big to get safely on and off Espoir, even with help from the squires. I hand-walked him or waddled around the meadows with Espoir until I couldn't.

I was getting close to giving birth and had no news. The queen had sent over a midwife. But I thought if I cannot have my Lavinia I would rather send for Gawain's mother. I trusted Lady Morgause over Queen Guinevere any day. I could only sleep on my side and with difficulty. I moaned half the night to the point that Gawain had taken to sleeping in our guest quarters. I understood one of us should be able to sleep but I resented him for it.

Summer had arrived in full force. I was sweating all the time. I could barely walk. I knew my baby was getting ready to come into the world. It was a matter of days. I was at my wits end when Gawain walked into our chambers. I needed help and asked him to send for his mother.

"Do not worry yourself, wife. Lord Gromer Somer agreed to let his midwife help you."

"When?" I grunted, rolling over to my side and to a sitting position.

"A couple of months ago," he answered.

"You've known all this time that Lavinia was coming, and didn't tell me?" My anger went from simmer to boil, and the runes leapt at the strong emotion. I savored their presence. They'd gone dormant with the pregnancy. Making a baby was woman magic, not rune magic.

"There was no point to inform you until now, until it was certain she would be here. I didn't want you to be disappointed if she didn't make it in time for the birth."

Are men that stupid? "No point? How about to relieve my worries on the eve of giving birth for the first time?" I was pacing, or rather wobbling, furious, and wanted to break things.

With his beautiful, worried eyes trained on me, Gawain said, "Calm yourself, wife, you will hurt the baby. That's what I've come to tell you. She has arrived."

"What?" I barked, like the beast I used to be.

"Your Lavinia is here," said my husband.

Before I had a chance to take in the news, there was a knock on the door and we both turned, shouting in unison, "Yes!"

The door opened and I cried out with relief, "Lavinia! Oh, my dearest Lavinia!"

I walked over because I couldn't run and endeavored to hug her despite my enormous belly. She held on to me then stood back to look at me. "It's so good to see you, My Lady, looking so well, and like yourself."

"I look like the barrel I bathe in," I quipped. "But thank you."

Lavinia laughed her deep throaty laugh, and I felt home for the first time in over a year.

She applied a gentle pressure on my big belly. "You are carrying low. It must be a boy."

"I know," I whispered, like a secret incantation, rubbing my hand over my belly.

"Do not speak of it," said Gawain, crossing himself. He was afraid that the Christian God would punish us, or the baby, for our hubris, claiming to know the sex of the child.

Lavinia spoke up. "Do not worry yourself, Sir Gawain. This is simple woman wisdom."

Gawain took in Lavinia's words and sighed. "So glad you are here." It was heartfelt. I had been difficult to live with during the pregnancy, even more stubborn and contrary than usual.

I introduced them to each other before Gawain left, relieved that I was in safe hands.

I wanted to hear all the gossip from home. But Lavinia shushed me and said she would make me one of her broths first. The dark circles under my eyes told her I hadn't been sleeping and that wouldn't do at all. "You need all your strength for the birth," she said.

We ordered boiled water, and I drank her herbal broth, then she massaged my lower back and within half an hour I was fast asleep. I woke up a while later, feeling better and calmer than I had in weeks. I looked around and saw her sitting by the hearth, knitting. My body felt more at ease, like warm water was running through it instead of the fire of the last few months.

"How is Hillel?" I asked.

Lavinia looked up from her knitting, "He is well."

"And you?"

"We are both doing well."

There was more to it, but she wouldn't say, and I didn't probe.

"Tell me, who persuaded whom to let you come?" I asked.

"I'm sure you can guess," she answered.

"My bet is on Lady Amunet getting her way."

"You'd be wrong," said Lavinia.

"Somer?" *He must know he'll be facing humiliation if he comes to the christening.*

"Your brother has grown tired of all the scheming. He wants to face the king."

"Lady Amunet must be displeased with that attitude," I said.

"The mood is very dark," answered Lavinia. "Many servants have quit Dinas Emrys."

"Oh dear. That must be hard on Hillel and on you," I said.

Lavinia smiled but I could see the worry lines between her brows, "We have each other," she said. "We are luckier than most."

"Do they know it's me?" I asked. I worried about that. I thought if she knew, Lady Amunet would be fomenting some new treachery.

"The baron has told them of a beautiful lady who mostly keeps to her rooms and rarely attends banquets. He has no clue as to who you are."

"But didn't the baron attend my birthing day feast?" I asked.

"It was one night. You were fifteen. You've changed," she answered.

"Have I?" I asked.

"You were a child," she said. "You are a woman now, and much more yourself."

"I can tell you it's very difficult to be yourself in a place such as this."

"No doubt." She smiled, commiserating with my plight.

I installed Lavinia in our guest quarters, and we spent every moment of the next few weeks together. When Gawain was home we would eat together, the three of us, in our rooms. Lavinia's presence made everything better. Even my relationship with Gawain improved. We laughed more. We were kinder with each other. Gawain was attentive, caring and not leaving so much. It was the best time of our marriage.

Some people came to visit. Myrddin came by as often as he could. Musicians came to serenade my baby yet to be born. My uncle Oeric visited as well and gifted us a handcrafted wooden cradle for the baby. Gawain discussed the merit of different woods with him and took my uncle to his rooms where he practiced and made his small carvings. I showed my little wren to uncle Oeric, and he was full of admiration for its precision and delicate rendering. I told him how much solace it gave me during my four-year ordeal. This acknowledgment in front of my uncle pleased Gawain enormously.

The sky opened up and a deluge fell over Camelot one late summer evening. It would have to be that night. The contractions came as if in rhythm with the thunder. Images of my mother pregnant in the rain invaded my mind and darkened my spirit.

"If I die, please take care of my baby," I uttered, breathless, between two contractions.

"You are not going to die," said Lavinia with utter conviction in her voice. "You are strong and so is your baby." She was firm with me and held my hand before ordering the servants to bring clean sheets and boiling water.

Giving birth reminded me of my ordeal with the priest and the doctors. It was painful like that, but this time, the pain had a purpose. I was bringing a new life into the world. And that gave me the courage to keep pushing, when I didn't think I could. It went on for a lifetime. Lavinia did not leave my side. She warned me that she could not give me strong herbs because it could affect the baby. But she gave me what she could to fortify me. She brought me several cups throughout the night, and I drank them all. I couldn't imagine what it would have been like without any herbs at all. My body felt ripped apart, torn in two. She kept encouraging me and singing to me, *Ragnella, Nella, Nella.* She timed it with my moans, when I pushed. Having that rhythm in my ear helped.

At last, the contractions came so close together, I could no longer find my breath. "I'm never doing this again," I screamed, grabbing Gawain by his shirt, tearing it in the process. He had made an unfortunate appearance at the worst moment. He stared at me and at Lavinia, wide-eyed, unprepared for the intensity of my outburst and retreated until after the birth.

The baby came with the dawn, as the first rays of sunlight pierced through the last remains of the thunderstorm and splashed across the bed. Lavinia cut the cord, bathed him, swaddled him and brought him to me. I knew he was a boy. I had known it for months. She put him in my arms. I set him on my chest so he could hear my heartbeat, as my mother had done with me, in the last moments of her life.

Everyone came to congratulate me and take a look at the baby. Gawain had tears in his eyes and kept repeating, *My son. My son.* He looked at me with such gratitude for he now had an heir. The king and queen came to visit, and their doctor examined the baby and pronounced him healthy. And Myrddin. He gave my son a charm which I put around his little neck immediately. The skin was so translucent, you could see the blood pulsing underneath. He looked so fragile, it made me nauseous.

Gawain carved a tiny dragon for our son. He painted it red of course, and we hung it above his cradle.

The queen sent one of her demoiselles, *to assist in binding the breasts*.

"No," I said, protecting my breasts with my hands. "Why would I do that?"

The demoiselle answered like I was the most dimwitted creature in Camelot. "To stem the flow of milk."

"Get out. Now," I shouted.

The demoiselle, incensed by my rudeness, left promptly. A nurse followed. I turned her away as well. This was unheard of at court. The nobility did not breastfeed. I assumed they preferred to keep their pretty breasts. But it made no sense to me. I had milk and I was going to feed my son, regardless. My husband knew better than to quarrel with me about it and Lavinia argued on my behalf that the milk of the mother was the one best suited to insure the health of the baby. Eventually they all left except for Lavinia and Gawain.

"I have a name for our son," he said, smiling. "He will be called *Le Bel Inconnu*."

"*The Fair Unknown* is a strange name for a baby boy," I said.

"He is beautiful and still unknown to us," he argued.

"Very true, husband." I smiled at Gawain. "I like it well."

There was a certain poetic violence to the name. It presaged an interesting life.

Lavinia helped me become a mother over the next weeks, showing me how to clean him, wrap him, how to go into the quiet of a daydream when I fed him. I was afraid to break him, terrified his tiny birdlike neck would snap if my hand slipped while holding his head. I would stare at him when he took a nap, afraid he wouldn't wake up, and probe his little body with my finger to make sure. I slept with my infant son on my chest, his ear against my heart so the rhythm of life would be stamped forever into his own heart. He would spread his body over mine like a little frog and we would spend timeless moments of blissful togetherness. I wanted nothing from the world but us.

Invitations were sent out for the feast that would follow the naming ceremony. I knew my brother was invited. Myrddin confirmed it.

"I feel a great deal of trepidation about this," I said to Myrddin, while picking up my baby from his crib. It was nearing his feeding time.

"You won't be alone. You'll be surrounded by friends," he said.

"You misunderstand," I said. "I'm not worried for myself. I worry about what my brother might do, if he is pushed too far."

Myrddin waited for me to say more. He always took the time to listen. It was one of the qualities I loved about him.

"He's become such a stranger to himself. He'll want to tear everything apart if he feels stripped bare, with nothing left to believe in. He could destroy everything around him."

"Like a dragon on a rampage," said Myrddin.

"Yes. Like that," I acquiesced. The comparison sounded plausible. When I remembered the poet and the scholar I cherished and how much he had strayed from himself, I feared a rupture of some kind.

"I don't think he will," said Myrddin. "He is not like you."

Like me. A temperamental beast? I thought.

"But I will convey your concerns to the king. He did offer him a pardon in exchange for your midwife, for Lavinia."

"Was that a genuine offer?" I thought it had been a pretext.

"Not a full pardon," the druid admitted. "King Arthur respects the knight's code of loving the enemy one has defeated, but it is a pardon with conditions."

"Somer has never been good at conditions," I said. I turned my thoughts back to my son. His violet eyes lifted my spirit. I concentrated on the only thing that mattered, feeding my baby.

"His name is the *Fair Unknown*," I told the bishop at our baby's naming ceremony, what Christians called baptism.

"That is not a name," he argued.

"Both his father and I agree on it," I said.

"I chose the name," said Gawain, interrupting the argument before it escalated.

"It was inspired, husband," I said to him. To be in agreement about our son was a sweet feeling and I slipped my arm through Gawain's.

The bishop gave in and poured the water on our baby. Fair wailed at the offence. The holy oils followed. The bishop made the sign of the cross over our baby. Our son's godparents were the king and queen. A great honor. Not my choice. And my dear Lavinia. I insisted.

That night, we took Fair into a grove of hawthorn trees for the druid's blessing. Lavinia and Morgause attended. Gawain, being his mother's son, could not refuse to participate, but his father had converted to Christianity, and I sensed much tension in him. He kept his eyes averted from the proceedings. Myrddin wove the runes around our baby into a mantle of protection, and I heard the Goddess Rhiannon hum a lullaby. Fair smiled for the first time, his tiny fingers reaching for the filaments flowing from the runes. That he could see them made my heart sing.

Chapter Thirty-Two

The official feast celebrating our baby's welcome into the realm was upon us. Dignitaries from other principalities, some of whom I knew from my travels with Myrddin, were in attendance. My brother and his wife had yet to arrive. I was on pins and needles and Fair sensed it. He was mad and refused to rest in his cradle.

"Get out of here," said Lavinia. "You are disturbing the baby. He will never sleep."

"I should stay," I said.

"He is fed, and burped, and he needs his rest, and you are not helping," she scolded me. "Go the feast. I'll be here if you need me."

I gave in and dragged my feet toward the Great Hall as if I was going to a funeral. Lavinia had said my brother wanted to make his peace with the king. But I worried about Lady Amunet, and her scheming. Part of me was fearful of what would happen upon seeing them and them seeing me. And curious, now that I was no longer a beast but a wife and mother to a newborn baby boy.

My mind was a jumble of admonitions and rebukes I had wanted to scream at Somer for years now: *Did you truly believe yourself as powerless in your life as a woman is? Was Father's power over you so destructive to your life that you could find no other solution than to poison him? Neither one of us could ever be enough for him. It was always about Arthur and Briton. How could you be so smart and so stupid? If you truly believed yourself excluded from the life you deserved, how could you inflict the same fate on your own sister? That I should live as a beast with nothing. I loved you. You were my family, and you destroyed all of it.*

For what? Power over other people's lives? Because you didn't believe you had power over your own? You made a beast of me and murdered our father. That's not power, it's a tragedy!

It was a plea for understanding. I caught myself mumbling. A couple of guards were staring at me. No one else heard, thanks be the Goddess. They were all gathered for the feast. I sounded full of bitterness even to my own ears. I couldn't stop my mind from ranting at Somer. *You killed the love in your heart and filled the void with what? An illusion. What kind of bargain is that? What is left worth living for, brother? What is left in your heart? A chasm. A void as endless as the starlit sky that no amount of power can ever fill.*

By the time I arrived at the feast, I was heart heavy, and my feelings were a tempest. I pressed my hand on the ruby necklace, and it calmed me a little. I was greeted by my husband who gathered my fingers away from my throat and pressed them to his lips.

"I was worried you might not come," he said. "Most of the kings from the other provinces have arrived. You've met them before?"

I nodded, "Yes, I did. With Myrddin."

I recognized some of them from my sojourn in Caernarfon. They didn't recognize me. I was now Gawain's wife, interesting only in relation to King Arthur. Except for Segon Fawr. He was there with his squire who had turned into a young man. They were both staring at me as if they couldn't believe their eyes. Myrddin must have told them who I really was.

Segon Fawr approached us, followed by his squire. "The Lady of Dinas Emrys, if I'm not mistaken." The Bear took my hand and kissed it.

Gawain put his arm around my waist.

"You are correct Segon Fawr," I said.

"You look transformed," said the Bear. "Congratulations on your wedding. And may I say, motherhood agrees with you."

It was all banter. I enjoyed the Bear. He was made all of one piece.

I turned to the squire. "Osian, isn't it?"

Segon Fawr jostled the youth. "Answer, you oaf. The lady is addressing you."

"Yes, My Lady," he said, blushing. "It's good of you to remember."

"You took care of my palfrey, Espoir."

"That's right." He smiled. "How is Espoir?"

"He is very well, thank you for asking." Osian's fresh face was a relief. I smiled back.

"Feel free to go say hello to him," I said. "That lovely grey mare is stabled with him."

Osian laughed. "I remember. Rhian."

"Yes. Go on," I urged.

Osian looked at Segon Fawr who gave him leave. The youth took off after stuffing several sweet and savory pastries in his coat pockets.

"What a sweet young man Osian has become," I said.

"Not a man. Only thirteen and already in love with you," said Segon Fawr, his eyes hungry, devouring mine.

"He's not the only one," said Gawain, with a proprietary squeeze.

We were still laughing when my breath caught in my throat. Gawain looked at me in alarm as I turned to stone in his embrace. His eyes followed my gaze to the entrance of the banquet hall. My brother was standing between the double doors, waiting to be announced by the herald. His wife was next to him, but they might as well have been miles apart. They were like strangers, ignoring each other. Somer was as pale as ever. I recognized the almond shaped eyes with their long fringe of lashes, but where there was fire before, I saw a vacant stare, an emptiness. He was always slender, but his skin was draped tightly around his skull like an old man's. A sheen of sweat smeared his brow, as if he had a fever. He reeked of ill health. The medallion on his chest looked like a boulder around his neck, too heavy for him. He stood tall in spite of it. I felt sorry for Somer. And despite everything, the girl I had been still loved him.

The herald announced, "Sir Gromer Somer and Lady Amunet of Dinas Emrys."

Somer took a step forward and froze. His eyes caught mine and couldn't look away. Everything slowed down. We were confined into a space made only for the two of us and no one else, a space where past and present collided. I saw the recognition on his face, the moment of joy wash over him like sunlight. His smile, like a hopeful child. I smiled back at him. I couldn't help myself. And then horror swallowed him up, devouring all the sunlight as it all rushed back in, all that had happened, all he had done. He stumbled, distress plain on his face, and the medallion cracked like a thunderclap. It fell from his neck, breaking into pieces on the stone floor. Lady Amunet cried out as if it hurt her. It was a faraway sound.

No one spoke. No one moved. Or I didn't hear them. Somer and I stared at each other for an eternity. Tears rolled down our cheeks, unchecked. I wanted to go to him, embrace him, tell him I forgave him, tell him I loved him, but it didn't matter. He could never accept it. What he had done was unforgivable and we both knew it.

My brother sounded worn out when he spoke the words, *Omnia Mutantur. Everything is transformed.* I answered as I did long ago when I clung to him as he left for Rome, *Nihil Interit. Nothing perishes.*

Our eyes were still locked on each other when Somer reached for his belt and pulled something too small for a sword. Those were forbidden inside the hall. The fatal glare of steel flashed between us in the torch light. He brought the knife to his throat. The blade sliced through his flesh, in one unerring, sharp move, like gutting a deer or a pig. The blood poured from my brother's throat, a thin red thread at first. It was beyond comprehension. But some visceral part of me understood what he had done. My eyes widened with the terror of it. I felt untethered from the earth as I flew to Somer, screaming his name. He fell all at once, like a puppet whose strings had been cut. His eyes fluttered between life and death as I held his head and pressed a piece of fabric torn from my gown against his throat, failing to stem the flow of blood. For a moment, I saw, still there, dancing in the depth of his eyes, unerring, luminous, the soul of the poet that was my brother, the one I loved, and would always love.

The next moment the dark pools that were his eyes filled with utter resignation, the irrefutable knowledge that his end was upon him. I peered into the midnight of my brother's death and was drawn in, compelled by the heady mixture of his love and his need. They were my love and my need too. I could have followed him. I knew it in my bones as they turned to ice. But the door to the infinite closed as quickly as it had opened. My body shook and shivered, like a dog getting out of the water.

Lady Amunet was watching us, paralyzed. I saw the fear in her kohl rimmed eyes. I had admired her like a Goddess as a child, but now I was filled with rage as I looked up at her and accused her, "This is all your doing! This is your fault!"

I wished I had my claws to rip her apart. She must have felt my hatred because she fell back on her heels and fled. No one stopped her. I didn't want to let go of my brother, but I could let the runes lose after her. I felt their power crackling through me, aching to be set free. I would've done it but Myrddin and Morgause held me back. I fought them.

Myrddin whispered, "You cannot do this, Dryw donn. You cannot use the runes for this. Someone else will deal with Lady Amunet."

"I will find her," said Gawain, kneeling at my side.

"Yes. Please husband. Go."

It was all the encouragement he needed. He was a knight on a quest. He would find her.

I pleaded with Myrddin to do something for Somer but part of me knew it was too late. My brother's life had already spread its wings and flown from his body. Somer was gone. I tore the ruby from my neck and wailed like I had not wailed since my father's death. I was not frozen in despair as I was then. My tears were fueled by rage, and it was directed at Lady Amunet.

I was in a state of pure unbridled emotion and Ehwaz, my spirit horse, leapt at it. I urged the rune to show Gawain the way. My eyes were Ehwaz's eyes. I barely heard Myrddin, trying to rein me in. It was pointless. I saw it all: Osian crying out. Espoir's feet dancing and Eira, the crow, a blur soaring over the woods. Espoir rearing up as Eira dove straight at him from the treetops. A figure falling off my palfrey and hitting their head on a rock with a sickening thud. Then nothing. I was panting from the rush of images and slumped over my brother's still body.

I looked up when Osian ran in through the double doors. He took in the still body in my lap and shook as he spoke, "I'm so sorry. I told the lady she couldn't take Espoir, that it was your horse, but she wouldn't listen. She pushed me and I fell, and she got on, but Espoir wouldn't have it at first. She kicked him so hard he had to go. But then this crow flew out of nowhere and Espoir reared up and the lady fell and hit her head. And then Sir Gawain arrived with his brothers and told me they would take care of her and to go back to the castle to tell you."

“Thank you Osian,” I said as calmly as I could. Osian was brave but so young still. “Is Espoir alright?” I needed to know.

“Yes. He heard the mare, Rhian, whinny for him. He was very agitated, but he listened to her and returned to the stables on his own.”

Segon Fawr took charge of Osian. “Good lad. You did well. Come.” They left the hall.

I was grateful for Rhian and her love for Espoir. I looked up at Myrddin, and he helped me to my feet. King Arthur ordered the guards to come and collect my brother and take him to the church. Somer would lay in the king’s chapel until his burial. Stunned guests slowly made their way out. I returned to our chambers. Lavinia had heard the dreadful news from a guard. She enfolded me in her arms.

“My brother is dead because the king wanted my lands.”

“It’s not your fault, Nella,” said Lavinia, stroking my forehead.

“Do not make up a story, Dryw donn. This is fate,” said Myrddin.

“Fate? the one you plot and plan with your king. I hate this place.”

“The blade was laced with poison, Dryw donn,” said Myrddin.

He was trying to tell me more, but it was all too ugly. I didn’t want to speculate on why or if the poisoned blade was meant for my brother or someone else. I would hear no more.

“I will not stay here. I’m going home, and I’m taking Somer back with me. I won’t have him buried here even if it’s in the king’s chapel.”

“I will arrange it, Dryw donn.” Myrddin was gentle, treating me like a bruised little bird.

“The red dragon goes free tonight. Or I will make a rampage.”

Myrddin did not try to placate me or convince me otherwise.

I was so besides myself I didn’t noticed Lady Morgause had accompanied us.

“I apologize, Lady Morgause. I tore your ruby from my neck.”

“I collected it. Methinks you do not need it anymore.” She turned to the druid. “She will make her own fate, Myrddin. You’ll see.”

She kissed me on the forehead and was gone. Myrddin followed her. The other servants left too. All the noise was sucked out of the room. I was alone with Lavinia and the baby who was thankfully asleep. It was as if he knew I needed to be the child right then, sobbing in Lavinia's arms as she sang the old lullaby, *Ragnella, Nella, Nella.*

The king kept his word, according to Myrddin, and liberated the red dragon in the middle of the night, away from prying eyes. He didn't want anyone to know the symbol of the country was gone. King Arthur also gave me his permission to return to Dinas Emrys. He knew I would have gone anyways, and I had the feeling he was glad to have me out of the way. I was a woman, too unruly for his court, and a reminder of an episode he and all of Camelot would rather forget.

At my urging, Gawain asked Segon Fawr if Osian could come back with us to begin his apprenticeship as a knight. All the men agreed it was a good idea, but I made sure to ask Osian personally if he would like it and to not feel obligated. He flashed such a smile at me as he agreed, that it assuaged all my doubts about the request. I wanted Gawain to have a young man to practice being a father and a mentor with. And I thought Osian would be a good friend to my Fair as he grew up.

We were a somber party leaving Camelot. Lavinia rode in a carriage with Fair. Gawain, Osian and I rode ahead. And trailing behind us, a pair of mules pulled the cart with Somer's body and his wife's, Lady Amunet. She had succumbed to her head injury that same night. The king's doctors had attended to her but couldn't help. She was always afraid of horses and had died trying to steal Espoir. In her case, I agreed with Myrddin. It was fated. He also swore to me that Eira had acted on her own. She had rescued Espoir from a stranger, answering the call of my runes, the druid believed. I saw her glide overhead as we departed and she spoke to me for the first time in my mind. *I did as Rhiannon asked, for her messenger.* Rhiannon. I had not thought the Goddess would interfere in this way, but I was glad of it.

My mind kept wandering back to the poisoned blade in spite of myself. I had no doubt it was Lady Amunet's work but whether she meant it for my brother, or someone else, I couldn't fathom. She must have been possessed by such a devouring need to bend the world to her will. It brought about disaster for us all.

I steered Espoir along the carriage carrying Lavinia and my son. "You knew Lady Amunet the longest," I said. "Why would she poison my brother's blade? She must have known nothing good could come of it."

"She anointed all of your brother's blades with poison. Death is what she knew best."

Lavinia was right. Death was Lady Amunet's constant companion, her way to navigate this world. She'd taught my brother the same. Somer's feud with our father and the cruelty of war prepared the way. My brother had loved Lady Amunet as much as he could love any woman. I knew that now.

Chapter Thirty-Three

As we left King Arthur's court behind, my spirits lifted, and I let my mind wander and daydream. My son would grow up in Dinas Emrys. I would tell him about my father, the great warrior Lord Vortigern, and teach him poetry, and play games with him, like the ones Somer and I had played. He would learn about crops and about the stars from Hillel, and I would teach him to ride. Gawain and Osian would help him become a gallant and honorable man, a knight.

The surprising part in all of this was that it happened much as I imagined it, except Gawain had to leave often to be at court and support his uncle. We had visitors. My Saxon Uncle Oeric and Lord Kay vied for my son's affections. I could see Lord Kay was revived by his visits with us and took advantage of my open-ended invitation. Gawain's brothers and Lady Morgause also stayed with us. She traveled regularly without her husband to visit her grandson.

Lady Morgause and Lavinia would go off into the woods, to Myrddin's circle of stones and practice the druidic ways. Gawain pleaded with me to leave them be and not get involved. It was hard for him to tread the line between the old world and the new with its Christian rules. Gawain wanted to belong to the new. *It is inevitable and we must adapt,* he'd say. I didn't want to fight my husband on this. I gave in and suppressed that part of myself, almost forgetting that I bore the runes, the chosen sign of the old Gods. Lady Morgause and Lavinia got along so well, I was a bit jealous of their friendship.

I loved my son as well as any mother and Gawain was devoted to him when he was home. Hillel received news from Myrddin through Eira but for the most part the druid stayed away. There were still too many shenanigans to contend with at court and beyond.

Fair was a happy boy. I remembered so many moments of my own childhood through him, though Dinas Emrys no longer held my heart in the same way since Somer's death. It had been a shock upon my return to see the extent of the changes Lady Amunet had made. All the women's quarters turned over to the apothecary trade. Halls growing plants indoors. Fields filled with herbs better suited for sunnier climates. Hillel had worked hard to keep enough crops so our people wouldn't starve. I slowly reclaimed my home but never slept in my childhood bedroom again. Gawain and I took over my father's old rooms.

I was not entirely surprised to find that Somer and Lady Amunet had kept separate rooms. Somer stayed in his old rooms, and the lady in hers. I took her book of spells, the one she used to curse me, and gave it to Hillel to hide. My runes tingled at the mere touch of its cover. On it, under the watchful eye of Horus, a leafless rose spread out its spine full of thorns with a bleeding serpent spiraled around it. A perverse version of the rod of Asclepius. This was a dangerous book. I didn't want it falling into the wrong hands, including mine.

My son loved the woods as much as I did. I took him to the hunter's cabin where I had lived as a beast. He had trouble understanding that I had been cursed and couldn't see me as anything other than his mother, but I wanted him to know as much of my story as possible. I didn't want to hide anything from him.

Fair began riding early, first with us and then on his own pony and by the age of nine was as fair a rider as his name. For his tenth birthday, my uncle Oeric gifted Fair a two-year-old colt. It was the last foal from his own mare and, if Oeric was to be believed, her best. Fair had the same bond with his horse as I did with Espoir. It was a pleasure to see them together as they both grew and learned. He called his horse *Plaisir d'Amor. Amor* for short. Gawain thought it was a silly name for a horse.

I raised an eyebrow at my husband. "Coming from a man who named his son the Fair Unknown? You will not say a word. That horse is our son's first love."

Gawain finally understood as he remembered his own devotion to his first horse.

Osian was attentive and as good a best friend and older brother as one could hope for, but he missed his family and after a few years asked if he could go home. He had given us so much, and though I was sad to see him go, we agreed it was time. Fair was devastated even though Osian promised him they would meet again.

My son took Osian's departure so hard, I worried about him. He stopped wanting to do anything, riding, reading, eating and would lay down in the hay next to his horse all day.

I asked Gawain to support our son through this loss and he did. My husband was granted permission from his king to return to Dinas Emrys for as long as was needed. My husband shared his love of wood and wood carving with our boy. Fair regained his *joie de vivre* under his father's tutelage. He showed an aptitude for wood carving which delighted Gawain. They spent so much time together in the part of the stables that had been converted into my husband's woodcarving shed, I'd have to send servants to remind them of supper. Fair would strut into the dining hall, eager to share his newly acquired knowledge.

"You must observe the direction of the grain closely and proceed with care and make use of the good knots," said Fair, in between bites of food. He was eating with a gusto I hadn't seen in a long time. "It's all about the grain of the wood before you can start carving at all. And you have your soft woods like pine, which are easier to carve than oak or linden wood, but not as durable. And there is always the trusted walnut, the wood father used to carve your little wren. Do you see, mother?"

"Yes." I nodded, exchanging a glance with my husband, who was glowing with pride.

It wasn't long before Gawain began to train Fair in the arts of chivalry, including sword fighting, jousting, and more. Fair embraced all of it and thrived. Gawain wanted another son, and we did try but to no avail. With Lavinia's help, I brewed herbs to fortify my fertility, but nothing worked. Gawain accused me of taking herbs to stop pregnancy.

"Admit it," he said. "You don't want another child. You said so when you were giving birth in the first place."

I stared at my husband, incredulous. "Anything I said while giving birth is meaningless. I was in agony, beyond exhaustion, in a way you can never comprehend."

"These herbs you are taking are not for fertility at all. Are they?" said Gawain, his face red with anger.

"That is nonsense, Gawain," I protested. "Has someone been feeding you lies? Have you been listening to a priest?"

Gawain jerked away from me as if I'd slapped him. His eyes veiled with a mixture of embarrassment and righteousness. *Not again,* I thought, Somer coming to my mind. *Not you too.* That was a blow. You can never tell what will bring about a rift in a marriage.

"Your disbelief is a break of trust between us, Gawain," I said. I shook my head, saddened, and walked away from him. We slept in separate rooms after that.

My son didn't need me as much anymore. His father had stepped in as he should. I began to feel restless, like I had more to do with my life and more to give but I didn't know how. When Fair turned fourteen, I knew he would be sent away to finish his apprenticeship. I asked Gawain if we could send him to Segon Fawr. It seemed like the right fit, a trade, to make up for taking Osian from him. We sent word to Caernarfon, and the answer came back with a yes. Fair was excited to go because Osian had secured a permanent post with Segon Fawr. My son would get his best friend back.

From the moment we got the answer from Caernarfon, I began to hear the Goddess Rhiannon again. It had been a long silence. It was not much more than a whisper, but I heard it. *It's time, it's time*. Like a lullaby, but instead of putting me to sleep, it woke me up.

I told Gawain I would travel to Caernarfon with them. He was surprised by my decision but didn't argue with me. He had learned long ago that it was fruitless. He came around to my thinking that it was a good family trip for the three of us.

I said my goodbyes to Lavinia and Hillel. They sensed something, but I didn't want to explain myself or alarm them. Especially when I wasn't sure of anything myself.

"I am entrusting my son, my husband, and Dinas Emrys to you both, as always."

Hillel raised an eyebrow, unclear on what I meant since I was traveling with my husband and my son. "Of course, My Lady, it goes without saying."

"Nella," asked Lavinia, studying me, "Are you well?"

"I am very well," I replied. I wasn't lying but I wasn't telling the truth either. "I love you both more than I can say." That was the truth. I hugged each one of them for a long time. They were both white haired and Hillel stooped when he walked. I might not see them again.

I packed very little for our trip to Caernarfon. My tartan, my cloak, my little wren, and Myrddin's gift, the rowan stick. It was all I needed. I wore one of the costumes made for me by Lady Morgause's seamstress. Espoir was getting older but had lots of energy still and was ready for a new adventure. I walked up the hill to the mausoleum. The garden was so overgrown, it looked like an enchanted forest.

Lady Amunet's parents had come to retrieve her remains when they were informed of her death. They wouldn't believe me when I explained that their daughter had been killed falling off a horse. They demanded to speak with Gawain. But he was gone on a hunting trip with my son.

"Our daughter would never ride a horse," said the father.

"It was the only thing she feared," said the mother. I could see the daughter in the mother's eyes, full of pride and fury, keen on vengeance.

"My brother taught Lady Amunet," I said. Since Somer was dead too they couldn't berate him and left but not before the mother insisted on seeing her daughter's rooms. She took all of Lady Amunet's jewelry back. She perused the apothecary books on the shelf.

"A valuable book is missing." She described the cover of the book of spells, with the eye of Horus at the top. A rose and a serpent intertwined below. I pleaded ignorance. That was easy because I had asked Hillel not to tell me where it was hidden. She glowered at me but said no more. My blank expression didn't fool her. She could tell I knew *what* the book was even if I didn't know *where* it was. I didn't care. I was glad to see the back of them.

It was only Somer and my father now in the mausoleum. It seemed fitting and I hoped they found peace resting here, together. But knowing them, they were probably still arguing.

It pleased me to show my druidic side to my son on our trip to Caernarfon. I used the runes to find our path and our lodgings. I insisted we stay in the old caves and hunt for our food. Gawain would have preferred to stay at the castles of his various friends from court, but also acquiesced this was a great adventure for our son.

Fair was fascinated. He wondered how I could light the fire without flint. I told him it was Rhiannon who lit the fire, not I. His violet eyes opened as wide as the sky. "The Goddess is your friend."

"I am her messenger," I said. "The only human who is her friend is Myrddin Emrys, and he is only half human. And I wasn't really human myself when she chose me."

No one spoke of the Gods anymore. Not out loud. Gawain was uncomfortable with our conversation and let me know. I wondered if he had become uncomfortable with my entire past. If the Christianization of the court exerted more pressure on Gawain than his father's conversion already did. And if it had made it easier to accuse me of taking herbs to prevent pregnancy.

I showed my son the runes on my wrist. I told him their names. That one of them was granted to me by a dragon thrilled him.

He asked, "Will I receive runes of my own?"

"I don't know," I answered. "You may have another destiny that is uniquely yours."

Later that night, when our son was asleep, Gawain asked, "Do you need to fill our son's head with all these stories?"

"It's my story," I argued. "And yes. I want him to know who his mother really is."

"It's not helpful," he said. "We live in a Christian kingdom now."

He worried for our son, but I did too, for opposite reasons. "Your Christian Kingdom. Not mine," I replied.

"You are my wife," he said, as if it explained everything.

Not for a long time, I thought. Apprehension coursed through me as I took a breath, "You once told me that my life was my own. Does that still hold true?"

Gawain answered warily, "I suppose it does. Why?"

"Because I have decided to leave," I replied.

"Leave?" he asked, unable to comprehend my meaning.

"Yes," I said. "Once we arrive at Caernarfon and remit our son into the capable hands of Segon Fawr, I will not return to Dinas Emrys with you. I will be moving on."

He searched my eyes in disbelief. He was like a wild animal in a trap, not knowing what to do but desperate to save his life. "You can't. You are my wife. We have a son."

"Yes," I replied. "I gave you both fourteen years of my life. It's time. You married a beast out of duty, Gawain. And I will always be grateful for your honorable nature. But I'm done."

"You are mad," he said between clenched teeth, repressing his urge to shout for our son's sake. "I forbid it."

"You have my lands, Dinas Emrys. It's all yours." I pressed on. "You gave me back my life then. Don't take it away now. Let me go."

Gawain was stunned into silence, glaring at the dancing light from the flames. We were but flickering shadows on the walls of the cave.

We didn't speak after that. Fair fretted about us. We had been quite merry up until then and I had broken us. When we arrived at Caernarfon, Segon Fawr received us like old friends. Things remained strained between me and Gawain. We were sharing the quarters I had once shared with Myrddin Emrys. It was full of memories including the Roman bath. I had been a beast then and I felt like one now, destroying my family. But I couldn't ignore the persistent voice telling me it was time to leave.

Gawain must have spoken with Segon Fawr, because the Bear asked me to take a walk. We marched the length and breadth of the castle. We conversed about Fair and Osian. About the latest rumors from court. Myrddin had taken on a new apprentice, Mordred, Lady Morgause's youngest son. There was talk about his parentage, whether King Lot was his father. The worst gossip concerned Queen Guinevere and Sir Lancelot while Arthur was away campaigning against the Normans.

I listened and waited until the Bear finally told me that I was making a horrendous mistake and how could I do that to Gawain and to Fair. "You don't mean it," he said.

"Have you ever known me not to mean what I say?" I asked.

He searched my eyes, frowning, "No. I haven't." He sighed. "Your husband will have to say terrible things about you to justify letting you go. That you are unfit, a harlot, that he had to cast you out and send you away to a convent."

"I'm used to terrible things being told about me," I said. "It won't be the first time."

The Bear gave up after that.

The hardest part was saying goodbye to our son. "Remember that I love you, that I will always love you."

He embraced me, beaming, as only Fair could. "I know that, mother." He knew he was loved. I had done something right. That was all that mattered to me.

"There are people who will say horrible things about me. Trust your own heart," I said.

His violet eyes darkened under his brow. "Mother, what is it? What's wrong?"

Gawain barged into the room and shouted, "Your mother has decided to leave us." He was unsteady on his feet and must have gotten drunk with the Bear.

Fair's answer took both of us by surprise. "I know. I heard you that night in the cave when you believed I was asleep."

"I'm so sorry, Fair," I said.

"Not sorry enough," barked Gawain. I knew it was the grief talking but I wished he behaved better for our son's sake. This disheveled man with bloodshot eyes and a snarl on his lips had been my dream come true at one time. But we had lived apart for a long time now.

"I understand," said my son.

"You do?" I wasn't sure I understood it myself.

"There is a new adventure calling to you."

I kissed my son on the cheek. "Yes, there is. As there is for you as well."

"Perhaps the Goddess needs her messenger," said Fair. For someone so young, there was a depth of understanding that astounded me.

"Do you know where you are going?" he asked.

The answer came to me, unsolicited. “The Isle of Skye.” I had not known it until that moment. The thought had been tucked away, hidden amongst all the memories of the island.

“Where the white dragon lives,” said my son, violet gaze shining with curiosity.

“Yes. That’s right,” I answered.

“I will come and visit you,” he said, with the certainty of a child.

“I hope so.” I wished I could take all the love in my heart and put it in his traveling pack like a loaf of bread that would sustain him without end, no matter how much he ate of it.

There was no sense in postponing the pain I would feel in abandoning my son and walking away from fourteen years of the life I had made with Gawain. I left the next day.

SOWELU

Chapter Thirty-Four

Espoir and I made our way to the white stone circle of Castlerigg. I missed Myrddin's company, especially when I was about to meet Rhiannon again. It unnerved me, the golden eternity of her on her horse, perfectly unchanged.

"Hello, Beast," she said. "It took you long enough."

I couldn't tell if the Goddess called me *Beast* as a sign of affection or a put down. The Gods are hard to read.

Rhiannon agreed with my decision to return to the Isle of Skye. "You can serve me there. Learn new things from the lizard."

It still distressed me to hear the Goddess refer to Dragon that way. I wanted to say so but didn't get the chance. With an impetuous gesture, and no preamble, Rhiannon threw us into the Fairy World, like flinging someone into a stormy sea to drown. I had to scramble with my runes to get us through to the other side. Myrddin's gift of the rowan stick focused the runes into one beacon that helped illuminate the path to the Fairy Garden. Dunvegan Castle was foremost on my mind and helped pull us through.

It was early fall and still thick with greenery and late blooms. I was grateful the image of the castle was so strong in me, but I couldn't understand why. Was it the Laird? The Fairy Garden? The last time I had seen the garden it was covered in snow. It had been the first real test of my relationship to the runes. Myrddin. *I would not be here now without the druid*, I thought.

Espoir and I made our way toward Dunvegan Castle. It had been fifteen years. Gawain was right. I must be crazy. I had this bad habit of plunging headlong into things before I evaluated the consequences properly. I was moved by my instincts. I had to be, as a beast. And they mostly steered me in the right direction. But I wondered if those instincts were about to fail me.

What would Laird MacLeod think? He would not know me. I was a stranger. He had only met the beast. It occurred to me that he might have taken a new wife, and she would not look kindly upon me, see me as an intruder, or worse. This new thought was so disheartening, I changed my mind and decided to go to Morag's cottage instead. *She'll take me in, teach me how to become a weaver. Yes. That's what I'll do*, I thought.

"Come on Espoir," I said, turning my palfrey around. "Let's go find Morag."

Espoir gave a neigh of approval. I felt more settled and confident with my new plan, as we headed toward the weaver's cottage. When we arrived, the door was locked, and Morag was nowhere to be found. I stood at a loss, holding on to my palfrey's reins. Even Espoir looked crestfallen. I was so certain this was the plan. *Now what? Where can we go?* I climbed back on my horse.

Ehwaz leaped forth, tracing her silver path toward the mountains and Espoir walked on with renewed vigor in his step as if he could see the rune. It finally occurred to me: we were heading to the Fairy Pools. *Dragon. Of course.* It seemed obvious now. Even Rhiannon had suggested I meet with Dragon again. And the dragon part of my heart had been calling me back to the Fairy Pools, but I had not heard, being more concerned with leaving where I was than where I was meant to go.

We arrived close to sunset. Dragon was there somewhere, still invisible in the light of the dying day. It was an odd sensation to be familiar with the awe I was experiencing all over again. As the moon rose high above the pools, I called Dragon to me with a song. I am no singer, but it came from the part of my soul which was like them. I waited. There were no Fairy Folk to be seen but Dragon emerged from the pools all at once, turning the darkness to silver. I was shaking with gratitude to witness their mysterious divinity once again, more ancient than the Gods.

"Dryw donn, it is good to see you again. Welcome home," they said in their exquisite multi-tonal vocalizing.

"It is good to see you too. Are you alright?" I asked.

"I'm not dead yet if that's what you're asking." Their chuckle blew waves on the surface of the pool.

"Did the red dragon come to you?" I asked. I wondered if the king had kept his promise.

"They came. And we both thank you." There was infinite tenderness in their voice. "They are not easily impressed but they held you in high esteem."

"Why?" I asked. I had barely managed to convince King Arthur to do the right thing.

"You didn't want anything from them. And you gave them hope. They died not long ago. Red Dragon was much older than we are."

"I'm so sorry," I said.

"They gifted me what was left of their essence. I am all of us now," they said.

"Like you did with me?" I asked.

"More or less." Their voices deepened. "Dryw donn. Listen well. More war is coming. And a plague will follow. It will decimate the human realm. Keep the people you love close."

"When?" I asked, throat closing with dread.

"Soon enough," they replied. "When there is a new emperor in the Byzantine world by the name of Justinian and the druid Mordred lies dead on the field of battle, at *Camlann*. The plague will sleep for a while, but it will wake again. It will endure for four hundred years and be known as the Black Death."

Myrddin's rowan stick, which never left me, began to burn in my hand. I looked and saw a new rune etched on its bark. It was *Sowelu.*

"Sowelu is a gift for you to grow into, the root and branch of wholeness, what holds our longing to live freely from the heart," said Dragon. "Red Dragon wanted you to have it. This is from all of us. It will protect you and your family from what is to come when we are gone. And so will the part of you which is like us."

When we are gone. *They know their own death, as well as the death that will follow.* I couldn't think of anything meaningful to say. "You didn't inscribe it on my body." It was a pointless remark, but they were generous with their answer. "That will come in its own time."

"Thank you," I said, shaken by the news. "What can I do?"

"Live your life," they answered.

Espoir and I left with the morning light. It was a bittersweet farewell. I hoped I would see them again. They had given so much to me, to the world. I let Espoir guide us through the rocky path. I let the mountains encircle me and the sky cradle me. I was oblivious to the present, consumed by my helplessness at what was to come, questioning the very meaning and purpose of my existence. Espoir neighed several times to get my attention. I looked up from my thoughts and pulled sharply on the reins. Espoir snorted his disapproval.

"I apologize, Espoir," I said, with a soft hand on his neck.

Two men were riding toward us. As they approached, my heart began to beat loud as a drum. My blood reached out to the runes and the runes reached back to me. I slowed my breathing and whispered, "Be still. No unruly displays of magic right now."

The Norseman was riding with a loose rein, confident, towering on his Shire destrier. I noticed some grey on his temples. I made a rapid calculation in my head. I was thirty-four. He was about ten years my elder. There was a young man riding with him who must have been about eighteen or twenty years old. His son by the Fairy Queen. The boy had the ethereal beauty of the Fairy Folk.

I caught the Norseman's eyes. He had been chatting with his son. They were both dressed for hunting, with leather breeches and boots. Woolen shirts. No surcoat, as the weather was mild for a Norseman. MacLeod stopped his horse, frowning. He took me in with a gaze that touched my entire being, Dragon included. His son was puzzled, his eyes darting back and forth between us. I waited, still as a stone, blood rushing through my body like a torrent. His smile lit up his whole face. He jumped off his horse, and I did the same. Macleod covered the space between us in three strides and lifted me into his arms.

"Changeling!" he shouted. "What a wonder you are."

He put me down, still gazing into my eyes. He had squeezed the breath out of me.

"How can you tell it's me?" A reasonable question, considering.

"I would know you anywhere, Changeling. Your innocent heart is the same it ever was, plain for all to see, in your eyes."

I heard the click then, the third turn of the key. The one thing Myrddin could not fathom, the final piece to my freedom falling into place: to be seen in my innocence, as I truly was. I stood there as myself. I was home. I always longed for home, for *hiraeth,* a special word in our Welsh language, both a yearning and a grief for the lost parts of a past I was no longer sure ever existed. I assumed home must be Dinas Emrys. And it was for a while. But I didn't know where home was because I hadn't come home to my own heart yet. Not fully.

MacLeod kept speaking about all the ways he could not fail to recognize me. "Not to mention your fearless spirit and the silver flame of your magic."

I laughed, holding back tears. He took my hand and introduced me to his son, formally.

"This is my son, Leod MacLeod," he said.

"Hello Leod," I said to the young man.

Leod kissed my hand like a knight would, his grace owing everything to his mother.

"And this is Lady Ragnell of Dinas Emrys," MacLeod explained to his son. "The one who came with Myrddin Emrys, that time."

MacLeod had told his son about me. Did he tell him about my drunken behavior as a beast? Or whispering on my hands and knees, trying to get Eira's attention? I hoped not.

I corrected MacLeod. "I'm no longer Lady of Dinas Emrys. It all belongs to Sir Gawain now, son of King Lot and Queen Morgause."

"The king's nephew." he nodded. "The wedding of Sir Gawain and Lady Ragnell is of note, even on our remote island."

There was so much to say. Too much. I stayed silent. He searched my eyes then turned to Leod, "Son, will you go ahead and inform the servants that we have company?"

Young Leod nodded. He jumped on his horse and galloped toward Dunvegan Castle. We followed at a more leisurely pace.

"Shouldn't he also inform your wife?" I mumbled, too embarrassed to ask the laird directly.

"There is no wife," he answered.

I breathed out slowly, and looked in Leod's direction, "A very handsome boy," I said. "He has the look of Fairy Folk."

A faint smile appeared on MacLeod's lips. "That, he does."

I was so nervous, Espoir snorted at me. I blurted out, "I have a son too, with Sir Gawain. He's fourteen." *There, I've said it.*

"And where is Sir Gawain now?" asked MacLeod.

It was a fair question. Women didn't travel without their husbands, if they traveled at all. We brought our mounts to a halt. They were prancing, reacting to our own trepidation.

"Back in Gwynedd," I answered. "Unless he extended his stay in Caernarfon with Lord Segon Fawr. We brought our son there for his apprenticeship," I explained.

MacLeod waited for me to say more.

"I asked Gawain to let me go. He married me under very unique circumstances, to save the king's life. He also helped transform mine."

"And did he? Let you go?" he asked, words slow on his tongue.

"Yes," I answered. "We had a covenant, that he remember my life belongs to me and no other."

"That must have been difficult for him," said MacLeod.

"It was," I acknowledged. "Very troubling."

"No man likes to lose what he values without a fight," he said. "He is honorable."

"One of the best men I ever met," I acquiesced.

"And yet, here you are," he said, staring into my eyes.

"Here I am," I repeated, like a dare.

That first night, with a twinkle in his eye, MacLeod offered me that most treacherous of drinks, mead.

"I am no longer such a naïve little beast as I once was, Laird," I said. "I have been to King Arthur's court."

His laughter melted my heart, but I resolved to stay strong. "You will not convince me to drink tonight. We are practically strangers."

"Not for long I hope," said the laird, kissing my hand.

In the days and weeks that followed, we devoted every moment to each other, discovering each other all over again and also meeting for the first time. The remnants of my unsatiable hunger evaporated, as body and soul remembered they loved each other. I was unafraid to be wholly myself with the Norseman. And he was always himself.

I learned that Morag's aunt had died, and Morag had replaced her as the head of the waulking community. She still went to the Fairy Pools with her linen weaving, but it was a rare event. The practice, like the Fairy Folk, was vanishing.

The conflict with the Normans, which started with raids, just like the Saxons, was turning into yet another large-scale war. The peace Britons and Saxons had achieved was soon forgotten. My part in it inconsequential. I was only a woman after all, not worthy of our historians.

Thanks to MacLeod's crows—not like having Eira around, but good enough—we could send messages and receive them from neighboring kingdoms and keep abreast of the various movements of the opposing armies.

My son was my primary concern. It is a harsh truth for a mother to accept that she cannot keep her son safe once he is gone from her. I pleaded with Segon Fawr to send my son to me. The message came back: *Osian will not leave my service. Fair will not leave Osian.*

These two had become even more inseparable than I knew. I had to trust Segon Fawr and Osian to protect Fair as much as they could. I hated feeling so helpless over my son's welfare. I didn't want war to harm him the way it had my brother. And I couldn't bear to contemplate the power of the plague to destroy all I loved. Part of me wished Dragon had not told me about this. It was a terrible burden to bear.

The Isle of Skye, being so far north, separate from the rest of Briton, was able to stay out of the fray. I worried for Hillel and Lavinia, but Gwynedd's western location helped place Dinas Emrys away from the brunt of the fighting as well. I sent one of Macleod's crows to Dinas Emrys regularly to make sure they were staying safe. I prayed to Rhiannon to protect them.

Knowing, as I did, that Mordred's death was a portent of even darker things, I waited and wondered when I would receive the news. When Myrddin Emrys arrived at Dunvegan Castle, unannounced, I knew. He was harried and worn out by the peculiarities of human beings and had decided to retire to Bardsey island, or Afalon as the druids call it. Myrddin felt he had made a grave mistake taking on Mordred as an apprentice. Mordred was gifted as a druid, but his mind was bent on destruction. He went to war against Arthur and burnt the castle to the ground.

"Did Mordred die on the battlefield at Camlann?" I asked.

"Yes," Myrddin answered warily. "Arthur still lives, though I don't know for how long."

My heart was breaking for the druid. "Dragon told me it would happen," I said.

"What else did they tell you?" he asked.

"A terrible plague will follow," I whispered.

Myrddin nodded, as if he knew already. His hand went to his chest and made a fist. He swayed for a moment, eyes closed, as if perceiving the devastation in his heart.

That night I received a message from Hillel. The plague, which began in the Egyptian port town of Pelusium, had reached Constantinople. Hillel had obtained news from a friend there. How long would it be before it reached the shores of Briton? A few months? A year? Two? I hoped it would be longer. The Black Death would devour whole cities in its wake, from Syria and Tunisia, to Hispania, Italy and Gaul.

Six months later Myrddin sent Eira to let us know he'd brought a dying Arthur back with him to Bardsey island. My sadness went to Myrddin. Arthur's death must have been like losing a son for the druid. And with it came a second death: that of his vision for an Arthurian Briton. Shrouding the end of his beloved king in mystery was the only thing he could do to keep Arthur's legacy alive for the glory of Briton. Lady Morgause also retired to Bardsey island after both her sons, Mordred and Gawain, died.

Lady Morgause bid Myrddin tell me of Gawain's death. I grieved for him. He was the most honorable of knights and father to our son. He had fought Lancelot and lost. It was over some treachery. Though Myrddin wouldn't say, I knew Gawain loved Arthur, not only as his uncle but as his king, and that it must be over Guinevere and Lancelot's unsanctioned love. What else could drive Gawain to fight his best friend to the death?

In the midst of all this death and uncertain future, I became pregnant for the second time in my life. Gawain and I did not have another child. He would never let me forget it, assumed it was my doing. Imagine my surprise when I got pregnant at the mature age of thirty-seven. It was such an affirmation of life, I could wish for no more.

Lavinia could not make the trip for the birth. Hillel was poorly and she wouldn't leave him. And travel was not safe. Morag brought her sister-in-law who was the local midwife, and we got through it well enough. I was in labor forever, like the first time. The dragon part of my soul remained a curious observer. Rhiannon stayed away, preferring to bring her blessing to the naming ceremony as she had once before.

I've never seen a man so besides himself as MacLeod. When I could catch his eye, it was wild with fear. It was MacLeod's first experience of a human birth. The Fairy Queen had not suffered so in childbirth. I had doubts as to whether MacLeod would be able to endure hearing me howl and watching me writhe in pain. But he managed in the end with copious amounts of mead. If I hadn't been in such devilish torment, I would have laughed about it. We had a baby girl. Flora wailed as fiercely as I did, entering the world.

MacLeod was smitten with his little girl and played endless games of peekaboo with her. It was quite the sight to see this giant of a man with his tiny daughter. As Flora began to walk and explore, she got herself into so many scrapes, despite the protection of the runes and MacLeod's vigilance, we got a sheepdog, named Nola, whose sole assignment was to keep track of our daughter. Flora ran the poor animal ragged. Nola would crawl in front of the fireplace at night, tongue lolling, as if she had been running sheep all day long. Flora's screams and squeals filled the castle and our hearts. She insisted Leod play the part of her pony, and he couldn't refuse her. He would gallop for hours through the castle, carrying Flora on his back. And when the son was tired, the father would take over.

Once men came to their senses and the war abated, the Normans became the latest allies of the Saxons and Britons. Fair and Osian came to visit at last. When they arrived, I hugged them both for a long time. They didn't mind. I didn't care if they did. I would tell them what was coming, much worse than any war, and bid them stay.

They immediately took to Leod and the three of them would go riding together. Leod unfurled the beauty of the island before them, the rugged peaks and the silver pools. He told them about the Fairy Folk, showed them the Fairy Garden. To the boys' ears, they sounded like fanciful stories and yet Leod's beauty, as unearthly as the landscape, made believers of them.

Flora insisted on tagging along, and the three boys would take turn, ferrying her on their horses. Our daughter was smitten with Osian, the oldest of the trio. She decided she would marry him. Osian was kind and played along but I could tell by the way they couldn't stop smiling when they looked at each other, brushed past each other, hands briefly touching as if by chance, Osian's heart already belonged to my son.

"I can see the tender regard you hold for Osian," I told my son one afternoon, as we took a stroll in the Fairy Garden.

Would he answer evasively or be defensive? But this was my son, the Fair Unknown. He looked me in the eye and said with a smile like sunlight, "Osian is the best person I know, mother. He's my best friend. I love him. Always have. Always will."

"Yes," I said. "I see that." What else could I say? *The world will be unkind. Make a different choice. Don't be yourself.* I would not do that to my son. I could not.

"I'm glad for you. Osian is wonderful." As I said those words, I felt my brother's presence around us, like a gentle breeze. I was giving my son permission to be himself, and Somer's spirit soared. A blessing.

MacLeod and I chose to marry on Flora's fifteenth birthday. It was a rather pagan affair with no church involved and the only binding that occurred that day. It was our gift to her.

Espoir's lifespan was unusually prolonged. Perhaps it was Dragon's presence in my soul, or maybe the trips through the Fairy World. I believe it was Rhian's presence. Myrddin left his mare with us at the end of his last visit. He sensed she would be safer and happier with us. Espoir was ecstatic. They stayed with us long past their allotted time. I was thankful for every moment I had with Espoir. And with Rhian, I had a beloved part of Myrddin Emrys with me. Eventually, Morag taught me how to weave the linen, and I'd stay in her cottage to work, often without her. There comes a time when solitude is not only a requirement but a necessity.

I was the last person to ever see Dragon at the Fairy Pools before they faded forever into the invisible realm, to live only through the fancy and skill of storytellers. It was inevitable that great darkness would follow such a great loss.

I have been a beast, a druid's apprentice, the messenger of a Goddess. I have shared my soul with a dragon. I have been a daughter, a sister, a wife, a mother, a lover, a friend to people, animals and Fairy Folk, and a linen weaver. I have seen men destroy each other in war, kingdoms burn to the ground, and the greater devastation of a plague.

It is this never-ending wheel of creation and destruction, we, human beings, get caught in. We want to control our fate. We believe it will help if we can control other people. But life will not be controlled. It wants to be lived and loved, as it is. It took me a long time to learn to love the beast I became, to understand that what I perceived as a curse was in fact a gift and my path to sovereignty. Only then could I love all there is to love. There is so much to love here.

www.ingramcontent.com/pod-product-compliance
Lightning Source LLC
LaVergne TN
LVHW090305210926
848480LV00001B/137
* 9 7 8 1 6 8 5 0 3 7 0 7 9 *